lso
he pr   u
man. .   ra
ter, his p   , hi
far as he had an /),   pr
documents clearly."
　　　—Franklin B. W
　　　University of   achuset

Robin F. A. Fabel is Associate Profes   i
tory, Auburn University.

Bombast and Broadsides

George Johnstone, 1730–1787 (Courtesy of the National Maritime Museum, Greenwich, Great Britain)

Bombast
AND
Broadsides

The Lives of George Johnstone

Robin F. A. Fabel

THE UNIVERSITY OF ALABAMA PRESS
Tuscaloosa   London

Copyright © 1987 by
The University of Alabama Press
Tuscaloosa, Alabama 35487
Manufactured in the United States of America

Library of Congress Cataloging-in-Publication Data

Fabel, Robin F. A., 1934–
  Bombast and broadsides.

  Bibliography: p.
  Includes index.
  1. Johnstone, George, 1730–1787. 2. Great Britain—
History—George II, 1727–1760. 3. Legislators—
Great Britain—Biography. 4. Great Britain. Royal
Navy—Biography. 5. West Florida—Governors—Biography.
I. Title.
DA501.J63F3   1987   941.07′3′0924 [B]   86-19348
ISBN 0-8173-0337-5

British Cataloguing-in-Publication Data is available.

Contents

Illustrations

Preface

It has been said, probably many times, that when historical topics have been "hitherto neglected," it has usually been for good reason. In the case of George Johnstone's life the most probable reason for the lack of a biography lies in the difficulty of finding the raw materials for the study of his many-faceted career. There is no collection of George Johnstone papers. The materials pertaining to his life are scattered because his career ranged wide, taking him from his native Scotland to England, the West Indies, Portugal, North America, and South Africa. Moreover, although he never went there, his connection with the East India Company involved him closely in affairs in India, and many documents relating to him originated there.

Not only did he acquire acquaintance with a broad variety of places but also with numerous circles of society: naval and military, plebeian and noble, literary and mercantile, diplomatic and legal. He moved particularly far in the political world, working amiably, at times, with the Opposition magnificoes Rockingham, Portland, Fox, and Burke, but at others giving welcome support to the treasury bench.

There is a note of amazement in J. K. Laughton's comment that "he is, even now, sometimes described as a politician,"[1] but the designation should have caused no surprise. Although he never held political office Johnstone commanded respect—fear would be more accurate in some cases—as an effective and influential backbencher of a type not unknown to the House of Commons in the 1980s. As this biography will demonstrate, his political fame rested on various types of expertise, but above all upon his forcefulness in debate.

Nothing is more ephemeral than a reputation grounded on oratorical thunder. Burke has retained something of his, partly because he made sure that his speeches were fully and accurately available in printed form. Johnstone did not, and most of his deliveries survive only through the chaotic methods of eighteenth-century reporters. Even where the words have been preserved, the fire he gave them has gone. At the time, nevertheless, it hurt grievously to be the target of a speech from Johnstone, as the testimony of Fox, Burke, North, and Townshend proves. Conversely he was an unusually welcome ally, "a powerful and active . . . friend," as Wedderburn put it, "who . . . does nothing feebly."[2] Most political memorialists of the later eighteenth century wrote of him, and none, as Laughton should have known, assessed him as a political nonentity.

Yet his celebrity faded. Except as a sailor Johnstone was forgotten. In the years following his death, few writers except the naval historians Beatson, Charnock, and Ralfe, all of whom found his conduct unforgivable, cared to remember Johnstone. His sin had been, on the basis of an unorthodox theory, publicly to denounce Admiral Howe's failure in battle and then, when he himself obtained a similar opportunity, to do no better.

In modern times there have been three biographical essays on Johnstone. Each is part of a larger work and none is a well-balanced study of his life. The earliest of these and already mentioned is by J. K. Laughton, yet another naval historian, who was almost exclusively interested in Johnstone's career in the Royal Navy: he accords, for example, not one line to Johnstone's work as a colonial governor. Dunbar Rowland, by contrast, wrote of him in 1911 in a preface to a collection of documents relating to West Florida in the 1760s.[3] Understandably, most of what he wrote concerned Johnstone as governor of that province. In the 1960s Ian Christie wrote an excellently researched study of Johnstone for Namier and Brooke's *The House of Commons, 1754–1790*. His emphasis was naturally on Johnstone's activities as a member of Parliament.

Nobody has attempted to trace his political work as a proprietor and director in that other pillar of eighteenth-century England, East India House, nor to plumb his role in the peace commission sent to the warring colonies in 1778. Most important of all, no historian has tried to assess the ways in which his various careers interacted upon one another and to portray the whole man.

Such a consideration is now attempted, greatly facilitated by documents unused in the existing published works on Johnstone, such as the Johnstone family correspondence in the Edinburgh University Library, Johnstone's letters to his brother William in the Huntington Library, San Marino, California, and one letter in particular in the Pennsylvania Historical Society Library, Philadelphia, which throws completely new light on Johnstone's view of the peace commission on which he served.

George Johnstone, nevertheless, remains an elusive figure. The surviving evidence is fragmentary and does not reveal all we should like to know. Who were the mistresses by whom he had five children? What did he actually say to the woman who accused him of trying to bribe congressmen? What made him so confident that he would be given cabinet office? The evidence does not say. If lacunae fail to answer questions, discoveries too can be disconcerting; such as that Johnstone had shared quarters with his one-time secretary for thirteen years.[4] No hint of the fact is contained elsewhere: we know next to nothing, therefore, about the relation between Johnstone and the man who was probably his best friend.

All the same, if incomplete, the surviving evidence, when pieced together, has some coherence and shows a colorful—almost polychromatic—man who had defects aplenty but also a driving force and ability which time and again made him a credible candidate for positions of responsibility to superiors who knew all about his record. Reconstructing his career also offers insight into the way in which colonies were administered, men advanced, bills passed, governments embarrassed, campaigns spoiled, as well as other processes in the bizarre, subtle, and vital society of Britain in the eighteenth century.

My debts to others in writing this biographical study are innumerable. My creditors range from William Hickey, who thought it worthwhile to record gossip about his contemporary, to my father, who helped me solidify my ideas on Johnstone by letting me chat about him. To the staffs of all the several libraries where I worked or from which I obtained research materials I am indebted. Without exception they were courteous and helpful. I ought also to say grateful prayers to those who conceived the interlibrary loan system. More specifically I wish to thank Maggie Fabel for her patience, Larry Owsley for his encouragement, Gordon Bond for his humor, Barbara Mowat for her professionalism, Joe Harrison for his erudition, and Bob Rea, who first drew attention to the need for a life of Johnstone, for his learning and wisdom. The interest of all of these in my efforts has sustained me. I also thank Auburn University for a research grant in the summer of 1975 which facilitated my quest for Johnstone material.

R.F.A.F.

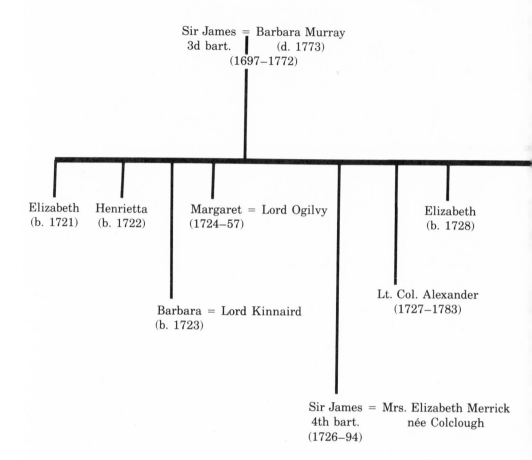

Sir James = Barbara Murray
3d bart.   (d. 1773)
(1697–1772)

Elizabeth   Henrietta   Margaret = Lord Ogilvy   Elizabeth
(b. 1721)   (b. 1722)   (1724–57)   (b. 1728)

Barbara = Lord Kinnaird   Lt. Col. Alexander
(b. 1723)   (1727–1783)

Sir James = Mrs. Elizabeth Merrick
4th bart.   née Colclough
(1726–94)

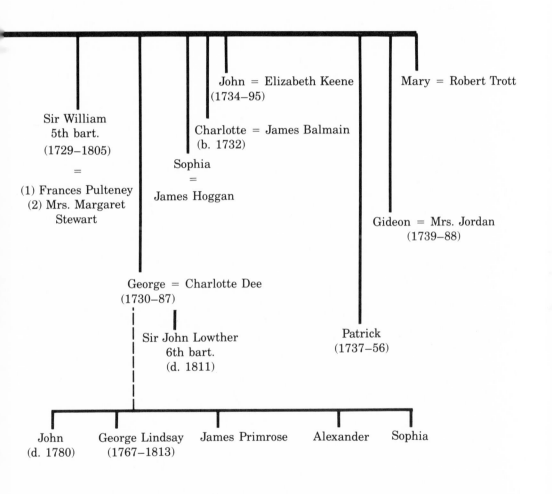

Sir William
5th bart.
(1729–1805)

=

(1) Frances Pulteney
(2) Mrs. Margaret
Stewart

Sophia
=
James Hoggan

Charlotte = James Balmain
(b. 1732)

John = Elizabeth Keene
(1734–95)

Mary = Robert Trott

Gideon = Mrs. Jordan
(1739–88)

George = Charlotte Dee
(1730–87)

Sir John Lowther
6th bart.
(d. 1811)

Patrick
(1737–56)

John
(d. 1780)

George Lindsay
(1767–1813)

James Primrose

Alexander

Sophia

Bombast and Broadsides

1. Man of War

Like the hero of a novel by Sir Walter Scott, George Johnstone was of an ancient but impoverished family of Border gentry. An ancestor, Sir Adam Johnston, had distinguished himself under the command of the Earl of Douglas at the notable Scottish victory of Sark in 1448. An elder son of Sir Adam was the founder of the famous Annandale branch of the Johnstone family, but it was from Matthew, a younger son, that the Johnstones of Westerhall, the line to which George belonged, descended. The winged spur, the heraldic device of his family, was assumed because several members, before the union of the crowns, served the Scottish king as wardens of the West Borders attempting, as their duty, to suppress the moss-troopers who ravaged the country near the boundary with England.[1]

The family moved from Lanarkshire to Dumfriesshire in the reign of James I of England, when James Johnstone, the sixth laird of Westraw, purchased the Glendinnings estate in Eskdale in 1624 and renamed it Westerhall. John Johnstone, his great-grandson, was made a baronet of Nova Scotia on April 25, 1700. Three years earlier another James Johnstone had been born. He was destined to be the third baronet and George Johnstone's father. In 1719 the future Sir James married Barbara Murray, daughter of the fourth Lord Elibank. The marriage, which lasted fifty-three years, produced seven daughters and seven sons, of whom George was the fourth. He was probably educated at home, since Sir James seems to have employed resident tutors for his boys.[2] But, as a cadet with almost no chance of inheriting the family title—although, against long odds, his son eventually did—George had to make his own way in the world and, at an early but not abnormally young age for the day, became a sailor. Many years later he was to tell the House of Commons that he first went to sea in 1744, but it could have been earlier.[3] When he took his lieutenant's examination on December 5, 1749, he offered evidence that he had served six years, fifteen weeks, and two days at sea in the king's vessels, and a certificate proving service in the merchant marine as well. Thus he could not have begun his official naval career later than 1743 when he was thirteen years old.[4] His first ship was a man-of-war commanded, we are told, by a relative. Almost certainly this kinsman was his uncle George, one of the Elibank Murrays, who at that time held the rank of captain, and who offered a place to his nephew, the first of many instances in which Johnstone's blood relationships with the Murrays served him well.[5] The wealthiest and most influential of the family was Patrick, the fifth Lord Elibank, who became rich through marriage to a Dutch nobleman's daughter who was ten years older than he but who owned large estates. Elibank liked his nephew George, knew many useful and distinguished men, and later worked closely with him in connection with Indian and Floridian affairs. All of this lay in the future. Initially, far from associating with the great, Johnstone served his naval apprenticeship in a series of humble positions—although he was lucky enough, according to an implausible rumor current in the later eighteenth century, to earn sufficient prize money on his first voyage to make himself independent of his father.[6]

During his first six years on royal ships he served as able seaman, midshipman, and, on the *Edinburgh,* captain's servant; he saw much action and demonstrated the rash bravery which was to distinguish him throughout his life. He is supposed, for example, after serving on the *Lark,* to have been refused a certificate by her commander, John Crookshanks, and in consequence to have challenged him to a duel. The captain accepted and received a ball in the neck.[7] The truth of this tale cannot be substantiated, but it is a fact that Johnstone served on the *Lark* as a midshipman for over a year and that, whereas other captains under whom he served provided certificates testifying to his competence and diligence, which Johnstone offered in support of his application for a lieutenancy, Captain Crookshanks of the *Lark* did not.

More creditable was the bravery which Johnstone is supposed to have shown while serving under Captain Brodie on the *Canterbury* during the attack on Port Louis, Hispaniola, on March 8, 1747/8. It is said that he boarded and attached a chain to an enemy fireship, thus enabling it to be towed clear of the British squadron.[8] Ships' logs are customarily laconic on such subjects, and the deed is not mentioned in the log of the *Canterbury* for that date.[9] It did occur, however, and required courage of the highest order. The boats detached to neutralize the fireship had to ply within the shadow of the fort at Port Louis. All involved ran the risk of extinction from the guns of the garrison or from small arms, for "musketry played very smartly" upon them, but none would attract more fire than the individual who hauled himself aboard the fireship. His identity was not specified in the official report of Admiral Knowles, the commander of the expedition. Knowles was, however, on Johnstone's ship, the *Canterbury,* throughout the action, and would have known if the hero of the day was not Johnstone, who could probably not have acquired a reputation for this gallantry if the credit belonged elsewhere.[10]

The navy was reduced after peace was made with France in 1748. Although Johnstone passed his lieutenant's examination in 1749, he was not given a lieutenant's appointment until war drums began to beat again in 1755, the prelude to the Seven Years War. Of his activities in the years between little is known. As a young man in his early twenties various social diversions no doubt occupied part of his time. In 1751 he used them as an excuse for not replying to a letter from "a lady of rank" in Scotland and referred, in his letter of apology, to his reading in both French and English as well as to his own attempts to write.[11] It was probably at this time that, in place of formal schooling, he acquired that acquaintance with literature and history which later affected his gubernatorial reports and parliamentary speeches.[12]

It is likely that he spent some if not most of his leisure time at Ballencrieff, the country seat of "my adopted father," Lord Elibank, in preference to Westerhall and the company of his true parents, of whose eccentricities Johnstone was well aware; his father was obsessed with speculation and his mother was highly temperamental.

For Elibank, by contrast, he felt such affection that he could not resist copying and sending to his brother William a long panegyrical passage from his reading which he considered descriptive of his uncle.[13] Patrick Murray was indeed a talented man. Witty and original, he was keenly interested in intellectual questions and as much at his ease in the company of women as of men. He was also extremely knowledgeable: even erudite Samuel Johnson told Boswell that he was never with Elibank without learning something from him.[14]

Elibank possessed every qualification to be a successful author except one—application. But, although he lacked industry, he loved literature and was rich, and made himself a noted patron of men of literary and oratorical promise, particularly of young clergymen. The liveliest company in Scotland met at the house of Elibank, who made it an outpost of the Enlightenment by encouraging unconventional theorizing and liberal sentiments. In matters of literary taste and composition Scotland was supposedly controlled by a triumvirate consisting of David Hume and Lords Elibank and Kames.[15] For Johnstone, acceptance into the Ballencrieff sphere, if he spent much time in it, would have been a more than adequate intellectual substitute, given the standard of universities then, for the formal education which he lacked. The young sailor never penetrated the inner circle of Scottish intellectual life, comprising the thirty members of the aptly named Select Society, which his uncle helped to found in 1754. Perhaps he might have done so had he been more firmly anchored in Scotland. But seafaring expeditions apart, he also involved himself in complicated amatory ventures in London.

Passing three days in the capital after an appointment in Woodford, Johnstone had met at the Mile End Assembly the twenty-two-year-old widow de Cour. He detailed her charms to an unnamed confidante, using the cliché-ridden vocabulary of eighteenth-century erotic literature, and asked for assistance. Perhaps it was as well, he added confusingly, that his heart was already given to a Miss Pratville.[16] Although the incident raises many questions which are not answered, it does confirm that he was "of an amorous complexion," a claim made by an anonymous writer of a biographical sketch of Johnstone which appeared in a gossip magazine in 1781.[17] It is a reminder too that among the fashionable in those days, a commitment to a lady of equal social class by no means barred a man from dalliance with a woman of inferior class: that Mistress de Cour had no elevated position in society is suggested by the location both of the assembly rooms and of her home, which was in Hackney.[18]

Diversion, however, was not Johnstone's sole concern at this stage of his career. A legal document of 1753 referred to him as "captain of *The Grace* bound for Jamaica."[19] This was, presumably, a mercantile interlude preceding his return to the king's service. The Admiralty appointed Johnstone lieutenant of the *Sutherland* in October 1755 but transferred him to the *Biddeford,* on which his younger brother Gideon was serving, in March 1756. Johnstone voyaged on the *Biddeford* once more to the West Indies where, not the only time in his naval career, he was court-martialed.[20] The incidents which led to his trial were trivial but illustrated Johnstone's penchant for quarreling and his concern for the rights of office to the detriment of more important considerations, both of which were to characterize his later career.

At four in the afternoon of February 20, 1757, the acting master of the *Biddeford,* George Roberts, took over the watch from Johnstone, who had been on duty with the starboard watch. The crew was depleted by sickness, a squall was brewing, and Roberts told Johnstone that William Preston of the starboard watch was, by order of Captain Digby, to be transferred to Roberts' own, the larboard watch. Johnstone refused to permit the transfer. He would obey an order from Digby in person or from what he called "a proper officer" but not from Digby through Roberts. Roberts simply repeated that these were the captain's orders. When Digby heard of Johnstone's pettifoggery, not, perhaps, the first example he had experienced of such uncooperative quibbling, he decided to court-martial him.

The trial took place on board the *Dreadnought* in Port Royal harbor, Jamaica, on February 22, and despite favorable evidence from the acting mate, Gideon Johnstone, the court found against his older brother.[21] Johnstone was guilty of disobedience, but in consideration of his former gallant behavior in the service, the officers sitting in judgment sentenced him merely to be reprimanded by the president of the court and to be returned to duty. This insignificant incident was subsequently used as a textbook example of "unmixed disobedience," in that there was no "admixture of insolence or drunkenness."[22]

Although Johnstone was transferred from the *Biddeford* on the day after his court-martial, his condemnation did not prevent his further advance in the naval profession. His next major appointment came late in October 1757, when he joined the *Augusta,* a 60-gun vessel of the line based at Jamaica. Her captain, Arthur Forrest, had obtained his first command in 1741, but years of experience had not dulled his dash. On October 21, 1757, the *Augusta* was cruising off the coast of Hispaniola in company with two other vessels of equal size, the *Dreadnought* and the *Edinburgh,* when the *Dreadnought's* lookout spied a large French convoy near Cape François. It was escorted by four enemy ships of the line and three frigates. Despite an obvious disparity in fighting force, Forrest, the senior officer, after the scantiest of consultations with his fellow commanders, decided to attack. The British took no prizes, but it was the French who had to break off the engagement after their flagship signalled that she would have to be towed out of the battle line. On both sides the warships had been badly mauled and had to retire to port to refit. Johnstone took part in this battle, which is remembered as "the action off Cape François," in the *Dreadnought*, to which he seems to have been temporarily attached and which had led the attack. Her captain, Maurice Suckling, wrote that Johnstone had distinguished himself in the action.[23]

Only afterward, and probably because one of the nine *Augusta* sailors killed in the battle was the first lieutenant, did he transfer to Forrest's vessel and consequently, in December, take part in a much more successful exploit. Prisoners from a captured French privateer had reported that a rich fleet of armed merchantmen was preparing to leave Port-au-Prince in Haiti for Europe. The commanding admiral at Jamaica detached the *Augusta* under Forrest to cruise off Hispaniola for two days before rejoining the rest of the squadron, which consisted of the admiral's flagship, the 90-gun *Marlborough,* and the 60-gun *Princess Mary.* Forrest sailed between Hispaniola and the island of Gonave, which was daringly close to the main island. He flew Dutch colors and disguised the *Augusta's* identity with tarpaulins. Passing up opportunities to make minor captures, he concentrated on finding and isolating the sloop escorting the awaited convoy after it left Port-au-Prince. He succeeded in taking her at night without an exchange of cannonfire, which would have alarmed other French vessels. Aboard this sloop, Forrest placed a lieutenant and thirty-five men. Their job was to prevent any fleeing Frenchmen from reentering the shelter of Port-au-Prince. Forrest then sailed through the night and caught up with the enemy convoy at dawn. *Augusta* went along its length, firing at each of its ships in turn. It sounds an easier maneuver than it was, for the convoy was not without defense. Between them the enemy vessels carried 112 guns. Nevertheless, before long three of the ships struck their flags and, with British prize crews aboard, were used by Forrest to subdue the remainder and to shepherd them back to Jamaica.[24]

Johnstone impressed Forrest as a "brave, active, diligent and capable officer,"[25] but he appeared in a quite different light to the rear admiral of the White, Thomas Cotes, who commanded all British naval forces on the Jamaica station. The trouble, as trouble often did, concerned the distribution of prize money. Under the Convoys and Cruisers Act of 1708, which was still in force in the 1750s, after the value of a prize had been assessed by an Admiralty court, the sum was divided into eighths. The commander of a captor ship received three-eighths, his commissioned officers, his warrant officers, and the flag officer over him received an eighth each, while the remaining two-eighths were shared by the crew members. It seems that Johnstone became incensed that Admiral Cotes had intervened to secure a share of the prize money earned by the *Augusta* off Port-au-Prince for her sister ships, *Marlborough* and *Princess Mary,* which were certainly part of the same squadron, but which had not been present when the convoy was captured.

When Johnstone was angry he had a tendency to use indecorous language, and the circumstances in which he used it matched his words on this occasion. He had attended a concert in Port Royal, Jamaica, on June 9, 1758, during which he had been obliged to go to the privy. There he fortuitously met a lawyer, George Lewis. They started to discuss prize money. The *Augusta* had initiated a case contesting the claims of the *Marlborough* and the *Princess Mary* to any share of the prize money arising from the affair off Port-au-Prince. Lewis represented the *Augusta* in the case, and Johnstone must have supposed himself safe when he told the lawyer that the intervention of Admiral Cotes in the business was "impertinent" and that he deserved to "have his arse kicked." He was mistaken. Cotes was in a position to intimidate Lewis into betraying Johnstone's indiscretions and must have done so extremely quickly, for on June 12, three days after his meeting with Lewis, Johnstone was summoned to Cotes' flagship. On arrival he found that the admiral had also called together all the captains under his command at Port Royal to inquire into Johnstone's behavior.

The occasion did not reduce Johnstone to deference. He stood with arms akimbo, which irritated the flag officer. He then placed them behind his back, but Cotes was not satisfied until the young officer was at attention with arms at his sides. The treacherous Lewis then presented a paper which revealed in full his conversation with Johnstone and included a list of questions compiled by Johnstone for Lewis' use in court in the prize-money case. The upshot was that Admiral Cotes suspended Johnstone from his duties as a naval officer: it was possibly the prelude to a court-martial.[26]

Forrest was disappointed that the Admiralty in London failed to share his belief that the *Augusta* alone was entitled to prize money for the captures off Port-au-Prince[27] and he regretted that, in suspending Johnstone, Cotes had deprived him of "a good officer."[28] In the long run, though, he came to the judicious conclusion that the young Scot was "incapable of subordination."[29]

Johnstone was long embroiled in a tussle over the legality of his behavior respecting Cotes. Ultimately he did not have to endure another court-martial but neither was he reinstated on the *Augusta* which, on July 16, 1758, exchanged lieutenants with the sloop *Tryal.* Johnstone, and perhaps this was the purpose of the exchange, which was no doubt ordered by Cotes, found himself serving under a martinet.[30]

Captain Thomas Cookson did not get on well with Johnstone nor, it seems, with any of his officers. The only evidence that he enjoyed any popularity with the ship's company is that once, when he ordered the issue of grog to sick men contrary to the instructions of the ship's doctor, the men cheered him. The long, uncomfortable, and dangerous journey which the *Tryal* made in 1758 from the West Indies to Plymouth engendered great bitterness between Cookson and those under him. If Johnstone's word is to be believed, the captain, while engaged in fraud himself, accused the innocent purser of the same offense, calling him "Dog, Rascal and Scoundrell." He caused the death of the mate by making him sleep in stifling heat when he was sick. In addition he flogged men without mercy for no reason, deprived the ship's surgeon of all assistance, intimidated sailors into spying on the officers and, once the *Tryal* was back in England, refused to allow his men, who were dying of scurvy, to go ashore or to receive fresh provisions. Incompetence was added to cruelty. The ship ran out of candles and oil and Cookson would not allow Johnstone to obtain any from friends in the fleet; when the *Tryal,* its maindeck awash, lost the convoy it was supposed to accompany, Cookson had the mate falsify the log. Johnstone's remonstrances were ignored. The whole of Cookson's conduct to his officers and men, wrote Johnstone in charges against his captain, "hath been one continual scene of meanness, avarice, ignorance, cruelty and scandalous behaviour, unbecoming the character of an officer & gentlemen." Cookson, however, took the initiative. Immediately upon arrival in England in December 1758, it seems, he lodged a complaint against William Thompson, the purser. The Admiralty ordered a court-martial on January 1, 1759, as a result of which Thompson was reprimanded for imprudence. In spite of a press report that Cookson, too, would be tried, for some reason he never was, and Johnstone, no doubt burning with unappeased resentment and with his reputation for trouble-making enhanced, was unemployed.[31]

Thus opened the year 1759, *annus miserabilis* for Johnstone. Perhaps because of privations endured on the *Tryal,* he was in poor health, to the distress of his mother who grieved for "my dutiful, my more than dutiful son."[32] This was scarcely how the Admiralty regarded him, and for some months he was kicking his heels in London. The philosopher Hume wrote his friend Lord Elibank in the spring to say: "I have seen pretty often your Nephew, Mr. Johnstone; & I think him a very gallant sensible young fellow. By the accounts I hear, he will soon be provided for, & have the Reward of his services."[33] Hume was too optimistic, but he was right in suggesting that Johnstone had patrons; without them he would have looked in vain for advancement.

One such patron was Hume's correspondent. Elibank had a link with a courtier, the earl of Guildford, who was close to Lord Anson, the first lord of the Admiralty. When Johnstone wrote a letter to Guildford, setting out the reasons that he should be granted preferment, he was able to enclose a supporting letter from Elibank. It is clear that the warmth of Guildford's reply to Johnstone derived from Elibank's endorsement of his application. He promised to speak to Anson in the lieutenant's favor.[34] Perhaps Johnstone also used as an intermediary that other uncle, now Vice-Admiral Murray, who had commanded one of Anson's ships on his most famous voyage. Whichever means were used, they proved effective. From a letter written by Sir Gilbert Elliot in November 1759, it appears that Johnstone had been given a promise of a command by Anson.

Elliot, another lord of the Admiralty, was inclined to help George because he was a friend of his brother James. His advice was that the lieutenant should ensure that Anson keep his promise by extending his convalescence and staying in England until he had secured his command. Even so, Sir Gilbert thought little of Johnstone's chances for promotion thereafter unless he got well away from Britain and rehabilitated his reputation through acts of gallantry in distant theaters.[35]

Johnstone's letters to his brother William from this period reflect boredom, worry, and the frustrated ambition of a young officer frantic for the command of a sizable vessel. Instead, the year 1759 saw him employed in a series of odd jobs. In July, under the direction of Commodore Boys, he was given temporary charge of an armed cutter, the *Prince of Wales,* operating in the Downs, one of several vessels on which he served at this time. Another was the 50-gun *Preston.*[36] In October he was shuttling between Dover and Deal. Mortified to learn that William had suffered a difference of opinion with Gilbert Elliot, he envisioned his patron's becoming his enemy. Although quite unconcerned for his mother, whose spleen, he coolly opined, would destroy her, he grieved for his sisters' prospects on hearing that his father was engaged in a speculative venture. With time on his hands, he summarized for his brother the plot of a novel which he had written, interesting only for its (limited) parallels with his own life: he foresaw that the hero would rise from lieutenant to admiral and end up being made an alderman and speaking nonsense in Parliament.[37] During this frustrating interval he managed only one coup of significance: the capture, while serving on the sloop *Viper,* of a Dutch ship carrying indigo and cotton.[38]

Finally on February 6, 1760, Lord Anson fulfilled his promise and Johnstone was given his long-awaited command, the sloop *Hornet* of 14 guns. Its main duties initially were as an escort vessel, first of a transport, the *Anne,* and a tender, the *Industry,* to Newcastle-on-Tyne, then of troop transports to and from Germany. It was while the *Hornet* was subsequently stationed at Yarmouth to protect the mackerel fleet that Johnstone first obtained promising opportunities to capture prizes. The French privateers which preyed on the fishing boats could usually outsail the *Hornet,* but her commander was able to report in June that he had captured the *Free Mason* of Dunkirk, a cutter equipped with a crew of fifteen hands and four swivel guns.[39]

Most of the difficulties with which Johnstone had to cope during this period were routine: the *Hornet* went aground off Yarmouth; several members of the crew deserted, while others fell sick. In September, however, he had to deal with a complicated and difficult problem. Employed once more on convoy duty, the *Hornet* was escorting a tender, the *James and Thomas,* when the 128 impressed men on it mutinied. With characteristic fortitude, Johnstone went aboard the tender, faced the mutineers, and tried to persuade them to submit to their lot; he then returned to the *Hornet,* leaving the *James and Thomas* in command of a Lieutenant Saxe. Once Johnstone had gone, the men climbed up to the deck from the hold on a ladder foolishly left there by Saxe, and promising the lieutenant that they would cause no trouble, talked Saxe into allowing them out onto the deck. Once on deck, the mutineers forced Saxe to leave the tender and tried to sail away to freedom.[40]

Johnstone acted effectively in the emergency. After firing a shot across the bows of the mutineers' vessel, he poured two broadsides into her. The tender hove to. The mutineers' defiance was not erased by Johnstone's gunpowder, however. Ten days later they tried again to get control of the tender by sawing through a bulkhead, but the attempt was discovered and Johnstone put two men in irons, transferring others to another tender. Finally the *Hornet* arrived at Sheerness on October 14 with all but one of the pressed men alive, although nine were wounded. Commander Johnstone had shown coolness and sense in retrieving a dangerous situation brought about, as he did not hesitate to point out, by a subordinate who had shown poor judgment and a tendency to panic. It was Johnstone, however, who was court-martialed; with justice he was completely exonerated.[41]

The *Hornet*'s next voyage was to Lisbon, and Johnstone had better luck with prizes. While still in the English Channel he took a French snow privateer with fifty-eight men on board.[42] He was able to leave her at Plymouth before continuing on his way to Portugal, during which leg of the voyage he captured the *Society,* a brigantine of 6 guns and a crew of sixty.[43] His good fortune was balanced by the mortification of seeing two other prey escape, for which he blamed the poor condition of the *Hornet.* For fourteen hours, he chased a snow among the Seven Stones, where she foundered as, almost, did the *Hornet.* Even more galling was his encounter with an 18-gun privateer. He chased her for twenty-seven hours, until his crew was dropping with fatigue, after which a lucky breeze enabled his opponent to escape.[44] Finally in company with the prize *Society,* the *Hornet* reached Lisbon on January 22, 1761.

Nobody could guess from what remains of Johnstone's letters written during his first tour of duty at Lisbon that Portugal was in the midst of a particularly interesting stage in its political development at the time of his arrival there. Dominant was the Marquês of Pombal, who had made his reputation in the wake of the great Lisbon earthquake of 1755 by energetically implementing his maxim of "bury the dead and feed the living." The subservience of King Joseph I to his premier gave Pombal full scope to pursue policies which politically owed something to the French—both to their *philosophes* and to Louis XIV—and economically to the British example. With speed and vigor he sought to cut back the power of the nobility, to curb the influence of the church, to reduce the Society of Jesus to impotence, and to foster Portuguese industry and commerce. It was Pombal more than another candidate, John V, who deserves the title of the "Portuguese enlightened despot" in that he achieved more, although, as with most enlightened despots, it is all too easy to discern facets of Pombal distinguished more by darkness than by light.

His policies provoked a fierce reaction. The Jesuits, furious that Pombal had freed the Indians of Brazil and had denied the right of missionaries to exercise the civil power over them, conspired with some of the Portuguese nobility to assassinate King Joseph in 1758. Thus indirectly had they intended to annihilate Pombal's power. Instead the attempt, being unsuccessful, enormously strengthened the minister. It enabled him to consign the nobles directly involved, both men and women, to the wheel and the ax and to fill the prisons with those less closely concerned, a process still under way while Johnstone was in Lisbon. The Society of Jesus was banned from Portugal in September 1759; the only members remaining in the country were those who had taken part in the plot against the king, for whom Pombal thought exile too mild a punishment.[45]

Britain had maintained close commercial ties with Portugal from the mid-seventeenth century, but after the signing of the Methuen treaty of 1703, the relationship became almost colonial. Sometimes depicted as mutually advantageous—the English learned to drink port and the Portuguese to wear Yorkshire woollens—Britain was in fact the prosperous senior partner who could and did compel the destruction of possible competitors like, for example, the budding Portuguese textile industry. The English factories in Portugal were not places for manufacturing but not merely depositories either. They were agencies for handling imports. Pombal saw correctly that Brazilian diamonds and gold were ultimately enriching British rather than Portuguese merchants. He began a policy of fostering Portuguese concerns and breaking the British monopoly of the wine trade in northern Portugal. Favoring colonial over foreign trade, he established companies to nourish business with Portugal's possessions abroad both to the east and to the west.[46] This economic policy had already begun when Johnstone arrived in Portugal but, like another of Pombal's favorite schemes, the rebuilding of Lisbon, it took time to fulfill.

Lisbon in 1761 was probably the least prepossessing capital in the world. As yet, almost no reconstruction of public buildings had followed the great earthquake of 1755, the bizarre exception being a gigantic arsenal. The squeaking wheels of the primitive ox-carts in the Lisbon streets offended the ears: their superstitious drivers would not grease their axles because they believed the noise kept away the devil. To this noise an Italian traveler, Joseph Baretti, preferred the stench from the piles of refuse blocking many of the capital's thoroughfares. Manufactures of any quality, even of simple items like shoes, were all imported and consequently expensive. The cost of living was high: although fish was cheap, board at an inn of moderate quality cost a guinea a day. Visitors noticed and often deplored the dominance of the Catholic church in Portugal. Although Pombal had expelled the Jesuits, the Inquisition was still active in persecuting Jews who, in defiance of the law, continued to practice their religion. The presence of subjects who were Jewish by race, together with many blacks, mestizos, and mulattoes, gave Lisbon an exotic character which could be either exciting or alarming. The Portuguese were suspicious of foreigners and in rural areas were known to stone them.[47]

Johnstone had not wanted to be sent to Portugal from England because he rightly believed that only in London could he effectively practice the reminding, cajoling, and pleading which were the tactics of the successful post seeker. Nevertheless, once in Lisbon, four months after Baretti's departure, the Scotsman found that banishment had its compensations, one of which was the winter sunshine that provided, as he gloatingly wrote to his brother William, "the most temperate serene air of genial warmth." He lodged with a Mr. Mayne, whose house he considered the most agreeable in the entire city. A fellow lodger, Thomas Pasley, was a good friend. The British envoy at the capital treated Johnstone as a relative and while he was in port he enjoyed good company every day and "a round of pleasure every night." He found the ruins of Lisbon "romantick," the women pretty, and the people as a whole strange but with a novel charm.[48]

By August the pleasures of novelty had quite worn off and Johnstone was exclusively obsessed by schemes to obtain his post captaincy. It was important that he should be recalled before peace came or, as he preferred to put it "the everlasting gates of Jacinus shall turn on their Hungry Hinges."[49] He suggested two methods. The first was to have the *Hornet,* which was old, leaky, and foul, ordered back to England for careening, a reasonable proposition in that she could escort a convoy from Portugal on the voyage and it would cost the government less to clean the *Hornet* in a royal dockyard than in Lisbon. If this scheme proved infeasible, Johnstone suggested that a replacement for the *Hornet* might be sent to Lisbon and the *Hornet* permanently retired from the Portuguese station. Lest neither device to get Johnstone back to England succeeded, he suggested a third possibility—that he should be appointed post captain to a ship in England without actually being on the spot. He wanted his brother to remind Sir Gilbert Elliott of the promise he had made to help make Johnstone a post captain before peace came, apparently abandoning his original hope that he would obtain advancement through Anson's influence.[50]

A few words on the significance of the promotion to post captain may be appropriate here to account for the intensity of Johnstone's anguish in having to wait for it.[51] The post captain stood to make much more money than a junior officer, however competent. "Being made post" brought appointment to a larger ship of at least the sixth rate. As captain of a frigate Johnstone would be able to outsail and beat vessels which the *Hornet* could not hope to catch or outgun. This fact alone would improve a new captain's income from prize money; but of more importance was the established proportion of the value of a prize which a captain received. Whereas a lieutenant on a vessel which took a merchantman would be given only one-eighth of its value, which he would have to share equally with the master, marine officer, and physician, a post captain was entitled to at least one-fourth of its value for himself alone, and in some circumstances as much as three-eighths.

Important as the remunerative implications of a post captaincy were, particularly for one with Johnstone's nose for profit, they were a minor aspect of the rank. The greater advantage of the promotion was that it placed an officer on a ladder which led surely, if he survived without disgracing himself, to flag rank. Whether employed or not, the post captain would move up its rungs. It was a flawed system resulting in admirals too old for efficiency, as Britain was to discover to its cost in the American war. Yet Johnstone's anxiety to obtain a post captaincy as soon as possible is understandable: without it he had no future in the navy.

He was destined to wait a long time for it. Meanwhile he benefited both his reputation and his pocket through action. Quite apart from the vessels which he captured en route to Portugal he took at least five more prizes after he arrived there. They were small vessels—snows, brigs, a sloop. With a better vessel than the *Hornet* he could have captured more of them and have aspired to hunt bigger game, but it was also no doubt with his recall in mind that he stressed, in correspondence to the Admiralty, that the *Hornet* was sixteen years old and, because her stem was split, in need of not just careening but major repair.[52]

To counteract her poor sailing qualities Johnstone resorted to disguise. He stepped the mizzen mast of the *Hornet* and took measures to conceal her guns and the size of her crew. Instead of vainly trying to outsail the French privateers which so often eluded him, he tried to lure them to close quarters where the *Hornet's* superiority in men and metal would tell. He seems to have succeeded on one occasion.[53] His captures may have been small but were profitable, even if he had the chagrin of sharing his prize money with others. A brig from Martinique which Johnstone took, for example, was sold for £5,000, of which he received £400.[54]

Johnstone's small captures harmed Britain's enemies only minimally; of more service to his nation was the use to which he put one of his prizes. As soon as he learned that Britain had declared war on Spain on January 4, 1762, he dispatched a captured French privateer under John M'Laurin, master of the *Hornet,* to convey the news of the Spanish war to British naval units in the West Indies.

George Rodney, who commanded in the Leeward Islands, made good use of the intelligence. He at once sent messages to Jamaica asking the British admiral responsible for the western Caribbean to seize all Spanish ships at the island and the governor to embargo all Spanish trade. Rodney knew that officials in the Spanish colonies had received no notice of their country's entry into what became known as the Seven Years War and attempted to prolong their ignorance by deploying cruisers to capture the packets which had left Spain bearing the war declaration. He asserted that his ships took every one of them—with the result that knowledge of formal war was denied the Spanish colonists for months. Sir George Pocock and the British invasion fleet were in sight of Havana before the governor of Cuba knew with certainty that the British were his enemies. Had it not been for Johnstone the British in the West Indies would have foregone exceptional opportunities, since Rodney was not officially informed from London that Spain was at war until after successful offensives were well under way.[55] The admiral was grateful to Johnstone and their friendship proved lifelong.

Portugal was to be important in Johnstone's life. For a time during the American war he was to command all British naval forces on the Portuguese station and to use Lisbon as a base for diplomatic and intelligence ventures. In that he found in Lisbon the woman destined to become his wife, Portugal eventually would radically affect his domestic life. At this early stage of his career it was probably the social opportunities afforded by Lisbon which did most to offset his professional frustration, although he may also have formed commercial connections there. Most of those in the English community in Lisbon were associated in one way or another with the English factory, which contained "a set of dissatisfied, restless, proud and extravagant fellows" whom Johnstone probably found congenial company. The Portuguese king had given the factory a privileged position and business was brisk, because in 1762 Anglo-Portuguese trade was only just beginning to decline from its peak for the century.[56] That the Scot may have had a commercial link with the factory was hinted when he wrote to the Admiralty that "I shall ever remain in my private Capacity as bound to the Factory of Lisbon," although the phrase is ambiguous and may simply have meant that he had friends there.[57]

Before returning to England in May, 1762, he managed to take one more vessel. A brigantine, the *Fox Hunter,* belonging to a convoy out of Oporto, was abandoned by its Portuguese captain and crew because it seemed on the point of sinking. Johnstone placed a lieutenant and eighteen volunteers on board, who succeeded in pumping her out and sailing her most of the way back to England, although she had to be towed by the *Hornet* in the final stretch of the voyage.[58]

Once home, Johnstone was promoted to captain but could not assume command of his new vessel, the 24-gun frigate *Hind,* because of an accident that befell him one Saturday night in August when he was walking away from the "Barrick" of a future political associate, Isaac Barré. Without mentioning his sobriety (or lack of it) Johnstone explained that "the weather being extremely dark, and not being acquainted with the ground, I had the misfortune to walk over a precipice" seventeen feet high. He sprained the ligaments in his right leg and suffered bad contusions elsewhere. Of an irascible temperament, he was probably furious at being confined to bed and unable to take over his new ship. In October he wrote to the Admiralty for the discharge of several men from the *Hornet,* presumably so that they could be reappointed to the *Hind.* They were his black servant, Michael Arselin; a cook, Thomas Ginnear; his steward, James Johnstone; and a midshipman, "my relation," Henry Crawford.[59]

Thereafter his convalescence lengthened surprisingly. In November he asked for leave to follow medical advice and patronize the "Hot Pump" at Bath. In December, in reply to Admiralty orders to rejoin his ship, he pleaded that he was having to walk with a stick and that his surgeon and physician agreed that violent exertion might lame him for life.[60] In spite of his condition he was prepared, he wrote, to join his ship, but he gave the impression that he no longer wanted to. The *Hind* sailed without him and he was appointed to the *Wager* in December, but he never walked the deck of either.[61] Of course by the winter of 1762, with peace impending, there were few professional prospects for any naval officer to look forward to in the immediate future. But in this instance one suspects that Johnstone had scented more exciting possibilities connected with the promotion of a fellow Scot, John Stuart, earl of Bute, who became first lord of the treasury on May 26, 1762.

Precisely how Johnstone was able to move into Bute's orbit effectively enough to be offered high preferment is not known. But Barré conceivably, Elibank probably, and John Home almost certainly, had something to do with it. As has been mentioned, Johnstone was associating with Isaac Barré, who enjoyed high favor with the Bute administration, receiving the adjutant generalship of the British army in March and the lucrative governorship of Stirling in May of 1763. He was not necessarily in a position to ask for preferment for Johnstone, but George's uncle, Lord Elibank, was. Bute thought so highly of him that he intended Elibank to fill a vacancy that had occurred among the sixteen Scottish peers in the House of Lords. John Wilkes spoiled this scheme by publishing a letter, written as if by the Old Pretender, the septuagenarian Stuart claimant to the British crown, from his exile in Rome, in which great satisfaction was expressed at the intended appointment because of the debt owed to Elibank for his services to the Stuart cause. Few readers could have taken the letter for anything but a hoax, but the doubts raised about Elibank's loyalty may have been taken more seriously, for his brother Alexander was an undoubted Jacobite. It was as though a potential Reagan appointee were plausibly charged with Communist sympathies. Some members of the House of Lords raised objections to him and Elibank was not made a peer.[62]

Perhaps more important for his nephew's future was the fact that Lord Elibank had been a patron of John Home when he was a struggling dramatist.[63] Home's influence derived from his position as Bute's private secretary. His friend, Alexander Carlyle, suggested that in the distribution of government patronage, Home's power was exceeded only by that of the earl himself, when he wrote that he was "the second man in the kingdom while Bute was in power."[64]

A strange turn of fate had brought the secretary to eminence. He might well have lived and died in the obscurity of a Scottish manse had he not written the successful tragedy *Douglas*. The consequent notoriety outraged the elders of the Church of Scotland, who compelled Home to resign his living. Thereafter he had little luck in interesting theater managers in subsequent plays until in 1757 he became, at the age of thirty-five, Bute's secretary and tutor to the future George III.[65] James Boswell thought that *Douglas* was Home's only commendable play and its writer, although "an ingenious and really good man," something of a coxcomb. Boswell's close friend George Dempster considered foppery Home's dominant trait.[66]

Johnstone evidently found it possible to forgive the personal foibles of the secretary, to whom he was perhaps introduced by his uncle although as fellow members of the Scottish expatriate community in London they might easily have met by accident. Both, for example, are known to have dined at Lord Eglinton's London house, where James Boswell and Johnstone met on one occasion.[67] Johnstone did not captivate the diarist, perhaps because of his reservations about one of Boswell's poems, but he seems to have impressed Home, who according to Carlyle was "easily deluded by pretences, especially to those of romantic valour" and used his influence with Bute to advance to wealth or power "friends" with such pretensions. Barré's colorful military career would have qualified him as one of these. Although Carlyle does not mention Barré, he specifically cites Johnstone as an example.[68]

Johnstone could congratulate himself on a most adroit use of patronage. Bute appears to have done Johnstone several favors, perhaps even arranging for his promotion to captain, but the chief favor which dwarfed all others was to nominate him to a colonial governorship.

For a young naval officer with a spotted career behind him, who had just attained his captaincy after twenty years at sea, whose father had no peerage, and who was a Scot, this was an immense upward leap. Scottishness, normally in the eighteenth century a grave disadvantage, was the very qualification which helped him most, for with the accession of Bute to power the earl's fellow countrymen found preferment. All four of the governorships made available by the gains of the Paris peace treaty of 1763—Canada, the Caribbean islands ceded by the French, and the two Floridas—went to Scots. It is customary to blame Bute for this national bias, but it should be remembered that Home, too, was a Scot and the probability is that it was he who mentioned Johnstone as a possible governor. There is no evidence that Bute was close to Johnstone at this time, and he could have claimed that any obligation that he owed Elibank was discharged by the appointment of the peer's brother, James Murray, to the governorship of Canada. Johnstone, however, was a genuine friend of Home—Carlyle's skeptical use of quotation marks around the word was unwarranted. The naval officer and Home traveled to Scotland together in 1763, and twenty-three years later Home was described in Johnstone's will as "the most worthy of the human race."[69] The probability is that it was thanks to this friendship that George Johnstone was to be governor of West Florida.

Or so he had been promised. He much preferred West Florida to East Florida and had been at pains to point out on a map the difference between the two to Lord Bute! His disappointment was great when he discovered that Lord Egremont, the secretary of state for the southern department, thought Johnstone more fit for the eastern province on the flimsy ground that he was a suitable man "to find out harbours amongst dangerous rocks and shoals." The secretary was notorious for his vehement opposition to the continued exercise of influence by Bute after he had resigned from the premiership on April 16, 1763. Nevertheless the captain begged the fallen earl to intercede for him to ensure that he be sent to West Florida which, he reminded him, was as much a maritime province as East Florida.[70] His plea was successful and he received the royal nomination to the governorship of West Florida on July 14, 1763.[71]

John Home was delighted. From Leith he wrote Bute a letter which makes it clear both that he had never directly asked Bute to give a governorship to Johnstone and that he very much had wanted his friend to have one. It seems doubtful that the earl did not know of Home's preference. Lord Elibank also wrote a grateful letter, as well he might, for Bute had promoted his nephew and his brother, too, to colonial governorships.[72]

When these and other similar nominations were made public, Bute received the full force of vitriolic obloquy for partiality to his fellow Scots in the distribution of governorships. The attack, which also dilated on the tyrannical tendencies of Scots in authority, appeared in an extraordinary issue of John Wilkes's *North Briton* dated September 17, 1763. Johnstone lacked the disposition to bear such treatment passively. His letter of remonstrance was construed as a challenge by the author, who claimed that he would entertain challenges solely from Bute and only if the earl declared Johnstone his champion would he break a lance with the governor. Johnstone replied that he would break no lances with a knot of thieves who were strangers to honor and truth. His intention rather was to break a cudgel over the head of the writer. Then, having persuaded himself that the scribbler of the offensive and anonymous article was a certain Mr. Brooks, Johnstone visited the journalist at his lodgings on October 14 and first punched him and then, to use the vernacular of the day, rubbed him down with an oaken towel. When the weaponless Brooks grappled with him, Johnstone even drew his sword and made two passes at the wretched journalist before being restrained by outsiders attracted to the scene of the brawl by the noise. He was subsequently arrested and released on bail. According to another version of this affair, Brooks was not alone when Johnstone appeared in his room, but was instead attended by two barbers. The governor warned them to keep clear when they attempted to help Brooks, saying that he had already lowered himself sufficiently in chastising their master without the necessity of kicking his footmen too. The affair attracted popular attention and ironical speculation on the prospect for West Floridians.[73] Moreover, it cost Johnstone a great deal of money to extricate himself from the legal consequences of his rashness.[74]

The incident revealed Johnstone's taste for violent solutions and a disregard, in certain circumstances, for his own dignity of which, in other situations, he was inordinately careful. The Brooks affair did not, however, indicate any permanent enmity toward Wilkes, nor did it hinder the confirmation of Johnstone's governorship.[75] His commission was issued on November 21, and his instructions followed on December 7, 1763.[76]

Leisurely as the pace of administrative formality had been, Johnstone, though a man of action, tarried in assuming his governorship, not actually landing in Florida until October 21, 1764. The reason for the long delay was not, probably, so much the legal aftermath of his assault on Brooks, as has been alleged,[77] but rather and almost certainly that he found it impossible to leave unresolved a trouble in which his brother John had mired himself in Bengal.

Exerting influence in the affairs of the East India Company was a good deal easier than obtaining power in English politics in the latter half of the eighteenth century and required only a moderate amount of money. The company's executive board was composed of twenty-four men, but their will could be overruled by the vote of a simple majority in the company's

General Court of Proprietors. To qualify for a voice and a vote in the court one had to possess £500 worth of company stock. George Johnstone had purchased this necessary minimal amount on February 26, 1763, and was thus in a position to use influence in the court to compel the directors to restore his brother to favor.[78] Thus began that deep involvement in the affairs of the East India Company which was to preoccupy Johnstone for the remainder of his life. He never went to India, but several other members of the family did.

Providing for his younger sons was a problem which Sir James Johnstone, like many an eighteenth-century father, solved through the opportunities offered by John Company, as the East India Company was familiarly called at the time. Sir James had seven sons: his eldest, James, was heir to the estates and the baronetcy. He purchased a commission in the army for his second son, Alexander, who for many years held a lieutenant colonelcy in the Seventieth Regiment of Foot. The other five sons were all involved in the East India Company, although George initially looked elsewhere for his career and William became deeply committed only after he became a wealthy man in 1767, when the wife he had married seven years before unexpectedly inherited the fortune of her uncle, the earl of Bath.[79] The remaining three sons, Patrick, Gideon, and John, all went to India as writers, or clerks, in the company. Patrick was unlucky enough to be caught by Siraj-ud-daula's troops in Calcutta in 1756 and perished in the notorious "black hole." Gideon began, like George, as a sailor, turned subsequently to India, where he was a writer between 1765 and 1767, and then went back to the navy, rising to the rank of captain before his death in 1788. His closest approach to fame was when he married a young actress who, as Mrs. Dorothy Jordan, later won notoriety as the mistress of the future William IV.[80] It was the predicament of John, however, which brought George's involvement with the company and it is necessary here to digress into a discussion of John's career if his plight is to be understood.

John Johnstone saw more of India than any of his brothers and was the only member of the family who qualified for the pejorative if envied title of "nabob." Appointed a writer at Fort William, Calcutta, in 1751, he was an assistant at Dacca when the Seven Years War broke out. Like Patrick he was captured, but his imprisonment ended quite differently. Sharing his internment was a Miss Warwick, the elderly daughter of a rich merchant, who thought so well of Johnstone that, shortly before she died, believing that none of her family still lived, she willed him her fortune of £100,000. Released from captivity, John Johnstone, planning to leave India and to establish himself as a substantial landowner in Scotland, sent instructions to his relatives for the purchase of a suitable estate. His intentions were thwarted by the unexpected appearance of a brother of his benefactress. Johnstone at once turned over his new inheritance and cancelled his passage home.[81]

Having renewed his contract with the East India Company at a time of exceptionally favorable opportunity for the able and energetic, John Johnstone secured swift promotion. As a lieutenant fireworker he was in charge of a gun at Plassey on June 23, 1757, when Siraj-ud-daula was defeated. Briefly transferring back to the civil from the military branch of the company's service, he became a factor, then accompanied an expedition to the Northern Circars as paymaster of Francis Forde's troops, after which he went as secretary to Sir Eyre Coote on his campaign to track down the last French force in Bengal. Subsequently he became resident at Midnapore in 1760, chief at Burdwan in 1763, and finally a member of the Bengal council.[82] All the while it appears he was endeavoring his utmost to replace the wealth snatched away from him.

There never was a better time than the late 1750s and early 1760s for shaking the pagoda tree and there never would be again. The era of license ended in 1765 when Clive, posing as a reformer, returned to India. Meanwhile there were some in the employ of the East India Company who did not scruple to exploit unprecedented opportunities for enrichment.

Ever since the foundation of the company it had been tacitly understood that its servants might indulge in private trade as long as they fulfilled their official obligations. The tiny salaries which the company paid—£5 a year to a writer, £15 to a chief factor—made extra income a necessity. The advantageous commercial position which these wretchedly paid underlings were almost compelled to exploit derived from the *dustuk*. This was the privilege which a Mogul emperor had granted to the company of transporting its goods without payment of duty, provided that they were imported from or to be exported to Europe. The *dustuk* was customarily abused and, with the connivance of willing *gomastahs* (Indian agents), many goods belonging to private individuals, both English and Indian, were borne on boats and carts enjoying the protection of the company flag.

While the company remained essentially a mercantile concern, operating by permission of the native political power, there were limitations on the possible degree of exploitation. The situation began to change in the 1740s after the Marquis Dupleix of the French *Compagnie des Indes* demonstrated that the assistance of a European company's army, even if small, to the local political powers might have a disproportionate effect and could decide who was to rule.[83]

A period of rivalry between the French and English companies followed. The outcome would decide not only which European power would be forced out of India but also which Indian potentates in the subsidiary states of the decaying Mogul empire would hold nominal political power. By 1757, the year of John Johnstone's release from captivity, the result of the contest was settled in favor of the British. Thenceforth, until the British government was able, by the parliamentary acts of 1773 and 1784, to exercise authority over it, the East India Company was in a position of nominating the rulers of the states in the vicinity of its factories, and company servants were able to extort whatever privileges they wanted. At this period of great political change in India local rulers began, moreover, the practice of making enormous money gifts to company men as reward for their support.

Robert Clive was the most notorious beneficiary, but there were many others like John Johnstone who amassed fortunes in India which they enjoyed in Britain and who, as a class, were called nabobs. Probably John Johnstone's greatest coup was one of his last; it was a conspicuous royal protection racket. As head of the delegation which negotiated the accession of the sixteen-year-old Nujum-ud-daula as nawab of Bengal in February 1765, he received £27,650. A junior member of the delegation was John Johnstone's younger brother Gideon. As a newly arrived writer his services were unlikely to have been crucial to the success of the negotiations if they were, indeed, even noticeable. Yet Gideon was given £5,833 for his contribution, a sum which, for purposes of comparison, most colonial governors would have been happy to have been paid for half a decade's work.[84] John Johnstone's rapacity, however, had become infamous long before 1765. In collaboration with a fellow councillor, William Hay, and an able rascal, William Bolts, he had formed a trading combine.[85] In the situation which existed in Bengal at that time such a commercial organization could ignore the nawab's officials and exploit to the full what had always been forbidden, the immense profits of what was referred to as the "inland trade." Johnstone and his associates, among others, cornered salt, betelnut, oil, and rice. Indian peasants were forced to buy at monopoly prices. From this and other sources, chiefly land speculation, in which he used his position to intimidate competitors, John Johnstone managed to accumulate £300,000 before he left India in 1765.[86]

The activities of the nabobs were bitterly resented in Bengal. Mir Kasim, the nawab, was outraged when a compromise treaty on trade and duties which he and Henry Vansittart, the governor at Fort William, the English factory at Calcutta, had agreed to in 1762, was repudiated by a majority of the governor's council, including John Johnstone. He determined to assert his independence and amassed treasure, artillery, and a large army trained by European adventurers. By June 1763 Mir Kasim was ready to strike. Using force, subornation, and treachery the nawab overwhelmed the company factories at Patna and Cossimbazar and massacred a party of company servants at Murshidabad, in spite of the safe-conducts he had given them.[87] Subsequently, brilliant military performances by Majors Thomas Adams and Hector Munro would recover all that was lost and destroy Mir Kasim, his army, and his allies. But in the winter of 1763/4 the only reports that reached London were of economic chaos and military disaster.

As the first bad news arrived in December, the price of East India stock dipped alarmingly. The company directors, headed by Laurence Sulivan decided that the four mutinous councillors, including John Johnstone, who had refused to accept the treaty negotiated by Vansittart, were culpable and dismissed them in January 1764. George Johnstone placed the blame elsewhere: Vansittart had been weak, Mir Kasim treacherous, and the directors cruel. He urged his brother William to come to London to lend weight to his own activities in the Court of Proprietors on John's behalf: "I can get you a qualification," he wrote confidently. For over a fortnight, he alleged, he had been giving his whole time to making war on the directors, in which campaign pamphlets in favor of the deposed councillors seem to have been among his chief weapons.[88]

One of these literary attacks got him into trouble. On February 2, 1764, the Court of King's Bench issued a rule against George Johnstone to show cause why an information should not be exhibited against him for publishing in the London newspapers of January 28 a letter reflecting adversely on Vansittart's conduct in Bengal.[89] This legal process, of which the outcome is unknown, would have delayed Johnstone had he been itching to depart for Florida, but clearly he had no intention of leaving until the fight to reinstate his brother John was decided.

Another Johnstone who became involved in the struggle was the military Alexander. "We are making a great push," he wrote, "to turn out one O'Sulivan [*sic*], a Damned Irish Scoundrel," but there was no doubt as to who commanded the India House group. "George has certainly no equal on Earth," continued Alexander admiringly.[90]

To extricate his brother, if possible with his loot intact, was evidently a more pressing duty for George Johnstone than assuming his appointment in West Florida. In doing so he displayed a talent for organizing effective opposition to authority. In the navy the exercise of such an ability could lead only to unpopularity, trial, and punishment. In Johnstone's new sphere of activity it could lead to a reputation as a "man of business" which, in its turn, could and eventually did bring him lucrative employment.

In the 1760s East India House was an unprepossessing stone building in Leadenhall Street in the City of London. To the right of the corridor which ran the length of the building was the directors' court, containing a horseshoe table, seating the twenty-four directors, and also Johnstone's theater of operations, the proprietors' court, usually referred to as the General Court. Here debates of as high a standard as those in the House of Commons took place.[91] Here, quarterly in quiet times, qualified proprietors voted at their regular meetings. Here, most important of all in connection with the internal company struggles of the 1760s, a majority of the proprietors could summon an extraordinary meeting and reverse the decisions of the directors, although, when numbers justified it, such meetings were sometimes held in South Sea House or Merchant Taylors' Hall in Threadneedle Street.[92]

What gave Johnstone the opportunity which he needed to rehabilitate his brother was the rivalry between Robert Clive and Laurence Sulivan, who had triumphed over Clive in a contest for control of the directors in 1763. The result of that election made it only a matter of time before Clive was deprived of the most cherished privilege which he had acquired in India, the famous *jagir,* whereby in 1760 the nawab of Bengal had ordered that the annual sum of £27,000 which the company had, till then, paid as rents for lands near Bengal should thereafter be paid directly to Clive in remuneration for a sinecure to which the Mogul emperor had appointed him.

The anarchy in Bengal bred a demand in England that the victor of Arcot and Plassey should return to India to restore order. Clive determined to use the occasion to secure his hold on the *jagir,* but he needed every ally he could recruit to obtain the necessary majority in the General Court of Proprietors. George Johnstone, Lord Elibank, and their Scottish supporters offered to help Clive achieve his end, evidently on the understanding that he would help them achieve theirs—the reinstatement of John Johnstone.

Clive's coterie, reinforced by the Johnstone group, called for an extraordinary meeting of the General Court on February 27, 1764, to consider "the present dangerous and critical state of the Company's affairs in Bengal," but they were unable to outvote the Sulivanite directors. At another meeting of the proprietors' court on March 23, Clive arranged to be asked to return to Bengal as governor and commander-in-chief. His reply was that he would do so only if directors satisfactory to him were returned at the forthcoming election of directors on April 12. When pressed to clarify his statement, Clive said that he really did not mind who sat on the board of directors, provided that one person in particular—all present knew he meant Sulivan—was not on it.[93]

Before balloting day Clive managed to enlist the support of the Grenville government. Treasury funds were made available to buy stock entered in the names of Clive supporters. Johnstone also helped by supplying him with the names of men willing to purchase stock on their note of hand who could be trusted to vote according to Johnstone's wishes, which meant, for the time being, in the interests of Clive. Initially he furnished a list of twenty-seven names. It included few of his relatives—they were already stockholders[94]—but several naval, Scottish, and lawyer friends and at least seven who were destined for residence or office in West Florida.[95] The willingness of the would-be Floridians to buy stock did not necessarily spring from friendship but, perhaps, derived instead from fear of the consequences of refusal. Edmund Rush Wegg, for example, was to prove one of Johnstone's chief opponents once installed in West Florida as the colony's attorney general. On March 8, 1764, Johnstone supplemented his original list of names with a second suggesting another seven suitable purchasers.

Without the docile platoon of some thirty-four voters supplied by Johnstone, Clive would certainly have failed miserably in his attempt to supplant Sulivan's influence with his own in the April election. The contest was close. Sulivan was reelected as one of the twenty-four directors, although in circumstances that tempted him to resign immediately. Had the vote of one proprietor, Mrs. Drummond, wife of the archbishop of York, not been disqualified, Sulivan would have been defeated.[96] Nevertheless, in spite of Sulivan's narrow reelection, Clive achieved his main purpose: his henchman, Thomas Rous, displaced Sulivan as chairman of the court. So close had the issue been, however, that Clive seems to have decided that he could not risk pressing immediately for the reinstatement of John Johnstone.

Undeterred by Clive's bad faith, the Johnstone group attempted to secure its end by guileful manipulation of the factions which met in yet another session of the General Court on May 2. The main purpose of the gathering was to vote on Clive's *jagir,* but before that subject was broached a proprietor, normally a Sulivanite but primed on this occasion by the Johnstone group, stood up and introduced a motion for the reinstatement of John Johnstone in the company. The supporters of Sulivan, scenting a possibility that the Johnstones were transferring their loyalty to him from Clive, did not oppose the motion, while the supporters of Clive knew that to oppose it would be to forfeit the votes of the Johnstone group on the more important question of the *jagir.* So it was resolved "in consequence of the former services [of John Johnstone, in praise of which his brother had been eulogistic] and those of which the company had lately received advice" that it be recommended to the Court of Directors "to reinstate Mr. Johnstone in the Council of Fort William." The directors had no alternative but to comply.

George Johnstone had not realized all of his aims in connection with East India Company business. John still lived under the threat of legal action for his questionable conduct in Bengal, and George nourished a vengeful desire to make Clive pay for evading his obligation to his brother. To this end he called, in collaboration with nine other stockholders including his old associate Isaac Barré, for a vote on the "Instruments to be executed by the Civil and Military Gentlemen in the Company's service" on May 18.[97] This attempt to hobble Clive failed, but Johnstone was characteristically persistent in his enmity and tried again twelve days later. At a meeting of the Court of Directors on May 30, he and George Dempster tried to obtain admittance to the court in order to argue the case against giving extensive powers to the select committee consisting of John Carnac, C. B. Sumner, Francis Sykes, and Henry Varelst, which was the broom which Clive preferred to sweep up the mess in Bengal. The directors refused a hearing to the protesting proprietors. Even at this early stage in his career Johnstone evidently knew that he was more persuasive in person than on paper; nevertheless, when the directors would not listen to him he insisted on presenting a memorial to them which probably had little effect on directors who had clearly made up their minds on the subject of the committee but which, reproduced in the press as it was, possibly swayed some of the public against Clive. The main argument of the memorial was that the effect of conferring wide powers on Clive's committee would be to place Bengal under military despotism.[98]

In 1764 the time was not ripe for bringing Clive and the select committee into disrepute. At least, however, John Johnstone was back in the Bengal council, thanks in part to his brother George, who was now at liberty to take ship for Florida.

2. "Emporium of the New World"

Johnstone's governorship of West Florida has evoked no eulogies from historians, although the more perceptive, like Lawrence Gipson, have praised some aspects of his administration.[1] That a man appointed to govern any American colony in the 1760s should fall short of triumph need surprise nobody. The times were not propitious for success. The treaty signed in 1763 brought peace only with France and Spain; its sequel in America was not tranquillity but turbulence. Indians forcefully resented the activities of the colonists; the colonists likewise resisted the activities of the agents of the British government and parliament. The years of Johnstone's governorship coincided not only with these types of turmoil but also with oscillations in imperial policy resulting from the instability of ministries in Britain.[2]

The times alone would have made the task of governorship difficult even if Johnstone had been appointed to an established colony accustomed to British institutions and with a substantial British population. West Florida was not such a colony.

As an entity it did not exist before 1763, but was created then from part of Spanish Florida and from all that portion of French Louisiana which lay east of the Mississippi River, save for the "island" of New Orleans. Its eastern boundary was the Chattachoochee and Apalachicola rivers. The northern boundary, initially, was thirty-one degrees latitude. The European inhabitants, before the arrival of British occupation troops, comprised 350 Frenchmen who had remained at Mobile. With the arrival of the British all the Spaniards left Pensacola, the other West Floridian port on the Gulf of Mexico, which was the southern boundary of the province.[3] Most of those who lived within its borders were Indians of the Creek, Choctaw, Chickasaw, and other, smaller, tribes. This Indian preponderance meant that the fact that Johnstone was a governor in the age of Pontiac was more significant than that he governed in the Stamp Act era; not that anybody in Britain, including members of the government, could accurately assess the significance of anything as it affected Florida at the end of the Seven Years War. Almost nothing was known about the province.

Soon after Spain legally ceded it and before occupation forces were landed or governors appointed, the ministry in London received a detailed, informed, and optimistic memorandum entitled "Thoughts Concerning Florida." It is unsigned and is not in Johnstone's hand but was certainly written with his knowledge. Because it anticipated so many of the principles and schemes which he subsequently advocated, it seems likely that it was dictated by him or, since there is no idea in it that is repugnant to opinions that he expressed at a later time, that the author thoroughly converted him. The more likely alternative is that Johnstone had a hand in its composition and that the document strengthened his candidacy for a Floridian governorship.

The first necessity, it was argued, was for a "judicious person," preferably a naval officer, to explore the country and to survey the coast and currents in the adjacent oceans. "For Commerce as well as Command" a good port should be established on the Gulf of Mexico. If the coral at its harbor mouth were torn up or crushed, Pensacola could be such a port, particularly as it would be a suitable base from which to attack Spanish Louisiana, Cuba, or Mexico in time of war.

In peacetime, however, trade with the Spanish should be cultivated. They would certainly want to buy European manufactures imported via the new province. Florida itself could produce topmasts, tar, and fish for them. Florida could also supply British Jamaica with hides, deerskins, indigo, cotton, tobacco, and Indian corn. The other West Indian islands would import Floridian lumber. As more distant projects it would be possible to produce sugar, silk, oil, and wine in the new possession.

No economic schemes would get far without people, and the writer of the memorandum considered several means for increasing the working population. Encouraging foreign immigrants, taming the Indians, introducing slaves, and persuading existing residents to stay should all be attempted. Whether plans to populate Florida succeeded, the writer believed, depended on the government there. Justice should be strictly administered and religious toleration should be practiced. There should be a public system for securing the property of those who died according to the example—and here may be a clue to the author's identity—of the East India service. A "well digested distinct Code" of laws for the colony should be established. Initially the governor ought to be given wide discretionary powers, as well as a 20-gun ship and a sloop. He should establish good relations with the Indians. If he did, no slaves would ever escape from their plantations. When occupying soldiers were sent in, continued the memorialist, they should be seasoned troops, perhaps from Havana.

Finally, the author of "Thoughts Concerning Florida" suggested a prompt start to populating the province by sending in 800 men and 500 women as soon as actual, as opposed to legal, cession occurred. "If Captain Johnstone is thought deserving of this appointment He is confident he could carry 300 Worthy Men from Britain and the West Indies who on the smallest encouragement from Government would follow his Fortune."[4]

If the "Thoughts" memorandum was really a disguised request for preferment it was an unusually substantial one and, despite a tendency to gloss over difficulties, impressive as positive analysis. Its enthusiasm for Florida's economic future was reproduced in similar but even fuller detail when Johnstone penned an encomium on his province on November 1, 1764, a few days after his arrival there. He intended to lure immigrants and, perhaps with the residents of the sickly West Indies in mind, commended above all and quite falsely the healthiness of the climate in West Florida. Evidently an efficient publicizer, he ensured his brochure's appearance in such diverse periodicals as the *Georgia Gazette* of January 10, 1765, and the *Scots Magazine* of the following month.

Johnstone's comparison of Pensacola with Venice and his slogan that West Florida would be "the Emporium of the New World" may smack of a certain more modern type of Floridian land salesman, but it should not be forgotten that there was much truth in what he wrote. West Florida's position was promising. The province was full of unrealized potential and the governor's enthusiasm was not affectation. Nearly eighteen years later, on February 17, 1783, with reunited Florida again in Spanish hands, he would regretfully tell the House of Commons that "ministers knew not the value of that province, either in point of situation, or of commercial produce; there was a bay in it, called the bay of Espiritu Santo [Tampa], that was one of the finest harbours in the world."[5]

If the profitability of Florida, a note repeatedly struck by Johnstone, sounds a little harsh, a touch ungentlemanly, it was music to British governments daunted by two products of the Seven Years War, an enlarged empire and a national debt of unprecedented size. The new governor's concern with commerce was dominant even when he wrote like a proconsul: "the first object in every Community is the internal Police of the Country. . . . The next object is Security from External Enemies. . . . The third object is, the commercial interest of the Society, Internal and External."[6] Although commerce had an apparently low priority, it was still, for Johnstone, the most important of the three objects. Order within and safety from outside foes preceded it, but only because they were the necessary prerequisites for commercial prosperity.

A concern both with the success of his province and with personal gratification are discernible in Johnstone's activities in the long interval between his appointment as governor and his arrival at Pensacola. Fighting his brother's battles in Leadenhall Street and the Brooks affair by no means fully occupied him.

An early concern was to recommend congenial candidates for positions in the new province to the secretary of state. On July 20, 1763, he proposed that Lord Egremont should find employment for James Macpherson, a celebrated literary figure believed at the time to be the discoverer and translator of the Gaelic epic *Ossian*. Johnstone thought he might do as secretary, register, treasurer, or naval officer. Eventually Macpherson did become secretary, but the governor's suggestion that the chief justice of the colony should be a lawyer named Kiliken was ignored.[7]

An expensive scheme by which he proposed, a few days later, to transport Dutch, Norwegians, and inhabitants of Massachusetts and Jamaica who were prepared to make a home in West Florida was similarly received. Settlers and traders, he suggested, should be given one or two slaves, skilled workers a bounty of £20. No doubt the lords of trade doubted Johnstone's optimistic estimate that a quitrent of sixpence on every Floridian acre granted would pay for the scheme.[8]

When he recommended that the boundary of his colony should be pushed northward to the 34th parallel, on the specious ground that the existing border did not include Mobile in the province, he was more successful and, in accordance with an Order in Council of May 9, 1764, a line drawn due east of the confluence of the Mississippi and Yazoo rivers to the Apalachicola became the new legal boundary.[9] The new territory included Natchez, the fertile soil of which was more likely to attract farmers than were the sands of Mobile and Pensacola.

Johnstone personally attended on the lords of trade several times before embarking for America and wrote to them even more frequently. Future dealings with Indians preoccupied him; more than once he devised lists of presents in addition to the inventories compiled for him. He suggested that the gifts might accompany him and his staff in the vessel which, in January 1764—just before his delaying involvement in John Company affairs—he was urging the Board of Trade to obtain from the Admiralty to convey him to Florida.[10] His last appearance before the board prior to sailing was, it seems, on May 28, 1764, when he applied for the use of an official sailing boat.[11] This wish was granted and the schooner *Patty* would see much service on the inland waterways of West Florida before his tour as governor ended.[12]

He found time too, before his departure, to apply to the crown for land. On June 19, 1764, in association with an old mercantile acquaintance, Samuel Hannay, and the Indian trader John Mackintosh, he applied for a joint grant of 20,000 acres in West Florida.[13] The result of this particular application is uncertain. What is sure is that Mackintosh acquired a Pensacola town lot in 1765 and, in 1766, 5,000 acres near the Iberville, a river which once joined Lake Maurepas and the Mississippi: at the same time Hannay was awarded 5,000 acres in Natchez. While he was governor Johnstone obtained for himself three minor tracts totaling something over 280 acres,[14] but in the year following his return to England he was to receive a substantial grant of 10,000 acres at Baton Rouge, a holding which would attract purchase enquiries as late as 1776.[15]

Finally, in the second week of July 1764, Johnstone left England on what was to be an unusually long voyage to Pensacola.[16] With him went his "family" of civil officers, his servants, army medical assistants, ordnance stores, and, as he had requested, a load of Indian presents.

At first the going was swift and by August 4 his vessel, the transport *Grampus,* had reached St. Christopher in the Leeward Islands. Presumably while the ship was anchored in the sea road off Basseterre, for St. Christopher had no harbor, he wrote an optimistic dispatch to the secretary of state.[17] Thereafter the governor's progress was slow because of his justifiable insistence on being landed in Jamaica. The master of the *Grampus,* Thomas Fortune, had once overturned a boat there and refused to place himself within the jurisdiction of the Jamaican courts. Johnstone, however, considered it of the utmost importance to obtain a supply of rum to supplement his Indian presents. Without it the gifts would be of no avail, he argued, and so he had Fortune land him at the east end of Morante Bay on either the thirteenth or fifteenth of August.[18] In addition, the governor realized that West Florida would be heavily dependent on sea communication and he wanted to meet Sir William Burnaby, the commander of the Royal Navy squadron at Jamaica, to ascertain what support he could expect from him.

Insistence on visiting Jamaica meant that Johnstone had to wait for a ship to take him to Pensacola. He used his time in buying 1,328 gallons of rum, in collecting a hundred varieties of vegetable seed for planting in West Florida, and in recruiting several settlers for the province.[19] Time passed and the packet for Pensacola, which had left England only a few days after him and which was supposed to stop at Jamaica, still did not come. Johnstone was alarmed by travelers' reports that there was a chronic shortage of specie in West Florida. He cashed a check payable by the treasury in London to make sure that he at least would arrive with ready money to get his government established.

There is no record of how Johnstone amused himself socially while in Jamaica. He had visited the island before in both the merchant and the king's service. That he certainly had friends on the island, although not perhaps high in Jamaican society, is suggested by a letter written in 1763 to a Miss Balfour. It is worth quoting for a combination of warmth and wit rarely found in letters of commendation:

> Dear Katherine,
>   Some people recommend Ministers and Dukes to Kings, others send young Buckara Man to Collonel Price & Colonel Farson. But I more simple and sincere send an Honest Sailor to Black Kate of Port Royal desiring she will help him in selling his little adventure to the best advantage: His Name is Peter Fife. He was with me in the Hornett, an Honest Sober Lad & I beg you will be kind to him.
> God Bless you Kate.[20]

After lingering in Jamaica for seven weeks, Johnstone evidently despaired of a passage on the Pensacola packet and went instead on Burnaby's sloop *Nautilus,* after arranging for the twelve puncheons of rum which he had bought to go separately. He landed at his capital on October 21.[21]

The condition of West Florida before his arrival may be judged from the reports of various military men concerned with its occupation and initial administration, Lieutenant Colonel Augustine Prévost and Major Willsom Forbes at Pensacola, and Major Robert Farmar at Mobile. They were factual and, when not condemnatory, cool in tone and without that ebullient optimism which invariably characterized Johnstone's appraisals. Naturally they were mostly concerned with military aspects of existence in West Florida, for soldiers formed the bulk of the early British immigration and their forts were the most important buildings in the province. Whether put up by the French or Spanish these forts and the surrounding buildings were now in decay. On two sides swamps hemmed in both Mobile and Pensacola, which, elsewhere, was almost engulfed by forest. While both outposts had commodious harbors the bar at each forbade entry to large vessels. These reports were fittingly much concerned with Florida's defensibility.[22]

A more balanced description was made by Lord Adam Gordon, an entrepreneur who hoped to make money from organizing emigration to Florida, and who visited both Pensacola and Mobile between August and October 1764, immediately before the arrival of the governor. He found the fort at Pensacola unfinished and primitive, consisting of a double stockade and a very narrow ditch. The governor's house within it, two-storied, shingled, and balconied, was the only tolerable house in town. For miles around deep white sand seemed the only soil. Apart from fish and some hogs, goats, and poultry kept, for fear of theft by Indians, within the stockade, the only source of fresh meat was the distant Mississippi shore or Mobile, sixty miles away over trackless land, which supported some cattle.

Nevertheless, although Gordon rated Pensacola "a poor place," he compared it favorably with Mobile because it was healthier. Mobile's Fort Charlotte was partly of brick, its streets were well laid out, and its soil was more fertile than Pensacola's, but almost everybody there was sick with fevers, agues, and fluxes. Gordon seems to blame the local drinking water, which, he acutely noticed, French Mobilians of longer residence than the British were at pains to avoid.[23] Having assessed the region, he subsequently preferred to pursue his Floridian emigration scheme in the more easterly sister province rather than in West Florida. Further information on the condition of that colony at the time of Johnstone's arrival is contained in an anonymous account by an emigrant who possibly traveled most of the way there in the same ship as its governor but who did not dally in Jamaica. Arriving at Pensacola on September 1, 1764, he felt deceived. He had been led to expect a "terrestrial paradise." Instead he found "the most sandy, barren, and desert land . . . not capable of producing a single vegetable, nor the least prospect of improving it." With turkeys costing fifteen shillings, chickens five shillings and eggs sixpence each, and even fish, for lack of fishermen, expensive, life would have been impossible for the soldiers had it not been for their rations of salted meat. Without exception their quarters leaked, and even those provided for officers would have been considered unfit for dog kennels in England. The author believed that the Spaniards had used Pensacola as a penal colony and that the only reason Britain had accepted it was for its strategic use in the event of war with Spain. The writer, one of at least a hundred disembarking from the same ship in Florida, stated that his own disillusion and pessimism were shared by all his fellow passengers.[24]

Governor Johnstone's outlook was quite different. Arriving the following month amid the same barren squalor, he retained, if his writings are any guide, his buoyant optimism about West Florida's economic prospects, particularly now that military rule was about to give way to civil government.

His long voyage had given Johnstone a chance to become acquainted with some of his principal subordinates among the civil officials of West Florida, a sparse bureaucracy by modern standards, consisting of a chief justice, an attorney general, the secretary and clerk of the council, a land surveyor, two parsons, a provost marshal, and what today would be called a registrar, then styled register.[25] All were paid from the royal treasury, but none so munificently as Johnstone himself, the size of whose salary, at £1,200 a year, excited comment from Lord Adam Gordon and compared favorably with that of, for example, the governor of Georgia, who received £1,000, let alone the governor of Nova Scotia, who had to manage on £500 annually.

The officers of the civil government were, like Johnstone himself, appointed in England in accordance with the patronage system and not necessarily because of suitability for colonial administration. Simon Amory, to take one egregious example, "had been educated in a very low situation of life, having lived as a Retailer of Pins, Needles, and Grocery, in Taunton," and was a septuagenarian when appointed naval officer and register of West Florida.[26] The governor was empowered by his commission to appoint "necessary Officers and ministers . . . for the better administration of justice and putting the laws into execution . . ." in his province.[27] Nevertheless he could be overruled in his appointments from London, although he used his authority with discretion. When the register, the aged Amory, died in 1765, Johnstone replaced him in the post with John Hannay, son of a family friend, but sought confirmation from the secretary of state in most conciliatory terms and asserted that he had refrained from nepotism: "If private views could have determined my Conduct, I have a Relation in my Family, besides my Private Secretary, to whom it would have been more natural to have offered it."[28] In this case Secretary Conway did not accept Johnstone's recommendation—he appointed a Sir Richard Murray to the registership—but he did not overlook Hannay, with whose family Conway also was acquainted, and advised the governor to prefer him to the post of provost marshal.[29] If Johnstone did not always see his appointments endorsed he could and did remove officers when they failed to support him. On his outward voyage to Florida the governor could scarcely have anticipated how much he would need support.

Heterogeneous as Johnstone's team was, it did, on the whole, back its captain. Exceptions were the lawmen: James Clifton, the chief justice, and Edmund Rush Wegg, the attorney general. The lieutenant governor, Montfort Browne, joined this dissident couple when he at last reached Pensacola to take up his duties in January 1766. Johnstone, backed by a council which, subject to Board of Trade approval, he himself appointed, and which consistently supported him, would have experienced no difficulty in coping with recalcitrants had they not found extremely powerful allies in a place where he had evidently expected no opposition—the army.

Thanks to Johnstone's tardiness in taking up his appointment as governor, West Florida had lacked civil government for over a year when he arrived. During this period the autocratic Major Robert Farmar had taken over Mobile and adjacent forts from the French with only minor difficulty[30] and then ruled as de facto military governor.[31] He had done well in the role; he handled the thorny problem of transferring private land to the British with practical common sense; he had also successfully presided over an Indian Congress at Mobile designed to secure the goodwill of the local tribes. Although there were vague allegations of oppression, which invariably accompany military rule,[32] the most discreditable specific charge against Farmar was that, with dubious ethics, he had obtained a large tract of land east of Mobile Bay from the Creeks. Probably the greatest balancing tribute which may be paid to Farmar and his various counterparts at Pensacola is a negative one: during the period of military government, when further north the violence begun by Pontiac reached its height, in West Florida there was no war.[33] Successful as military government on balance had been, the transition to civil government upon Johnstone's arrival in October 1764 had to be made, and perhaps unfortunately, the change could not be accompanied by the reduction or evacuation of troops.

Because of the unique situation of West Florida, close cooperation between the military and civil powers was essential if Johnstone were to achieve his aims in the colony. As a frontier province, its danger from external enemies was great. The Spanish were slow to replace the French in Louisiana: both nations were thought to harbor resentment following their defeat by the British in the Seven Years War. The Indian tribes in West Florida, moreover, had known grievances and were subject to incitement by the French, with whom some had been on good terms, or by

Pontiac, who had been active among southern Indians early in 1764.[34] United in a confederation hostile to the British, they could pose a formidable threat, since, if Johnstone's estimate was at all accurate, they could muster ten thousand warriors.[35] The military might also have to cope with serious internal disorders in the colony, since the existing population was unused to British rule, and new arrivals were, in the governor's phrase, "the refuse of the Jails of great Citys, and the overflowwing Scum of the Empire. . . ."[36] There was, of course, no police force in West Florida; even in Britain, Fielding's Bow Street Runners were, at this period, merely a promising experiment in law enforcement. For internal and external protection everything depended on two depleted infantry regiments.[37] Apart from ensuring the survival of the colony, the military was necessary to give the protection without which, thought Johnstone, the French, German, and Swiss immigrants, whom he hoped to lure from New Orleans once it fell under Spanish rule, would not come.[38] Likewise the governor's schemes for the expansion of trade and the extension of settlements would benefit greatly from the assistance of the army.[39]

Desirable as such cooperation might be, it never materialized for a variety of reasons. The first was Farmar's inability to get on with Johnstone, an explanation for which must remain speculative. Having enjoyed the exercise of power, Farmar probably resented having to surrender some of it. Farmar, moreover, was testy and could scarcely have enjoyed Johnstone's refusal to allow him to keep either the land he had acquired from the Creeks, or Dauphin Island, which he claimed to have bought from the French.[40] Farmar may also have shown the prejudice against Scots prevalent in the 1760s. Perhaps, too, he was moved by the simple jealousy of the passed-over for the preferred or by the complementary antipathy of Smollett's Hawser Trunnion: "he and I could not abide one another . . . because, d'ye see, I was a sailor and he a land-man."[41]

Certainly as important as the personality clash between Johnstone and Farmar in creating friction was the fact that the comparatively large military units stationed in West Florida were there primarily to serve the needs of imperial policy rather than those of an individual colony. Johnstone never saw this clearly. The grandiloquent phrases of the papers which conferred authority on him must bear some of the responsibility for this defect of vision.

The commission appointing him "Captain-General and Governor in Chief" of West Florida required and commanded "all officers and Ministers Civil and Military and the other inhabitants of Our Said Province to be Obedient Abetting and Assistant Unto You the Said George Johnstone. . . ." Furthermore, in order to resist enemies the Governor was given full power "to Levy, Arm, Muster, Command and Employ all persons whatsoever residing within our Said Province . . . [and] to March Embark or Transfer [them]." In time of invasion he was empowered to execute martial law.[42]

As a result Johnstone conceived that he had extensive authority over the army units in West Florida and was shocked when officers denied him even access to the forts in the province on the ground that they were exclusively under the authority of Major General Thomas Gage, the commander of all British regulars in North America.[43] The governor asked the new secretary of state to clarify the extent of his power over the army. Halifax replied that in all military matters the commands of Gage or of his deputy, the brigadier general in the southern department, were supreme. In the absence of any such specific commands the governor could, through the senior officer on the spot, "give Orders for the Marching of Troops, the disposition of them, for making and marching Detachments, Escorts, & such purely Military Services, within his Government." He had the right, too, to be informed of "the State and Condition of the Troops, Magazines and Fortifications."[44]

Gage, who never ceased to accord imperial needs priority over the claims of this governor of a single colony, preferred to base his counterclaims on custom and refused to be impressed by scraps of paper:

> I am well aware of the inferences that may be drawn from the Circumstances of Parole [he wrote, referring to Johnstone's commission]; but I am to acquaint you, that it is in the King's Power . . . to give that Show of Command by way of Compliment to any Person he chuses, and at the same time limit and circumscribe his Power as to many Essentials. . . . no Governor upon this Continent . . . ever had any Command over the Troops during Ten Years that I have served here. . . .

Gage in fact was not willing to let Johnstone give orders to officers save in insignificant matters:

> No disputes should be had on account of such a Trifle as an orderly Serjeant or any thing of the kind, if at any time the Governor desires such a thing.[45]

The game Johnstone was trying to play was in one corner of Gage's continental board. The trouble was that he had no pieces of his own and refused to recognize that the ones which existed belonged to Gage. As the man who had to cope with Pontiac, Gage's reluctance to share control over the troops was understandable, but the general was wrong to deny Johnstone's claims by reason of what was customary in other colonies. West Florida was no normal colony: it was too young and poor and underpopulated to have a colonial militia. The governor could do nothing, therefore, in time of emergency, if he were denied all real authority over the British regulars.

Johnstone, however, showed a deplorable ignorance of reality in his preference for confrontation, in his sarcastic letters to Gage, and in his penchant for committing officers to trial. The only possible way to have made the military more amenable to his wishes would have been through the application of diplomatic skill and by demonstrating both a willingness to compromise and an understanding that the problems of West Florida were not the army's sole concern.[46] What Johnstone needed was more common sense and less legal punctilio. David Wedderburn judiciously commented that the governor "imagined that his Commission and Instruction gave him more Power, than I think he has. Major Farmar, and the officers, would not allow him the power, which he undoubtedly has."

In a struggle between the civil and military authorities, the soldiers were sure to win, since Johnstone could count consistently only on his supporters in the civil administration to press his claims: this meant pitting the unarmed against men with muskets. His sole military adherent, Lieutenant Colonel Wedderburn, who considered Johnstone "meek, moderate, patient and ill-treated," was promptly disciplined by Gage when he accepted the governor's authority.[47]

Foregone though the conclusion was, Johnstone never ceased to advance his pretensions against the military during the twenty-eight months of his active administration. As has been seen, the quarrels began over Johnstone's right to enter the fort where he lived and continued with the question of the governor's right to review lawsuits decided during the period of military rule. There followed arguments on his right to give orders to soldiers and to move bodies of them, to appoint town majors, to allocate barracks, and to impose duties on the military. The rivalry is a saddening tale containing episodes of spite, pettifoggery, stupidity, spleen, and black humor. Incidents illuminating Johnstone's character rather than a comprehensive treatment will be given here.[48]

Johnstone, furious that his pretended right to issue passwords and countersigns was challenged, defiantly continued to do so, using the risible words "Bedlam" and "Lunacy."[49] After he had been denied authority over the fort at Pensacola by Captain Mackinnen, commander of the fort, who had had no orders from Gage on the subject, Johnstone wrote: "it is the first Settlement of any Colony since the beginning of the World, where somebody on the Spot had not the general Command of the whole Military force within the Province."[50] Johnstone believed that the army had determined to harass him by unjustly punishing his servants. After one had been beaten in his presence by a sergeant major and another was court-martialed and condemned to four hundred lashes while he was absent in Mobile, he, too, acted vindictively. When Major Farmar, in order to acquire specie, which could not be obtained in Florida, for an expedition to the Illinois country, proposed to sell skins in New Orleans, Johnstone charged him duty on them and otherwise tried to obstruct him.[51] Later the governor brought charges against Farmar for embezzlement.[52] When Johnstone temporarily acquired sufficient force to back his will, thanks to the complaisance of Admiral Sir William Burnaby and of Lieutenant Colonel David Wedderburn, he compelled Captain Andrew Simpson to yield the keys of the Pensacola garrison.[53]. When he attempted, a year later, to repeat this coup against Simpson's successor, Lieutenant Colonel Ralph Walsh, the governor, this time lacking armed backers, rashly climbed into the fort accompanied only by his secretary, James Primrose Thomson, whose sword was soon busy fending off sentries lunging at Johnstone with bayonets.[54] The governor subsequently arrested Walsh for high treason, but Chief Justice Clifton dismissed the charges, whereafter Johnstone suspended the judge.[55] In an official report the governor blackened the reputations of two enemies at once by insinuating that Walsh had accepted a Huguenot immigrant as his concubine and that Lieutenant Governor Montfort Browne was the donor.[56] When Johnstone left Florida in January 1767, he was still at odds with the army; the final dispute was over Indian problems, the generals favoring a diplomatic, the governor a military, solution.

One of the significant consequences for Johnstone's career of his experience with the army in Florida was a set of political attitudes—to call it a political philosophy would be to overdignify it—which he expressed in the debates on the American colonies prior to the Revolution. The essence of his posture was distrust of unfettered military power. As early as 1764 he had argued for the subordination of the military to the civil power, on the ground that "Imperium in Imperio cannot exist in a Commonwealth," and in 1765 he asserted that the exercise of government bred delusions of superiority in the military.[57] There is a direct link between these sentiments and those he voiced in the debate on the Boston Port Bill in 1774 when he deplored that Governor Hutchinson was deprived of military authority "so that in truth he remains an insignificant pageant of State, fit only to transmit tedious accounts of his own ridiculous situation: or, like a Doctor of the Sorbonne, to debate with his Assembly about abstract doctrines in Government." It was not that Johnstone objected to coercion to secure political ends but that under every establishment obedience could be secured by force only if "conducted with wisdom."[58]

In a colony, as he conceived it, wisdom would reside in the governor in council; that was where provincial sovereignty should reside. Johnstone was careful to obtain the backing of his council in whatever he did, but he was autocratic by nature and when a council member like Clifton thwarted him, he obtained his removal. Opponents, with some justice, claimed that he "collected a Council Subservient to his Purpuses."[59] Moreover, although, in accord with his commission, he did summon an assembly to supplement the rule of the governor in council shortly before he left Florida, he was a man of his time in distrusting the generality of the people: "I have found, by fatal Experience, since the Stamp Act, that the ultimate Law of Kings [i.e., the use of force] is the first Law with the Populace."[60] It was perfectly acceptable, however, for Governor Johnstone to resort habitually to the ultimate law of kings, since his primary task was that of "establishing an European Colony, which is generally made up of the overflowing Scum of all other Societies, who can only be held together by coercive Means."[61] That Johnstone should have cited the Stamp Act riots when denigrating the mob is curious, since, although Johnstone claimed to have lost popularity by enforcing that particular law, he was able to do so with minimal resistance, in part, admittedly, because of his own firmness: those who refused to pay the tax on land grants, where it most commonly applied in West Florida, were dispossessed.[62]

Contemptuous as Johnstone was of the colonists in West Florida, he did enjoy some popularity. "The poor ignorant North Americans," he wrote in 1766, "would willingly have gone to Death in my Service Six months ago," a boast supported by some independent testimony. The French Protestant colonist François Caminade, for instance, called him "our beloved and Wise Governor" and "the ablest of any in a similar position; nobody ever knew one of greater integrity nor one who better understood the interests entrusted to him." James Adair, the Indian trader, thought him "Sagacious and gallant" and believed that "all the western Indian nations bear the highest regard to that paternal governor and plain friend of the people."[63]

Johnstone was widely read and was something of a literary name dropper. In official correspondence he alluded to Molière, *Hudibras, Candide, The Tale of a Tub,* Greek and Roman history, as well as to more pertinent reading, such as the statutes of the realm, Foster's legal commentaries, and the *Articles of War.* Most frequently of all he cited Montesquieu.[64]

From Montesquieu the governor could derive support for his ideas on the constitutional role of the military force in the colonial body politic. On the subject of the government of the provinces of the Roman Empire, Montesquieu had written that "in a Commonwealth the same magistrate ought to be possessed of the executive, civil as well as military."[65] Johnstone seemed but to paraphrase the French philosopher's words when he wrote:

> There must be an ultimate Power lodged Somewhere in every Community. That the military is not distinct from this Power, but a necessary Part of One great whole, the Commonwealth; That, in the Civil Concerns of the Community, the Power is generally lodged with certain Numbers of Men. In military Matters, it can only, with Propriety be in One Person. . . .

If the military were allowed to be independent of that one person "who can be supposed to have the Prosperity of the Colony most nearly at Heart" then it would be "the greatest solecism in Politics, which must either end in Anarchy on the one hand, or despotism on the other."[66]

Johnstone when governor never mentioned the best known of the principles advocated by Montesquieu, that of the separation of powers; certainly there was little sign of it in West Florida. Johnstone dismissed judges who displeased him; he summoned no legislature until the tail end of his governorship and sought to maximize the power of the executive, which he headed. If had he cared to, he might have comforted his conscience with Montesquieu's belief that different climates and different conditions made a variety of governmental forms appropriate.

In summary one may say that in the years when Johnstone was governor of West Florida, before he became one of the most outspoken of champions for colonists' rights, his ideas on colonial government were traditional and autocratic. A colony like West Florida was part of a transatlantic community. Parliament had a right to legislate for the colony, and its governor was subject to the king's authority through royal ministers. Under this restriction Johnstone thought that a governor should rule with more despotism than enlightenment: from Montesquieu's philosophy there is no evidence that he derived anything except what would confirm his existing views. In word and deed Johnstone showed his belief that both the garrison and the council of the province should be under the governor's authority. It was essential for a governor to use force, though exercised with wisdom. Lack of necessary strength among the king's representatives, he believed, had caused troubles throughout the British empire.[67] Force was particularly necessary, since colonists, about whom his repeated use of the word "scum" is revealing, did not know what was good for them. "One must do Good to the People like administering Phisic to a Child," he wrote.[68] If his attitude was essentially paternal, he was a father who had favorites and believed in firm discipline.[69]

Johnstone was not necessarily wrong in believing that what a pioneer frontier colony like West Florida needed was strong government, at least in its early days. Although he never secured what he regarded as "sufficient Authority to inforce . . . Regulations," a necessary prerequisite for internal policing, "the first object in every Community," he did his best with limited powers and West Florida was not a lawless community.[70] Moreover, the governor's running legal fight with the military did not nullify his pursuit of what he regarded as a community's second object, "security from external enemies."[71]

Of these, the Indians posed the gravest immediate threat. Johnstone had the chance, before leaving England, of reading Farmar's copious papers to the secretary of war, which revealed both the fluid state of Indian affairs and also the wretched condition of the British defenses in West Florida.[72]

The underlying difficulties making it almost impossible for the British to establish satisfactory relations with the Indian tribes are well known.

The intention of the proclamation of 1763 was to replace, in the trans-Appalachian area, the authority of separate colonies with the single authority of London and to protect the Indian hunting grounds from invasion by settlers. However desirable this might be for the Indians, for English fur-trading interests, and for an imperial government looking to avoid the expense of war, it was unwelcome to men on the spot with superior force and was a denial of perhaps the most potent trend in the history of North America.[73] Furthermore the proclamation did not protect the Indians from traders; on the contrary it gave traders a new freedom to peddle their goods. Illegal rum and muskets did nothing to preserve peace. Ministerial changes during the 1760s resulted in a wavering Indian policy.[74] It was actually contrary to the principles implicit in the royal proclamation that the British government should endorse the aggrandizement of West Florida, situated as it was, west of the Appalachians; that it should subsidize the emigration there of Huguenot settlers; and that it should approve extensive land grants and the establishment of a fortified post, not on the coast but in the interior of the province. Yet it did all of these things during Johnstone's governorship.

Major Farmar had taken action to conciliate the Indians before Johnstone's arrival. He continued the French custom of supplying them with presents and at a congress with the eastern Choctaws at Mobile on November 14, 1763, shrewdly contrived under joint Anglo-French sponsorship, Farmar explained the transfer of West Florida to English rule. By January 24, 1764, he had also formally informed the Alabamas and Creeks of the new British supremacy in the area. Meanwhile all his officers were under instructions "to Cultivate and preserve a good understanding with the Indians."[75]

Less successful had been the efforts in 1763 and 1764 of the successive commandants at Pensacola—Prévost, Forbes, and Mackinnen. A Creek conference in that town had been stultified by the absence of some of the most influential tribal leaders, particularly The Mortar, their chief.[76] Nevertheless it was to the credit of the British officers commanding at Mobile and Pensacola that the tribes in West Florida neither involved themselves nor imitated Pontiac when Indian rebellion crested in the north.

As Johnstone was well aware, pacification was incomplete and the danger of war still great when he landed in Florida in October of 1764, and he at once concerned himself with establishing a stable peace with the Indians.[77] That he was at all successful resulted not only from his own talent—he showed a diplomatic flair when negotiating with Indians quite absent from his dealings with the British army—but also from the considerable assistance of two talented men.

The first of these was John Stuart, superintendent for Indian affairs for the southern district, who was well qualified for his post by experience in the backcountry in peace and war.[78] High among his credentials for getting on with Johnstone would have been his Scottish blood and his naval experience—he had gone around the world with Anson. But probably much more important than either was his evidently innate ability, attested by his dealings with Farmar, Gage, and the Indians, to establish satisfactory relationships with other human beings.

Another whose help to Johnstone in Indian affairs proved invaluable was the Chevalier Montault de Montbéraut. At one time a soldier in French Louisiana, a linguist with influence among Indians, the chevalier was tempted, thanks to the fortune of war, to stay in what became after 1763 West Florida in order to safeguard his estates there.[79] Montbéraut was a quarrelsome man; in time past, Governor Kerlerec of Louisiana and M. d'Abbadie, the French commandant there, as well as the Society of Jesus, had all had differences with him. In future time he would earn the detestation of French *habitants* of Louisiana when he adopted the uniform and views of a Spanish colonel.[80] In the interval between serving the kings of France and Spain he worked under Johnstone. Ultimately they were to have a monumental dispute. Temporarily, though, when his undeniable talent for handling Indians was most in demand by the English, he was cajoled by Stuart and Johnstone, in spite of his misgivings, into being useful to the British crown.

The problems which the West Florida Indians posed for Johnstone were manifold. Not only did he have to make the several tribes refrain from war, but he had also to persuade them to meet with him, to agree to forsake any lingering French loyalty, to surrender land to the British, and finally, to allow royal officials to live among them.

None of these tasks was easy. The Indians were well aware of Pontiac's cogent arguments for driving the white man into the sea. Because of Florida's weak defenses and debilitated regiments, nowhere could the plan stand more chance of success than West Florida. The French connection, moreover, was not lightly severed; not only had the tie been built up over decades, but some Frenchmen had evidently assured the Indians, not implausibly except in hindsight, that they would be back.[81] Lastly the cession of land and the acceptance of British commissaries in their midst could clearly end in enslavement and the destruction of the Indian way of life. In favor of accepting British demands Johnstone could pit only alcoholic entertainment, the allure of cheap gifts like blankets, medals, tomahawk pipes, tinsel-adorned suits—and deft diplomacy.[82]

Of the two Indian congresses which Johnstone succeeded in convening in 1765 the easier to arrange was the first, since one of the invited tribes, the Chickasaw, was traditionally friendly with the British. It took place in Mobile during the ten days which ended on April 4.[83] Stuart's experience and Johnstone's loquacity both, no doubt, contributed to the success of the congress, which concluded with the signature of a treaty ceding to the

British a strip of land extending twelve leagues northward from the sea and eastward as far as the Creek territories. And in spite of Johnstone's homily on the evils of liquor, rum too, which Chief Pouchama blatantly demanded "in return for the Lands," no doubt helped bring agreement.[84] But the treaty might have quickly become meaningless had it not been for Montbéraut. Latecomers to the congress, the representatives of the eastern Choctaws, did not arrive until April 22. They refused to give up their French medals, symbols of allegiance to a European sovereign. Stuart failed to dissolve their surliness with threats. It was Montbéraut who, more subtly, expatiated on the honors and favors which those Choctaws who had already accepted English medals might expect and persuaded them to change their minds.[85]

To have secured the allegiance of those who attended the Mobile congress was a noteworthy feat. This was particularly true of the old chief of the Alabamas, Mingo, whom Johnstone regarded as one of three "very Superior Characters, in their way" who had conspired to unite all Indian tribes in common enmity to the British.[86] The other two were Pontiac and The Mortar.

It was the allegiance of the latter which Johnstone sought at the Pensacola congress held between May 27 and June 24, 1765.[87] The initial difficulties of finding The Mortar, who was somewhere in the Creek hunting grounds, and of persuading him to come to Pensacola were solved by Montbéraut and his son Louis.

It is noteworthy, however, that Johnstone had a share in ameliorating the hostility of the Creeks and making them amenable to attendance at a congress. Within days of his arrival in Florida the governor dispatched a diplomatic delegation to the Creek country. It consisted of John Hannay, a family friend of the Johnstones, and Thomas Campbell, a marine lieutenant who had impressed the governor with his judicious remarks.[88] The pair were given their instructions on November 19, 1764, and set off the following day. They lived among the Creeks until May 1765, by which time they had so ingratiated themselves that "most of the Chiefs and Principal men of both the upper and lower Creek villages came down with us to the Congress held at Pensacola."[89]

Having arrived at Pensacola the Creeks proved obtuse. They began by refusing to enter the garrison; once coaxed inside the town, The Mortar feigned to see evidence of hostility in the red cross on the Union Jack: contact with more easterly colonies must surely have made the Creeks aware that the British national flag had no such symbolic significance. More ominous was The Mortar's initial determination to delay discussion of boundary definition.[90] Montbéraut again intervened effectively; privately he demonstrated to the Indians that the proposed boundary required no great cession of land but merely a strip some fifteen miles wide around Pensacola. The Mortar agreed to this cession, but refused a great medal: he had never found it necessary to have any medal when allied to the French.

Stuart used his understanding of the Indian mind to overcome the objection. When receiving The Mortar to discuss the matter he sat on a heap of French medals exchanged for English equivalents by other chiefs.[91] His pretense that he might not offer an English medal to The Mortar kindled the Creek's desire for one and of course his wish was granted. One final impediment to the success of the Pensacola congress was The Mortar's demand for low trade prices, which Johnstone could not promise. All negotiations might have been nullified had Montbéraut not used his influence to persuade the chief to trust the governor. The treaty resulting from the congress resembled that signed by the Choctaws and Cherokees, except that because of their sustained objections, the Creeks would have no British commissaries living among them.

Johnstone was jubilant. The report which he and Stuart composed reeked of self-congratulation.[92] Lawrence Gipson has written that "the two Indian congresses showed Johnstone at his best, which was very good indeed," and certainly, although Gipson's verdict smacks of hyperbole, in that the success of the congresses owed much to others besides Johnstone, the governor did deserve praise.[93] A president of the United States may claim credit for a foreign policy which would fail without the help of a gifted secretary of state. To the same extent and for the same reason Johnstone might claim credit for the congresses; whether his Indian policy worked or not, the governor was responsible. Besides this, it was he who recruited Montbéraut; he worked in harmony with Stuart; he, at Pensacola, modestly allowed Sir William Burnaby to make the major opening speech; he also arranged for the presents and entertainment, essential props for a successful production. In writing to Bute during the Pensacola congress, Johnstone likened it to a parliamentary election. "Suppose," he suggested to the earl, "the actors at an English election changed into shrewd, pawky, proud, barelegged Highlanders, all armed and reeling. The wives are exactly the same. It is impossible to overreach any of them, drunk or sober, or gain a point without a present." On the high cost of Indian congresses he again invited a comparison with an election. There was not a borough of equal numbers where double the cost of a congress would not be spent to decide the choice of a single member of Parliament. The result of the Pensacola congress was more significant. It secured peace with the Indians at least temporarily.[94] The way was thus open for the pursuit of the third of Johnstone's avowed objectives in the government of West Florida, "the Commercial Interests of the Society, Internal and External."[95]

The governor directly sought commercial prosperity through two main plans. Of these, unfortunately, he managed to obtain government support only for the one less certain to make his colony flourish. This was the attempt to divert all the trade coming down the Mississippi into the Iberville River, which branched off the more important waterway 102 miles above New Orleans. If the Iberville could be cleared, waterborne traffic using it could reach the Gulf of Mexico by way of Lakes Maurepas and Pontchartrain and save some forty miles of river travel. The prosperity enjoyed at New Orleans by the French or Spanish would pass instead to British traders in West Florida. A fort at the junction of the Mississippi and the Iberville would provide protection while clearing, dredging, and, finally, trading went on. Johnstone was completely convinced of the virtues of this plan. "There is nothing, on which I would pawn my Reputation so soon," he wrote and offered, if London would not advance money for the project, to have the expenses deducted from his pay until its benefits became manifest. Johnstone was not alone in his enthusiasm for the scheme and he certainly did not originate it. Sir Jeffrey Amherst had proposed in 1763 that a fort be built where the Iberville joined the Mississippi.[96] In January of the following year Major Farmar wrote of his intention to clear the Iberville to allow passage to boats with a draught of three feet; with undiminished determination in April he ordered Captain James Campbell of the Thirty-fourth Regiment to recruit New Orleans blacks to begin the work. Using not only blacks but also Frenchmen and even some English deserters, Campbell had already made good progress when Johnstone arrived in Florida in October; by December 12 he told the governor that within a month boats drawing eight feet would be able to go from the Mississippi to Mobile without passing New Orleans.[97] Strategic considerations moved Farmar; he wanted a base for an expedition to the Illinois country; he desired also to neutralize the Indians and to obviate the necessity of sailing under the guns of a potentially hostile New Orleans. Commerce was a stronger motive for Johnstone; nevertheless he and Farmar were in accord on the Iberville enterprise. On January 7, 1765, they met with Captain Campbell, Major Loftus of the Twenty-second Regiment, and Ensign Archibald Robertson of the Royal Engineers to decide on details of the fortifications to be built at Point Iberville. No doubt Robertson, already known as the architect of a new fort for Pensacola, was asked to give his ideas on what would be suitable for the Iberville. They were ambitious. The fort which he planned in collaboration with Elias Durnford would require great quantities of wood and 38,000 bricks and would cost nearly 6,000 Spanish dollars.[98] Initially the committee decided to content itself with a minimal defense structure, comprising a blockhouse and a small stockaded fort capable of housing fifty men. Johnstone promised naval cooperation; at the meeting he showed his colleagues a letter in which Sir John Lindsay offered the loan of the frigate *Nautilus*.[99]

Johnstone succeeded excellently in selling the Iberville project to the Board of Trade, which agreed to meet expenses already incurred and which approved an ambitious extension of "this useful Establishment."[100] And so the work of river clearing and of building the fort, which Johnstone named after his benefactor Bute, went on.

Progress was uneven. Great, perhaps too much, responsibility was placed on the shoulders of the junior officer Robertson. He was to get permission from the local Indians at the Iberville to build Fort Bute and was authorized, with the approval of Campbell and Stuart, to grant land to promising settlers near it but not in its immediate vicinity. The young engineer was provided with 500 Spanish dollars, bills against the British treasury with a nominal value of £1,000, Indian gifts, and a handful of gunners, but promised reinforcements to supplement his tiny command did not arrive. His vulnerability made the neighboring Indians bold. On August 27 fifty predatory Alabamas and Houmas arrived at Fort Bute looking for liquor and stores. Robertson did not know how to deal with them. For two days he and his men locked themselves in his room while the Indians roamed at will, taking all the weapons, powder, Indian presents, and drink that they could find. They killed the livestock and hurled the artillery pieces, such as they were, into the Mississippi. The plight of Robertson's party, alive but marooned in the wilderness, would have been serious had not kindly Frenchmen ferried them down the river back to frontier civilization.[101]

Johnstone was full of excuses. His orders to send reinforcements to the Iberville had been evaded by Farmar and blocked by the navy, which, now that his friend Lindsay had been replaced in Florida by Captain William Cornwallis, would not cooperate on the Iberville. The Indian attack, he darkly hinted, had been instigated by Montbéraut and a French trader called Du Part. Nevertheless he was determined to persist with the Iberville scheme in spite of all setbacks, and garrison troops would soon be arriving from the Thirty-first Regiment on board his schooner *Patty* and the transport *Prince of Wales* together with a detachment of the Twenty-first. All told they should number 120 men. Once arrived, communication between them and the larger English settlements in West Florida would be maintained, optimistically wrote Johnstone, by the *Ferret*, a vessel Lindsay would send from Jamaica. Orders to back these promises to Robertson were issued the following day.[102] Persistence was repaid. Fort Bute was restored and a garrison was installed by the end of 1765.

The governor's reports to England made small mention of the main hazard to the success of his project: the Iberville was navigable only when the Mississippi was in flood, and he showed in writing to his friend Lindsay that he knew full well that the water was high only in spring and summer, when it would bear vessels drawing six feet of water. Presumably he thought that these limitations would not prevent a lively commerce. He also knew that in September the bed of the Iberville was some twenty-four feet above the level of the larger river.[103] Keeping it clear of logs and other debris was expensive and tedious, and, if mechanical dredging were required, the available technology was insufficient. Nevertheless, the lack would be made good if labor were abundant and Johnstone never ceased in his attempts to attract immigrants. The best hope for success, as Thomas Gage appreciated, was "from the Mississippi striking with Force upon the Point, 300 yards above the Junction of that River [the Mississippi] with the Iberville."[104] Only the diversion of a natural force, in short, could turn the Iberville into a viable route for traffic. The expectations aroused in January 1765, when Lieutenant James Campbell "passed in a little pirogue from this river [the Mississippi] to Lake Maurepas" were never fulfilled. In the following year, Captain Harry Gordon, chief engineer for all British troops in the western part of America, wrote bitterly in his journal: "The free navigation of the Mississippi is a Joke, no Vessel will come to Iberville from Sea. It was once done and found merely possible at the King's Expence."[105]

Johnstone's ambitions for the post on the Iberville, which he had envisaged as a rival to New Orleans, were never realized. After all his expenditures the cost of completing the project was still estimated at £8,000 in November 1767, and it was abandoned in 1768 after his departure from Florida. His pursuit of the Iberville chimera, however, revealed some of his strengths.[106] He realized the need for speed, in that the Spaniards who were to succeed the French at New Orleans would probably try to hinder the project, and he acted fast. He secured cooperation for the project from the government and encouraged those who had to carry it out. Lastly he concerned himself in a practical way with necessary details and achieved some, though not all, of his objectives. The Iberville, or Manchac, district did attract population, enough by the following decade to send four members to the West Florida assembly: Fort Bute did become a minor trade center, and, although proof is impossible, its existence may have helped preserve peace with the Indians at a particularly dangerous time— certainly Farmar's expedition to the Illinois in December 1765 got through without hindrance after Fort Bute was established, although other measures by Farmar to ensure peace were probably more important.[107] The project ultimately failed, but it was more than a wild whim: Johnstone secured a wide variety of opinion in its support, and a decade later Thomas Hutchins, engineer and geographer, with some success advocated to the British government the possibility of a cut from the British posts on the Mississippi to those on the Gulf of Mexico.[108] Nothing was done at that time and while the superior technology of the nineteenth century would have made the opening of the Iberville feasible, the transfer of New Orleans to the United States made it unnecessary.

Apart from establishing the Iberville as a commercial waterway, the other main means by which Johnstone hoped to make the West Floridian economy boom was through participation in trade with Spanish America. The prospect was good. Lord Adam Gordon at Pensacola in 1763 wrote that "the Spanish Trade . . . will be more commodiously carried on here, than at any Port belonging to great Britain, particularly after that the Crown of Spain shall be in possession of all the East of Mississippi and New Orleans."[109]

What Johnstone tried to obtain was a relaxation of the letter of the Navigation Acts without violating their spirit and intended objectives. He was anxious to sell English manufactures to the Spanish in exchange for tropical raw materials and, in particular, for specie, since there was a chronic shortage of ready money in West Florida—"a thing incredible in a country surrounded with silver," complained the governor.[110] It would have been entirely legal under English law to carry on such a trade in English ships; unfortunately to do so would contravene Spanish laws, which were enforced with sufficient rigidity to make such transactions extremely hazardous. To carry on this type of trade in Spanish ships would be contrary to both Spanish and English law, but there were Spanish merchants and captains willing to take the risk. What Johnstone pleaded for was an easing of the British regulations so that Spanish ships which successfully escaped from Spanish ports should not be detained and held, as they were, by zealous Royal Navy commanders when they tried to enter Mobile or Pensacola.[111]

Johnstone had argued cogently for such a relaxation even before his arrival in Florida and he did not stop once he was there.[112] It was all to no avail. Perhaps he might have had more success had Lord Bute not been forced from office in April of 1763. Secretary of State Halifax, however, was cool to the point of not even bothering to present arguments for the maintenance of existing trade regulations; instead, in one short paragraph in a letter mainly about something else he stated that Spanish vessels might be admitted to the ports of West Florida only if they lacked food or water or were in distress. In no circumstances might such ships unload their cargo. Johnstone had the mortification of knowing that naval officers were unlikely to wink at the regulations, since a recent parliamentary statute had stipulated that two-thirds of the value of a smuggler's cargo as well as the entire value of his ship would go to the capturing crew.[113] So initially the governor was met by a complete rebuff in connection with Spanish trade.

In spite of all Johnstone's preoccupations and frustrations, his promotion of imaginative schemes for quick prosperity did not prevent his assiduous attention to the creation and running of the political and administrative institutions which consolidated the British grasp on West Florida and fostered slow but definite economic growth. Having appointed a council, he worked it hard. During the only two complete years of Johnstone's governorship, 1765 and 1766, the council met thirty-one and twenty-four times, respectively. By comparison, in 1767, when his successor, Montfort Browne, was for all but a few days governor, the council met only eighteen times and in 1768 only fourteen times.[114] Granting land was the council's main occupation.

Certain favored applicants were granted extensive tracts in the colony. On orders from London, large grants went to people with royal or ministerial influence. Among these were the Buteite earl of Eglinton (20,000 acres); Samuel Hannay (5,000 acres); the Indian superintendent John Stuart (10,000 acres); John Mackintosh (5,000 acres); Lord Elibank (20,000 acres), to whom Johnstone was both nephew and land agent; and the lieutenant governor, Montfort Browne (17,400 acres). These large grants were by order of the king in council. All the other seven hundred or so were less extensive, with the result that there is an appearance of rough equity in land distribution, especially as Johnstone, while governor, contented himself with a few hundred acres.[115] However, his nephew James and his supporters, Primrose Thomson, John Hannay, and Sir John Lindsay all received land, although his opponents fared less well. Apart from the lieutenant governor, the beneficiary of a royal order, only Walsh among them received a land grant and then only temporarily. Of the rest—Clifton, Wegg, Mackinnen, Farmar, and Lieutenant Colonel Maxwell—not one received cultivable land, as opposed to a town lot for an officeholder, until Johnstone had left Florida.

The council also did much to turn Mobile and Pensacola from military posts into towns and to facilitate communication between them. A member, Elias Durnford, surveyor general of the province, had laid out a plan for Pensacola by February 1765, which has given its stamp to the town even to the present day.

At the town center was the fort, adjacent to a wharf jutting into Pensacola Bay which was begun on orders from Johnstone's old acquaintance, Sir William Burnaby, in 1766. An area of some 200,000 square yards around the fort was kept free of all new building.[116] The two main streets, George and Charlotte streets (now Palafox and Alcaniz), named after the king and his consort, ran into this area on a NNW-SSE bearing and were paralleled by five others named after other members of the royal family, Gloucester, York, and Cumberland, and the early benefactors of the colony, Johnstone and Lindsay. At right angles to them were narrower streets, most holding the names of contemporary English politicians; starting with the more southerly, these were Pitt, Bute, Granby, Harcourt, and Prince's streets. Thus was the town divided into compact rectangular blocks, each of which was subdivided into twelve equal lots for allocation to private individuals. Durnford surveyed some hundreds of these and for each such town lot a complementary garden lot was available on the edge of Pensacola. Lots were reserved around the fort for the use of the military and along the waterfront for the navy. Other lots were reserved for the erection of public buildings and for the Anglican church; a lottery open to all determined the distribution of remaining lots. Johnstone himself chose no lot for himself until 201 lots had been disposed of by these methods; that is, one may presume, until everyone else in the community had been satisfied. It was an unusual display of disinterest and a shrewd one if popularity was any part of his aim.[117]

Manifestly in the allocation of land the public was given precedence over private interest. Johnstone alleged that he was guided by the system adopted in London after the Great Fire a century before, and his council followed his lead in making grants conditional on quick building and draining, on pain of forfeiture and penal quitrents.[118] The principles governing the planning of Pensacola provided a pattern followed at Mobile, Campbell Town, and Natchez.

Another conciliar activity was the drafting of regulations to improve order and health in the colony, many of which ordinances were put into legislative form after the first meeting of the assembly, to convene which Johnstone issued a proclamation in August 1766. After an election based on a comparatively wide franchise—the head of every household could vote—the fourteen members of the first assembly met in November, slightly more than two months before Johnstone left Florida, having firmly established government in a familiar and efficient form. This was a commendable but routine achievement, and though not easy, cannot be compared in difficulty with Johnstone's task of making his colony prosper economically.

Johnstone confessed, in an address to the Pensacola merchant community early in 1765, that a decision from London to relax the restrictions on trading with the Spaniards was the only thing that could make the colony "flourish in our days." He urged those merchants contemplating departure from Florida to have patience and to await a ruling on the restrictions kindlier to West Florida, which was the more likely because any such relaxation would accord with the spirit of the Navigation Acts and even, by his interpretation, with the very wording of the law. Meanwhile every man should act for the good of the colony according to his best judgment.[119]

The governor was already doing so. After placing his glowing description of West Florida's resources, climate, and opportunities with the British press, emigrants arrived in some quantity: an unofficial estimate placed their number for the year 1765 at 1,200.[120] He imported vine growers from Madeira in an attempt to stimulate viticulture and brought in blacks experienced in diving to fish for Mobile Bay oysters, which were believed to contain pearls as good as any from Brazil.[121]

Another product for which good commercial prospects were seen was the bitter wood called quassia, which was used medicinally against threadworm. As a general tonic, water which had been allowed to stand in a cup of quassia wood overnight was thought to be effective. In the eighteenth century Dutch Surinam supplied the world with quassia, but now it was found to grow in the western parts of Johnstone's colony.[122]

To offset such optimistic news was the discovery that the climate of West Florida had been overpraised. For many, especially new arrivals from England, it was deadly. In 1765 the seasoned garrison troops of the Twenty-second and Thirty-fifth Foot regiments were given deserved relief by the Twenty-first and Thirty-first regiments, who sailed directly from Britain for Mobile and Pensacola. Within six months the Twenty-first lost 3 officers, 62 rank and file, 13 women, and 23 children. Both their doctors fell ill. At Pensacola, which was by reputation the more healthy post, the Thirty-first lost 4 officers, 111 rank and file, 23 women, and a similar number of children.[123] This high mortality rate was probably paralleled by losses among the civilians who were also recent arrivals from Britain. The soldier who recorded these macabre statistics was probably not alone in thinking Florida "good for nothing but destroying Englishmen" and in abandoning previous thoughts of emigrating there.[124]

Nevertheless, the epidemic season passed with the arrival of cooler weather, and at the same time trade picked up, for despite unfulfilled hopes, money could be made in West Florida. There were contracts available from the army and navy and settlers to be clothed and fed; there was a certain, if disappointing, trade in deerskins with the Indians, and in spite of the formal hobbling of the Spanish trade, smuggling, both with Spanish Mexico and with the French at New Orleans. Charles Strachan, a Scottish factor, went to New Orleans in January 1765 and received orders for over £1,000 worth of cloth and glassware. During a year of trading he made a profit of 1,600 Spanish dollars, or about £350.[125] Johnstone told his superiors that he attempted to suppress the illegal traffic with New Orleans but that he lacked the means to do so effectively; in fact he probably did not try too hard. He gently suggested that official removal of the temptation would be more successful in ending smuggling than coercion. He clearly sympathized with the traders' dilemma. They could sell skins more quickly and for greater profit in New Orleans than by sending them to England. The subterfuge used to evade official regulations when clearing out of Mobile was to pretend that their cargo was destined for that part of West Florida nearest to New Orleans. This practice was perfectly legal and no duty was payable if British soil was their final destination. In fact the goods were then covertly ferried over to New Orleans.

In this way the sellers evaded payment of the export duties on their skins to which they were liable, but the practice did not seriously damage the main purposes of British trade policy. By contrast their custom of purchasing foreign manufactures while in New Orleans with the proceeds of their skin sales did, and Johnstone strongly objected to it. The manufactures referred to by the governor probably meant wines, liqueurs, and taffia, for the governor did not mind the importation of other New Orleans products—bricks, planks, and shingles—especially before the establishment of sawmills and brickworks in West Florida.

In general, though, there was, liquor apart, a shortage of manufactures in the European colonies in the vicinity of Florida, one that Johnstone was anxious to fill. He wanted to supply them not only with British products but also with the manufactures of continental European countries whose goods, especially linens, were on the whole cheaper than their British equivalents. To this end he proposed to his superiors that bonded warehouses be established in West Florida and suggested that European goods for reexport be imported into his colony in the regular packet boats visiting it and placed under bond of exportation.[126]

Since New Orleans had already been legally ceded to Spain, continued French government of the city was necessarily temporary. Once occupied by the Spanish it would be part of the Spanish trading system, which Johnstone constantly endeavored to infiltrate. There was abundant evidence that the Spanish themselves, whose need for European manufactures was quite unsatisfied by their own government's arrangements, were perfectly ready to be infiltrated. In 1765, a deputation of merchants arrived in Pensacola from Merida, the capital of Spanish Yucatan, to discuss means of carrying on trade with Florida.[127] Luckily, British naval officers seem to have lost some of their zeal in turning back Spanish vessels, and "several" small Spanish vessels visited Pensacola in the winter of 1765/6. "They only complain of want of goods for their cash," wrote a settler on April 1, 1766.[128] That the reason for the increased trade with the Spanish colonies lay in the greater complaisance of British naval commanders is supported by a report in the London press in December 1766 that seven Spanish vessels at once lay in St. Augustine harbor.[129]

It galled Johnstone in the same year that while his pleas for official modification of British trade regulations in favor of West Florida were ignored, both Dominica and Jamaica secured by act of Parliament the type of indulgence which he sought. The cause of this discrimination may undoubtedly be found in the existence of a powerful West Indies lobby in London and the lack of any comparable group to further the interests of West Florida.[130]

In spite of all setbacks the public works, population, and prosperity of the colony increased under the vigorous direction of its governor. One of the most obvious needs was for a road joining Mobile and Pensacola, which previously, as ports of different nations, had been unlinked. The governor boasted as early as February 1765 that he had opened such a road and had as well established a public mail service, two jails, the beginnings of a church, and a market.[131] One is obliged to wonder what he meant by "open," since, ten months later, his council was still debating how best to build the road, resolving, among other things, the absolute necessity of supplying the soldiers and sailors employed as roadmakers with half a pint of rum a day.[132] It had certainly been surveyed as early as December 1764 by the invaluable Elias Durnford, who went on to survey Pensacola Bay and then, in conjunction with a naval surveyor, George Gauld, and a military engineer, Philip Pittman, to perform a similar service at Mobile.[133]

In his efforts to stimulate economic growth Johnstone never flagged, even when his ideas were eccentric or when his own pocket was involved. In the spring of 1766 he begged the navy to provide transportation for two camels which he had been given in Jamaica and which he offered for service in the sands of Pensacola.[134] At the tail end of his governorship he offered a reward of 5,000 Spanish dollars to anyone who would introduce the manufacture of saltpeter to West Florida. The main ingredient of gunpowder, saltpeter also had a medicinal use which would make it doubly useful in the province.[135] If West Florida could become self-sufficient in powder, the supply of Indian presents, whatever happened, would never fail. In addition to Johnstone's readiness to finance the Iberville project from his personal funds, he also, it was reported, at his own expense imported experienced vine planters from Madeira and the Canary Islands.[136] He may have been stimulated to offer money prizes by the earlier proposal made by his lieutenant governor and rival, Montfort Browne, who had promised 500 Spanish dollars for the first ten pounds of cochineal produced in the colony by the French Protestant community at Campbell Town on the Escambia River, which was Browne's special interest.[137] However little Johnstone may have wanted the lieutenant governor to prosper, he certainly wanted to see Campbell Town thrive, for he valued the French immigrants highly, believing "two French worth four English."[138]

Though few of Johnstone's more bizarre schemes were heard of again after their introduction, his colony did expand. The extent of the growth is difficult to assess, since the main source of information remains the governor's own dispatches and invariably he minimized West Florida's defects and inflated his own achievements. In some ways the spring of 1766 was the zenith of his governorship. There was a lull in the ferocious personal quarrels dividing the colony, and the shadow of Indian war had not yet darkened the prospect. On successive days at the beginning of April, Johnstone, having been resident there for a year and a half, sent to the Board of Trade what was in fact a survey of West Florida's progress.

The population increase had been minimal. In February 1765, Johnstone had reported the colony's total population as 2,265, of whom 842 were black. On April 1, 1766, he described the population as "consisting of 1800 or 2000 inhabitants,"[139] although he probably excluded the two infantry regiments from his later assessment as he definitely did not from the earlier figure. Nevertheless, other aspects of the colony were more promising. Whereas in this earlier report Pensacola's residences had comprised 112 "poor despicable huts," fourteen months later he was able to gloat that 113 "good houses" had been built and that a waterfront lot without a building would now fetch 300 Spanish dollars. Along the coast near the town good clay had been found for making brick dwellings and inexhaustible quantities of marl for their kitchen gardens, which had sprung up in many places: "Beans and every vegetable of the vine flourishes here." Another source indicates that Pensacolans had indeed found their soil fertile and that they could also grow cabbages, citrus fruits, dates, apricots, coffee, and cocoa. In the countryside around the capital were eighteen farmhouses whose inhabitants were successfully growing grain. Fresh meat was plentiful, although still expensive. There were, Johnstone estimated, 7,000 cattle in West Florida. Indians brought them to Pensacola to sell along with deer and turkeys, which commanded 8 and 2 Spanish dollars each, respectively.[140]

This tale of abundance was echoed in an anonymous letter dated April 1, 1766, which subsequently appeared in the British press. Its optimistic tone is suspect, since it was probably written by James Bruce, who, as a member of the West Florida council and collector of the customs at Pensacola, may have considered it his duty to praise the province. As a staunch Johnstoneite, he possibly wrote it for propaganda purposes at the governor's request. The author of the piece stated that he had recently turned farmer and that he had already been offered £500 for his one-hundred-acre holding a mile and a half from the capital. "Our colony turns out beyond conception," he wrote. It produced superior cotton, its pine trees could each supply a barrel and a half of tar and, on that part of the province bordering on the Mississippi, the sugar plants were lusher than those of the West Indies. All that was lacking was labor to cultivate the cotton and sugar, to extract the tar, and, he added, to make bricks and distilleries to supply whisky and peach brandy to the Indians.[141]

Another nameless author gives information about the Mobile district in 1766, which by his computation included 140 houses and plantations and a total population of 860, of whom 360 were black. Like most contemporary observers he noted that Pensacola was healthier than Mobile for humans. But Mobile was healthier for cattle—he estimated their number at 8,000, even higher than Johnstone—and Pensacola had none except for some milch cows imported from Mobile. The latter, he also noted, still did more trade in skins than Pensacola.[142]

There is no denying that Johnstone glossed over many disappointments in his dispatches, the diseases, desertions, paucity of skilled immigrants, and after all his ingenuity, the failure of innovative crops and enterprises to generate wealth. In 1769, two years after Johnstone's departure, skins were still the only staple commodity of the provinces.[143]

Nevertheless, it does seem that Johnstone's efforts made his colony self-sufficient in food, and it may be salutary to recall the despair of early settlers who were convinced that nothing could flourish in the sandy soil to appreciate the beneficial aspect of the governor's energetic optimism. With respect to population it may be worthwhile to note that as late as 1771 the sister colony of East Florida had a population of only 1,188, including 900 blacks.[144] It should be realized, too, that, despite the high prices attracting Floridian smugglers to New Orleans, neighboring Louisiana was in a desperate economic plight. "Today there is no longer any money, any commerce," wrote its governor in 1765, and he resented Johnstone's success in drawing French citizens from New Orleans to Mobile.[145]

Comparatively, and considering for how short a time he had been bending his ingenuity to the task of making West Florida prosper, his achievement was creditable. It did not, however, outweigh, in the eyes of the ministry in England, the destructive effects of his abrasive relations with others in and around West Florida. The outcome was that Johnstone ceased to be a governor.

How and why this came about has always been misstated. "In January 1767 [runs an otherwise authoritative version], after he had begun to make plans for a punitive war against the Creek Indians, which ran counter to government policy, he was recalled."[146] Indians also figure prominently in other discussions of Johnstone's recall.[147] The fact of the matter was that the Indian war was not a reason for the governor's recall. It was an excuse for his dismissal and a very poor one, since the governor never did wage war on any Indians.

Circumstantial evidence suggests that Johnstone's fate was decided from the moment that William Petty, second earl of Shelburne, became secretary of state for the southern department on August 2, 1766, borne back to power in one of the several major ministerial changes of the decade. The earl was acquainted with the governor: when both were Bute supporters, Shelburne had presided over the Board of Trade at the time of Johnstone's appointment as governor in 1763; in the following year Shelburne, who was deeply involved in East Indian Company affairs, backed the loser and Johnstone the winner in the great rivalry between Clive and Sulivan.[148] After Shelburne left the Board of Trade in 1763 he abandoned his connection with Bute, became a disciple of Pitt, and considered imperial problems while in Opposition. When he became secretary of state he was responsible for colonial affairs. He was only twenty-nine but able, conscientious, and in the aftermath of the Stamp Act and Declaratory Act, against which he had voted along with only four other peers, convinced of the need to conciliate the colonies.[149] To this end he thought that in the existing situation, colonial governors should avoid treading on toes, and in September he wrote to every governor in the American continent "to behave with temper and moderation" toward the colonies in their charge.[150] He probably knew from personal experience that tact was a quality which did not come easily to Johnstone. If so, his first weeks in office would have confirmed that, in that respect, Johnstone's experience as governor had not changed him.

In August 1766, a letter reached England in which the attorney general of West Florida complained that Johnstone had suspended him unjustly; in September the news arrived that the governor had also suspended the chief justice. Simultaneously came a petition from twenty-two colonists complaining of Johnstone's "unjustifiable, arbitrary and Tyrannical Principles."[151] Shelburne must also have been aware of the long-standing feud which Johnstone had waged with the army. Clearly if Shelburne sought harmony in West Florida, and all the evidence suggests he did, then the first obvious step would be to get rid of the turbulent governor. Removal was easy. Friends, surely with Johnstone's approval if not at his urging, had petitioned Shelburne to grant him leave of absence to attend to his private affairs. The secretary wasted little time and on September 22, 1766, wrote simultaneously to Johnstone, giving him six months' leave, and to his lieutenant governor, conferring gubernatorial power on him.[152] That this was tantamount to Johnstone's dismissal is suggested by the fact that when Shelburne wished to replace Sir Francis Bernard as governor of Massachusetts in May of 1767, he drafted a letter granting him leave of absence.[153] If it may be accepted that September 22, 1766, was the real date of Johnstone's dismissal, then Shelburne recalled him at a time when he knew Johnstone had done much amiss but had not, as far as he could know, been unduly bellicose toward Indians.

Actually Johnstone had not, would not, and, without the cooperation of the military and the Indian superintendent, could not make war on the Indians. He was no pacifist. Neither were other British leaders in North America, who were united in support of the principle of "divide and rule," and who thus watched with complacency while a war developed between Creeks and Choctaws in the summer of 1766. Brigadier William Tayler, for instance, alleged that he preferred peace but thought that if the Creeks were to attack the British then his countrymen should combine with other Indians, attack the Creeks from every quarter and "put a stop at once to their Ill Conduct." John Stuart thought that "a war between the Creeks and Choctaws would be an Event rather advantageous to us than otherwise." General Gage himself did not want the English to make war on the Creeks: "we can never be gainers by a War with Indians." Nevertheless, the policy he advocated might well have brought one about. In alliance with Cherokees, Chickasaws, and Catawbas, he suggested, "to act against the Creeks, a few Provincials and regulars properly employed with their allies in their incursions . . . will soon bring the Creeks to reason."[154]

Johnstone's opinions on the Creek-Choctaw war were only minimally more extreme than those of his colleagues. He was proud of his contribution to the outbreak of intertribal hostilities: "tho' I claim some merit in this Transaction yet certainly their own passions chiefly operated to produce the Effect we wanted."[155] He went on a month later to propose to the government in London that the British should initiate war against the Creeks on a large scale. This farfetched scheme would have involved 1,700 British regular troops, 1,000 provincials, 400 marines and nearly 1,000 Indian auxiliaries.[156] That he should imagine such a plan could be welcome shows that Johnstone was losing touch with reality. His suggestion was contrary to the government's known preference for peace with the Indians; it was contrary to morality in that Johnstone advocated "destroying Men, Women, and Children"; and he proposed it at a time when the politicians in England were desperate in their attempts to reduce colonial expenditure. It should be noted that this wild letter did not reach London until October, after Shelburne's letter granting leave to Johnstone.

The governor, all the same, was not so out of touch with reality as to delude himself that he could wage war without cooperation: "I can do little more than represent," he wrote to Stuart. "The Management of the Indians is in you. The power to Chastise them and defend us is in the Brigadier."[157] The cooperation he sought was denied, but Johnstone did not stop "representing," and he drummed up support for a preventive war among his council, which joined him in urging Brigadier Tayler in October "that every Hostile measure permitted by the Laws of Nations, should be used against the Creek Indians."[158]

The wisdom of Gage and his subordinates in never allowing Johnstone authority over troops was now vindicated. Johnstone did not wage war on the Creeks, but the only reason that he did not was because he could not. And although Johnstone knew that without support he could not, the reports trickling through to Shelburne were alarming. Stuart forwarded to the secretary of state letters he had received from Johnstone. They contained sentiments which were not only of unabated bellicosity but which were also highly insulting to the ministry: "The Imbecility of Our Government," raved Johnstone, who was probably under the impression that only Stuart would read the words, would cause the murder of Englishmen by Creeks to be "huddled up by an Expensive tedious & useless Congress."[159]

The governor's belligerence did not result in war but did indirectly hasten his own downfall in that it provoked a general review of his conduct in office. Evidently convinced from his correspondence with Johnstone that a Creek war was imminent, Brigadier Tayler had applied to the

treasury for permission to spend extensively on the necessary preparations. The first lord of the treasury, the duke of Grafton, was aghast. He
became convinced that there must be no delay in sending out a replacement for Johnstone and raised the question in a cabinet meeting. There
followed a general consideration of Johnstone's performance as a colonial
governor, resulting, perhaps unfairly, in condemnation. There were no
cabinet members to emphasize the positive side of his governorship. In
general they were out of tune with his ambitions. Lord Barrington, for
example, the minister at war of the day, wrote in 1766 of West Florida that
"from the badness of the soil near the sea, and the unhealthiness of the air,
we should never attempt to settle or inhabit it."[160] They found that
Johnstone's conduct, irrespective of his dealings with the Creeks, was that
of "a Perfect Madman." All agreed that he should be replaced with "the
utmost dispatch." The king endorsed the verdict.[161]

Both his duty to his colleagues and obedience to his sovereign obliged the
secretary to dismiss Johnstone instantly. He probably did so willingly,
even though it put him in the irrational position of firing an official who, by
reasonable calculation, was already on his way back to England.
Johnstone had, in fact, left Pensacola on January 13 aboard the brig
Betsy,[162] in response to Shelburne's letter granting him leave, five weeks
before the secretary wrote him a tart dismissal on February 19, 1767.

Shelburne wrote as if Johnstone had actually begun hostilities against
the Creeks. At the time of writing he may have believed so, but he certainly
knew better later the same day. In a companion letter to the dismissal he
ordered Montfort Browne to take over Johnstone's responsibilities and to
put "an entire and immediate stop to hostilities." Before completing the
letter, however, he received word from Gage that Brigadier Tayler had
succeeded in preventing a Creek war.[163] Nevertheless, Shelburne did not
evidently find the news any reason to alter his letter to Johnstone and gave
his warmongering as the first reason for his dismissal. That he also
fomented the "Spirit of Disunion" in Florida was accorded secondary position. The loss of his governorship was probably unwelcome but not totally
unexpected. As long before as July 1765 he had written of his future plans
after his "unwearied toil and best endeavors have procured that dismission
which the fluctuating nature of our government bids every wise man to
stand prepared for."[164]

Johnstone's record as governor of West Florida was mixed. Inexperience
and temperamental unsuitability account for his failures. Prior to his
appointment, the result of the idiosyncratic patronage system, Johnstone
had borne no greater responsibility than the command of a sloop. The
difficulties of such a command, especially in time of war, may easily be
underestimated, but in one respect there was an axiomatic simplicity
about it; in all but the most extraordinary circumstances, the commander's

word was law and might not be questioned, let alone opposed. Johnstone had served no apprenticeship in government and never did seem fully to understand that to govern a colony was to preside over a much more complex political organism than a ship's company. Although the governor of West Florida was vested with considerable power, his was a circumscribed authority. Certain centers of power in the colony had to be conciliated rather than commanded. Johnstone, as his performance at the Indian congresses demonstrated, was not without conciliatory flair. He could also get along permanently with people, as his relations with Stuart, Wedderburn, and most of his council showed. What he found difficult to do was to sustain a conciliatory manner when he was thwarted or disappointed. The duels of his early naval career and the thrashing which he gave to the hack writer Brooks attest to his tendency, when frustrated, to turn to violence. They form part of a pattern repeated in West Florida. When the lieutenant governor objected to Johnstone's assertion that he was a swindler, the governor offered a challenge, to which, as Browne priggishly reported, he hoped he made a proper reply, that is, refused.[165]

In that it tolerated dueling, the eighteenth-century ethical code allowed the removal of an offensive person by killing, but only on the individual level. Johnstone, being an extreme man, extended this principle to an unacceptable length when he advocated the extermination of the lower Creeks. Even on his own figures—they had killed 138 whites in twenty-five years—the Creeks were a nuisance rather than a menace.[166] This drastic recourse to mass annihilation after the failure of conciliation was not an isolated quirk. A precisely similar pattern is discernible a dozen years later in Johnstone's dealings with the rebellious American colonists. His inability to sustain conciliatory efforts also resulted in the division into factions of theWest Florida community, where achieving harmony should have received high priority.

Johnstone had counterbalancing virtues. He was no absentee, and he was not lazy. He initiated action, interested himself in detail, and although his hopes of a swift, bustling prosperity in West Florida never materialized, his energetic efforts did help the establishment of political institutions, the orderly distribution of lands, the laying out of towns, and the creation of a viable commercial community, all in a sensible rather than a haphazard fashion and in a comparatively short time. His work in Florida was destined to be his most permanent achievement.

Presumably Johnstone thought well of his own record, since he was not ashamed to style himself Governor Johnstone for the rest of his life. Nevertheless his best gifts lay less in governorship than in opposition to the rule of others. His scathing invective, his flair for ridicule, his overstatements, and his talent for intrigue were all to find more effective employment in the irresponsible field of parliamentary opposition than was possible when he was a colonial governor.

3. The Guerrilla of Leadenhall Street

The political world of the later 1760s which Johnstone entered on his return from Florida had seen many changes in his absence. Grenville had been in power when the governor had received his commission, only to fall after the failure of the Stamp Act. Rockingham had temporarily seized the dropped reins but had been compelled to hand them over to Chatham, from whom George III hoped for stability at last. But in 1767, the year of Johnstone's return to England, the mind of Chatham began to give way and he could no longer hold together the diverse individuals who made up the "Tessellated Pavement Ministry."

The times were in turmoil. Victory in war had brought almost as many problems as defeat would have done. One was a national debt which, at £133 million, terrified many, and another was the administration of territorial acquisitions similarly daunting in scale. Meanwhile unprecedented economic events created puzzlement and alarm. The world's first credit crisis rocked markets in 1763, and in 1764 Hargreave's invention of the spinning jenny foretold massive alterations in the British economy.[1] In addition there was, in this disordered decade, a growing clamor for improvements in government, which were rightly thought necessary for a changing society. England was not ready for radical ideologues peddling new constitutions; there was, however, scope for the gifted demagogue who, even if he lacked traditional qualifications for political success, could work on public opinion which, in the 1760s, was growing rapidly as a factor in politics. It was the age of Wilkes.

The times were apt, too, for a Johnstone, who had discovered that he had a talent for mob oratory. We learn from Archibald Campbell, a literary friend of the governor, that in 1767 Johnstone was contemplating entry to Parliament and was speaking publicly in the *atrox genus dicendi* (literally, "fierce type of speech"). This mode, called by Cicero the *Vehemens Oratio*, was in Campbell's opinion "the only species of Eloquence worth a farthing, the only one which can force a man into power and acquire him a great and lasting reputation."[2] Presumably Campbell knew of Johnstone's speeches in the East India Company's Court of Proprietors.

It was natural that Johnstone should have perfected his oratorical and political skills in Leadenhall Street before graduating to Parliament, for he was already an established figure there. John Company, like so much in the 1760s, was undergoing great changes. The chief one, possibly, was that government was involving itself in company affairs with the hope of solving some of its own considerable financial problems by participation in the apparent prosperity of the commercial organization. The company's natural response was to attempt to protect itself against encroachment by increasing its representation and influence in Parliament. The administration could claim, quite legitimately, that closer supervision of the company had become imperative, since its servants had extended their activities into areas more normally the preserves of government than of a trading concern, particularly when Clive had accepted the *diwani* for the company from the Mogul emperor in 1765.[3]

The Johnstone group, which had supported Clive against Sulivan in 1764, had cause during George Johnstone's absence in Florida to reverse its allegiance. The reason lay in Clive's extraordinary prosecution of a double standard in company ethics. Having secured his *jagir,* the hero of Plassey hounded John Johnstone out of India in 1765, ostensibly for taking presents from Nujum-ud-daula, and the pro-Clive directorate resolved in 1766 to proceed against John Johnstone in chancery for his misdeeds in Bengal. The result was that the Johnstone group and Henry Vansittart, who had also felt Clive's displeasure, joined forces in support of Sulivan and tried to restore Clive's chief rival to the directorate. They were joined by those who, contrary to the wishes of Clive's director friends, wanted to declare an increased dividend for East India stock.

Thanks to his plundering in Bengal, John Johnstone was now a rich man and is supposed to have contributed £37,000 to the cause of the opposition party in the company. This money could be used for "splitting," the practice of dividing out £500 lots of stock to nominal owners, each of whom would have a vote in the General Court of Proprietors. Together with the votes created by their new allies, the Johnstones were able, at a General Court on September 26, 1766, to obtain a dividend increase from 6 percent to 10 percent but were unable to secure the abandonment of the case against John Johnstone.[4] The earl of Shelburne had deeply involved himself in East Indian affairs during 1766 and in September worked with the Johnstones in support of Laurence Sulivan. It is tempting to believe that when, in September 1766, Shelburne, as secretary of state, wrote to George Johnstone in Florida that "upon the Application of your Friends to me" he would give him "Leave to return to England on your Private Affairs for Six Months" that the "private affairs" were in fact East India Company affairs and that the "friends" would have included Sulivan, who was constantly at Shelburne's house at this time, and John Johnstone, whom his brother had once before helped out of a difficulty and now needed him again.[5] Another who may have asked Shelburne to bring George Johnstone home was George Dempster, who had ties with the governor but who was also acting as a liaison officer between the Rockingham group in Parliament, of which he was a member, and the Sulivanite opposition alliance at East India House.

Johnstone was back in England in March, in time for the election of directors on April 9, 1767, but even with his support the Sulivan coalition was not quite strong enough to overthrow the pro-Clive directorate, which nevertheless felt compelled to trim its sails to the wind then prevailing. In reply to a scheme which Sulivan had proposed in November 1766 for a negotiated sharing of profits and revenue between the company and the government, the directors approved, immediately before the April election, a similar counterplan of their own. Its essence was that in return for a renewal of the company charter and permission to raise money by loans, the company would pay a lump sum to the government and, after deduction of money for necessary expenses, share its income and profits with the government.

The Johnstones decided, before the negotiations between directors and government were complete, to press hard for their closest interest, the abandonment of the charges against John Johnstone. To muster sufficient strength they coupled this aim with another, which was unwelcome to the directors and economically quite unjustifiable but extremely popular with the rank and file of the proprietors—raising the dividend yet again.

Victory crowned their efforts; at a General Court on May 6, 1767, the directors' scheme for sharing profits and revenues was voted down, while William Johnstone Pulteney's motion to raise the dividend on company stock to 12½ percent was passed.[6] Another motion, "that the various Prosecutions commenced by order of the Court of Directors . . . against their former servants in Bengal . . . on Account of Presents received . . . be discharged" also passed.[7]

The ministry, now headed by Johnstone's old critic Grafton, was outraged. In order to avert what the duke was convinced would be a worse catastrophe than the South Sea Bubble, the collapse of which, forty-seven years before, had ruined thousands of speculators and brought down a government, he had a bill introduced into Parliament which would compel the company to rescind its recent dividend increase and to keep it down to 10 percent for at least a year.[8] Shortly afterward he instigated the introduction of another bill to prevent the practice of "splitting." In an attempt to persuade the ministry to abandon these bills, Sulivan mustered the support of a General Court on May 18 for a more generous profit-sharing scheme. The company would pay the government a fixed sum of £400,000 a year. The offer was accepted, but the ministry declined to thwart the passage of the bills against "splitting" and the high dividend. Thus, in exchange for John Johnstone's exoneration, the Johnstone group had helped to bring about a situation whereby the company offered to pay the government annually more than it could afford and to submit to parliamentary limitations on its internal operations.

George Johnstone's precise role in these events is difficult to determine. Contemporary newspapers were coy about using names when reporting East India Company affairs and the minutes of the General Court are terse. What the Johnstone group did is more ascertainable than the activities of any of its individual members. That the governor was in the forefront in prosecuting the self-serving destructive tactics of the

Johnstone group is so likely as to be almost a certainty. There is little reason to doubt the essential truth of an account of his activities during this period, which was printed in 1781, even if the laudatory interpretation placed on them may be questioned:

Upon his return from America the following year [1767], he made himself very conspicuous in the debates at the India-house when the late lord Clive found in him a formidable opponent. . . . The governor had, by this time, through great assiduity and attention, made himself a perfect master of the state of our Asiatic affairs; and we accordingly find, he did not confine his disquisitions upon this subject to orations at the India-house where he never failed displaying great force of reasoning, and a thorough acquaintance with the subjects under investigation, but he also proved himself a very able writer upon the measures in agitation. We are well assured he was the author of several pamphlets which appeared in vindication of his brother's conduct, who had been employed in the company's service abroad, and several other productions that were published, relative to Asiatic affairs. They were written in a masterly style and at once proved him the scholar and the man of business.[9]

Of the apparently numerous speeches which Johnstone made in the Court of Proprietors in the period between his return from Florida and his entry into Parliament, only one may be read in full today and that is possible only because he was proud enough to have it printed and sold for sixpence a copy. At eight thousand words, it was probably longer than his usual speeches, although there is no doubt that the governor was given to verbosity. There is in it no trace of humor; instead Johnstone strove, calamitously to modern eyes, for pathos, attempting the Ciceronian *Vehemens Oratio* which Archibald Campbell had so approved, of which the classic example outside of antiquity is Mark Antony's funeral oration in *Julius Caesar*. The technique in this mode is, while disclaiming any attempt to appeal to the hearers' emotions, in fact subtly to arouse their sympathy and then, when they are suitably moved, to capture their will with forceful argument. Johnstone's speech was so contrived that one might imagine the governor had, as he wrote, his Cicero open at the page where the Roman described the "three objects which alone have power to persuade . . . that the minds of the audience be conciliated, informed and moved."[10]

Primarily the speech was a plea to the General Court to compel the directors to pay compensation for private losses in the war against Kasim Ali Khan in 1763. The pro-Clive directorate had declared the war aggressive in that its purpose was to perpetuate the illicit inland trade in Bengal and had refused to compensate inland traders, including, it may be presumed, John Johnstone. In many places the speech was less a plea than an attack. Johnstone's particular targets were Clive, "a mock Pompey who reaps the Glory of the Conquests made by others,"[11] and a director, Clive's "man of business" in London, Luke Scrafton, whom Johnstone assaulted obliquely but venomously: "Judas too had his Reasons, and there is one among the twenty-four [directors] who has his Admirers." Hyperbole was not reserved for Johnstone's enemies; excessive praise was lavished on his friends. Adam Ferguson, for example, whose *Civil Society* Johnstone quoted, was "the greatest Author this Age has produced." Johnstone displayed a detailed grasp of Indian affairs, interlarding his arguments with excerpts from political theorists, from Plutarch, and from the jurist Vattel, but his oration had grave defects. It contained a lengthy extract from an opponent's pamphlet and several minutes worth of French—a most uncertain way of holding attention—and, moreover, it was long and obviously insincere. Not only was the speech couched in the language of the highest idealism, when in fact its probable object was the reimbursement of his rapacious brother, but also many listeners to his philippics against Clive would have remembered how, four years before, he had collaborated with Clive and Scrafton to pull down Sulivan.[12] Nevertheless *The Critical Review* thought well of his oratorical potential. Having advised Johnstone to prune the luxuriance of his verbiage, it concluded:

> This is a hint we should not take the pains to throw out to an ordinary speaker; but we think this gentleman's abilities would entitle him, with a little application, to a rank amongst the *diserti* if not the *eloquentes*....[13]

Soon afterward George Johnstone sought to enter Parliament, a natural stepping-stone for anyone wanting prestige, influence, and lucrative appointments. In addition, since the late 1760s was a period when the government and Parliament were beginning to exert authority over East India Company affairs, it was logical that Johnstone, in order to increase his influence and to protect his family's interests in the company, should seek, like so many of his stockholder allies, a seat in the House of Commons.

An attempt to secure one while he was still governor of West Florida had come to nothing. John Johnstone and William Pulteney had approached John Home in the hope that he would persuade Lord Bute to use his influence in the Aberdeen Burghs to secure the election of their brother George. Home was confident that Bute would recommend Johnstone if he recommended anyone at all, but the influence of the "Favourite" in Aberdeen was not as great as that of the earl of Panmure, who preferred, in the election of 1767, the probable date of Home's efforts for Johnstone, to help Sir John Lindsay obtain a seat for the Burghs.[14]

Johnstone found a more effective patron in Sir James Lowther. This young baronet, "the great Prince of the coalpits" as Walpole called him, was enormously wealthy, having inherited estates worth £2 million before he came of age. Riches gave scope to his least desirable traits; he was "a domestic bashaw and an intolerable tyrant over his tenants." His wealth also enabled him to indulge a passion for electioneering. Known as a "shameless political sharper," he was ambitious to control all ten constituencies in the counties of Cumberland and Westmorland.[15] To get what he wanted involved overturning the considerable entrenched interests of the earls of Thanet, Egremont, and Carlisle and of the duke of Portland. Ultimately he controlled a body of M. P.s called "Sir James' Nine Pins," a motley group which included various undistinguished members of his family but also some of the ablest politicians of the century: John Robinson, Charles Jenkinson, and Sir George Macartney. William Pitt the Younger too, although never one of the "pins," was given his first parliamentary seat by Lowther.[16] Johnstone, who was a "pin," probably made the acquaintance of Lowther before he became governor of West Florida, when he was on the fringes of Lord Bute's entourage, for Lowther too had links with the "Favourite"; he was one of his doughtiest political supporters and, in April 1761, had married Mary, Bute's eldest daughter. The bond provided by a common political affiliation to Bute was frayed by 1768 and what probably most commended Johnstone to Lowther was the forensic talent which he had shown at India House and, possibly, Johnstone's Grub Street productions. What Lowther needed in 1768 were advocates for his side in one of the most celebrated legal disputes of the age, one which spilled from the courts into Parliament and onto the undignified battlefield of pamphlet warfare.

The case was complex. It derived from an attempt by the duke of Portland in 1765 to punish his rival, Sir James, for infringing his fishing rights. Lowther then discovered that the duke occupied lands as his own which had not been specifically granted to his forebear, the earl of Portland, by William III in 1686. In a legal counterattack he petitioned the crown for, and was granted, those same lands, most of which were in the Carlisle area. Friends of the duke riposted by introducing the Nullum Tempus bill into Parliament, the principle of which was that there were time limits on royal claims, so that royal sales, such as the one by which Lowther had recently acquired land at Carlisle, might be declared illegal. Sir James denied the principle, the bill initially failed, and Lowther's claims were temporarily sustained. In his triumph he evicted three hundred of Portland's tenants, but he knew that his rights were debatable and during the years when his case was in dispute he needed spokesmen of Johnstone's caliber.

The matter seemed to be settled in 1771 in favor of Portland when the Court of the Exchequer ruled that the crown grant to Lowther was invalid on the technical ground that the quitrent payable was less than one-third of the annual value of the manors, lands, and messuages, and the grant thus contravened a statute passed in the reign of Queen Anne. But Sir James was tenacious. Although his own claim was quashed, the legitimacy of the duke's title still remained in question. Perhaps in the hope of ruining Portland, whose resources, as Lowther knew, were, though large, less ample than his own, Sir James persisted in expensive litigation to prove the duke's title. The affair dragged on for years.

By 1776 Lowther evidently thought that legal battering had brought Portland to the point of exhaustion and proposed negotiation. He would drop legal proceedings, he told the duke through his agent George Johnstone, provided that he might buy all of the disputed land. Portland's representative, John Dunning, replied that part but not all of the land might possibly be sold but only at a price that would give his employer a handsome profit. Johnstone thought that the basis for a compromise transaction existed, but Lowther was intransigent. He wanted all of the land for a price set, not by the duke, but by arbitrators. The negotiations thus broke down, but Johnstone remained optimistic that they might be reopened. In the summer of 1776 he traveled to Carlisle in the hope of talking about an accommodation with the duke. On the way he stopped at Wentworth to visit Rockingham and so impressed the earl with the sincerity of his intentions that the peer seems to have urged Portland against dismissing Johnstone without a hearing. The duke was quite prepared to receive overtures: he thought that to do otherwise might damage his interest in Carlisle. And there was, even on August 6, a price at which he was prepared to sell out. Only a few days later the lengthy trial ended and the Court of the Exchequer confirmed Portland in the possession of all his lands around Carlisle.[17]

If, in the long run, Lowther failed to secure his end, he failed in the short run too. Evidently impressed by Johnstone, the baronet decided to use him to complete the political control of the borough of Carlisle which had long been the object of his ambition. He had begun inroads on the duke of Portland's traditional domination of the city in 1763 by becoming an alderman. In 1765, after a severe contest with a nominee of the duke, Lowther was elected mayor and at once initiated a program for reform designed to shake the hold of the Blues, Portland's supporters, and to enhance the influence of his own, the Yellows. He broadened the qualifications necessary for city bailiffs, hitherto chosen exclusively from the corporation, so that all freemen became eligible, and secured the removal of several Blue aldermen. In addition he instigated a thorough examination of corporation accounts, and it was discovered that grave irregularities had occurred during the years of Blue domination. The city was in debt, and it was found that illegal land grants had been made to Blue aldermen. Sir James reformed the city finances to such good effect that by 1767 Carlisle was almost solvent again. To complete his work he hoped, in the general election of 1768, to run Yellow parliamentary candidates who would defeat Portland's nominees. He chose two naval captains, John Elliot and George Johnstone.

Elliot had enjoyed a similar but more fortunate career in the Royal Navy than his running mate. As a brother of the influential Gilbert Elliot who became a lord of the Admiralty in 1756, he had enjoyed swift promotion, rising from midshipman to lieutenant in 1756 and obtaining a postcaptaincy in 1757 at the age of twenty-five. He had obtained celebrity in 1760 by pitting three frigates against a French squadron of similar numbers and compelling its surrender off the Irish coast. Under Lowther's patronage he had become M.P. for Cockermouth in 1767.[18]

Sir James liked to reserve seats which he completely controlled, like those at Cockermouth and Appleby, for weaker candidates whom he favored, such as members of his family. Often, too, he would run a friend for two constituencies, one doubtful, the other a safe Lowther seat. If successful in both, the candidate would retain the doubtful seat, allowing Sir James to dispose of the other as he pleased.

Despite Lowther's gains at the municipal level, he would be lucky to add Carlisle to his parliamentary collection. Nevertheless, he evidently considered that Elliot and Johnstone, with his ample backing, would be strong enough to defeat their Blue opponents, Lord Edward Bentinck, the duke of Portland's brother, and George Musgrave, a member of a family which had often represented Carlisle in the House of Commons.[19]

The 1768 campaign for the borough was an active one. The Reverend Alexander Carlyle, who was present, tells of the skill with which Johnstone managed to pacify a drunken squire who had been punched by one of the minister's friends, an incident worth recalling in view of Johnstone's reputation for violence.[20] Drunks were probably a common sight in Carlisle at the time, since the Scottish candidates practiced to extremity the crudest and most usual method of securing the goodwill of the freemen. The liquor bill which they ran up in twenty-two public houses at Lowther's expense totaled £3,781. 18s. 10d. On the night before the poll, Lowther resorted to a drastic device to influence the outcome of the election. The Carlisle corporation created thirty freemen, all of the Yellow faction, but refused a similar enfranchisement to twenty-two Blues with equal claims. Lowther's vast expenditure and "dirty tricks" proved in vain. It is the destiny of ninepins to fall at times and the result of the election was that Bentinck secured 387 votes, Musgrave 385, Elliott 309, and Johnstone 307.[21]

Lowther seems to have continued to trust Johnstone's political ability in spite of his lamentable showing in the Carlisle election. Himself elected for one of the Cumberland seats by a margin of only two votes and by the most dubious of methods, Sir James employed Johnstone to approach his defeated and indignant opponent, Henry Fletcher, in order to work out some kind of compromise so that Fletcher would accept the electoral result as it stood. After meeting his supporters at the King's Arms public house in Carlisle and discovering their opposition to any such arrangement,[22] Fletcher persisted in his determination to have the House of Commons investigate the election, as a result of which Lowther was eventually unseated.

In spite of this further failure of Johnstone, Sir James continued to show partiality for the Scot and swiftly provided him with a substitute for the seat which he had failed to win at Carlisle, much to the fury of Sir James's brother-in-law, the duke of Bolton, who wrote that he had always feared "that some evil genius would persuade you to take part with the family of Johnston[e]." He was sorry that Lowther "should be so governed and persuaded by that Captain Johnston[e] to act so contrary to your own interest." If he had sponsored a more suitable candidate, Carlisle could have been won. He foresaw correctly that Lowther would be out of Parliament "to bring in Johnston[e]" and promised that he would not work politically with his relative as long as Sir James allied himself with the Scot.[23] According to Alexander Carlyle, the indulgence shown to Johnstone was the work of John Home, "who prevailed with him to prefer George Johnstone . . . to Admiral [actually Captain at the time] Elliott for one of his seats in Parliament, though he was by no means the best man. . . ."[24] The seat found for Johnstone was Lowther's pocket borough Cockermouth. At the time of the general election in March 1768, Jenkinson had been nominated for it, but since he was also elected for Appleby, he gave up Cockermouth to Johnstone. On May 24 the governor was elected with, as was usual in pocket boroughs, a minimum of formality; without delay he turned to the affairs of the East India Company.

The recent act of Parliament against "splitting" had sought to discourage the practice by stipulating that individuals in the company's Court of Proprietors might vote only if they had held £500 worth of stock for over six months. Its only effect was to bring the "splitting" season forward from the winter prior to the annual directorial election in April to the previous summer. "Splitting" was practiced even more extensively than before; there were 1,400 qualified voters in 1769 compared with 700 in 1768. Since John Johnstone had decided to be a candidate for the directorate in April 1769, his family had to busy themselves in 1768.[25]

The group had altered its allegiance yet again. Rather than Sulivan, it was Sir George Colebrooke, a director who strongly opposed all ministerial encroachments on the company's affairs, whom they supported in 1768. Nevertheless, the family did not rely on Colebrooke's followers and made a considerable effort to increase the number of voters whose allegiance was exclusively to the Johnstones through "splitting" stock. The capital used was John Johnstone's. George was not wealthy, neither buying nor selling any company stock in 1768, but he probably served his brother's cause by recruiting and instructing reliable supporters of the protean Johnstonian strategies.

It was probably in 1768 that Johnstone wrote a bitter letter to Pulteney accusing William of estranging himself from his brothers after his wife had inherited the Pulteney fortune in the previous year. He was contemplating negotiations, almost certainly in connection with East India House tactics, and wanted William to lead them: he was deliberately vague as to who was involved, but he did write emphatically that his old enemy Shelburne and Lauchlin Macleane, his "man of business," were not.[26]

How William replied to his brother's letter is unknown, but he did cooperate with the ambitions of his brother John by selling him £5,000 of East India stock on August 23, 1768. Broken up into ten £500 lots these shares were sold to supporters on October 1, 1768, which was, significantly, a few days more than six months before the directorial election of 1769. The ten new owners were three of the lesser Johnstone brothers, James, Alexander, and Gideon; George's friend John Home; John Robinson, George's colleague among Lowther's "nine pins"; David Wedderburn, the governor's military supporter in West Florida; Alexander Macpherson, who may have been another of several Macphersons with whom Johnstone was friendly; as well as John Dingwall, Hugh Lawson, and Peter Ramon, whose connection with Johnstone is unknown. In addition to these newly qualified supporters of the clan there were others of longer standing, like Johnstone's literary acquaintance Archibald Campbell, who sold out as soon as the 1769 election was over.[27]

The result of all this activity was disappointing for John Johnstone, who, in the fiercely contested and evenly balanced directorial election of 1769, was unsuccessful, securing only 689 votes when 775 was the minimum obtained by a successful candidate. Nevertheless the role of the Johnstone group was crucial in the election. According to a contemporary account:

> The most extraordinary piece of jo[c]keyship was practised on this occasion, that perhaps was ever attempted. No less than 13,000 l. capital stock i.e. equivalent to 26 votes, issued out to qualify by *one set of gentlemen*, was employed by him to whom the management of it was entrusted, to make votes for *the other*, and on this Machiavellian finesse, the grand point of election turned.[28]

What this meant was that the Johnstones reverted to their old allegiance to Laurence Sulivan and caused voters whom they had created with directorial money to vote against the existing directorate, an interpretation confirmed in a letter from John Robinson (who had every reason to know all about it) to Charles Jenkinson.[29] Despite the *Gentleman's Magazine*'s deliberately obscure language it is probable that he "to whom the management of it [i.e., the splitting of votes] was entrusted" was George Johnstone.

He had something, too, of a reputation as a "man of business" in the pamphleteering world at this time. When the duke of Queensberry wanted a pamphlet written in defense of Archibald Douglas' claim to his inheritance in an eighteenth-century *cause célèbre* he wrote to Johnstone as a man who would know someone who could do it.[30] In addition, Johnstone himself wrote pamphlets, two in 1769, the first of which was probably designed to enhance his brother's chances in the April election. The second was more general, a plan of constitutional reform for Indian possessions, the essential principal advocated being that the rule of the governor in council should be subject to minimal interference from London.[31]

After his election to the House of Commons, Johnstone did not initially attract much attention there, although he spoke against Wilkes in January 1769 and voted for his expulsion in February; then, apparently reversing himself, in April he voted for Wilkes or, perhaps more particularly, for the rights of the Middlesex electors.[32] It is true that debates were reported in desultory fashion at the time, so much so that the body of M.P.s elected in 1768 are described as "the unreported parliament," but the epithet applied most aptly to the period after 1771.[33] The debates of 1768 and 1769 were quite fully reported. It is surprising, therefore, that no record exists of the speeches which George Johnstone might have been expected to make in debates on, for example, the East India Company or the Nullum Tempus bill. The first parliamentary speech of Johnstone's for which a record exists was delivered on May 8, 1770. It was a lengthy and artificial disquisition on his King Charles's head, the desirability of colonial governors' control of the military power, and it can have done little either to impress hearers or to help solve American problems.[34]

There occurred a violent interlude before his next major speech. With extraordinary nonchalance he provoked and fought a duel with the American secretary, Lord George Germain. In a speech to the Commons, Lord George, who was notorious for alleged cowardice at the battle of Minden in 1759, claimed "that what he had been urging was for the honour of the nation, in which . . . he greatly interested himself." This unctuous puffery was forgivable, but Johnstone's reply was not. "He wondered that the noble lord should interest himself so deeply in the honour of his country, when he had been hitherto so regardless of his own."[35] The reason behind this very cheap gibe may have lain in Johnstone's desire for the inevitable publicity which would accrue either from openly insulting Germain with impunity or from dueling with a member of the administration. He may, on the other hand, have done it as a service to Sir James Lowther. Edmund Burke wrote that "they [Johnstone's clique] confess that the attack was in revenge of what Lord George had done upon the Cumberland Election."[36] This may be the most plausible reason—Johnstone's coolness in the duel smacks of the hireling—although Germain's offense must have been a sin of omission; Brian Bonsall's detailed study of the election, at any rate, makes no mention of him.[37] Whatever it was, it was not personal animus which motivated Johnstone. His duel with Germain was a most affable affair.

As second, Germain chose Thomas Townshend, a good friend of Johnstone, who failed, however, to persuade the governor to retract his insult to the secretary.[38] Johnstone said that the time and place of the duel should be specified by Germain, who mentioned the Ring in Hyde Park and the present time as suitable. Johnstone said that he was at that moment sitting on a parliamentary committee which was discussing a subject of particular interest to him, petitions relating to the embankment at Durham yard. Would Lord George mind delaying the duel by one hour? Germain asked whom Johnstone would have as a second. The governor suggested that Townshend might double for them both and asked "as at that time he had an open wound in his arm, and his legs were very much swelled" if they might use pistols. Germain agreed and at the time appointed, Johnstone, his committee work over, arrived at the Ring with his friend Sir James Lowther, whom he had happened to meet on the way. At Germain's request Johnstone chose the distance, twenty paces, that should separate them. The secretary invited Johnstone to fire first, but the governor refused, and Germain going first, the pair exchanged shots. Both missed, as did Germain's second ball. The shot which Johnstone fired a moment later shattered his opponent's pistol-butt as he lowered his arm.

"Mr. Johnstone! You have hit my pistol."
"I would rather that, my lord, than your body," called the governor.
"I am obliged to you, sir, for your compliment and I am myself fully satisfied," replied Germain.

Johnstone afterward said that he had never found a man behave with more courage and coolness than Lord George. The king, however, sourly remained convinced that Germain lacked resolution and had been pushed into fighting by friends, but Johnstone's verdict was echoed by Horace Walpole and Edmund Burke, and was probably general. Johnstone, who had acted with equal *sang froid* in the duel received little credit for it. Walpole called him "bully" and "ruffian," while Burke praised only the courage of Germain.[39] Johnstone, nevertheless, undoubtedly got much publicity from the incident, and, coincidentally or not, from the time of his duel onward, more notice was taken of his parliamentary activities.

Over a period of time he became a frequent and able speaker in the House of Commons. Practice endowed his style with flexibility. In the early 1770s, his speeches seem to have been careful but artificial, as though overly attentive to classical models. These early examples also tended to reflect too closely his own personal interests: the legal rights of Sir James Lowther, the privileges of the East India Company, and—a lost cause if ever there was one—the inadequacy of the authority conferred on colonial governors. Only when he subsequently became a champion of colonists' rights against the pretensions of Parliament and the crown did Johnstone achieve celebrity as one of the leading speakers in the House of Commons.[40] He did not quickly reach that position, and in the early part of the decade his reputation in Parliament probably rested on his expertise in Indian affairs and on his adherence to Lowther. Since self-interest was all too obviously engaged, his arguments in debate might well have been discounted. Actually he was not a slavish follower of Lowther although Sir James usually exacted a high degree of subservience from M.P.s for whom he found seats. In a speech much resembling a lawyer's brief, he delivered on February 11, 1771, a long and able defense of Lowther's position in the Nullum Tempus controversy. He did not always vote the same way as Sir James, however, and, like his fellow "pins" Robinson and Jenkinson, eventually broke with him.[41] In connection with Indian affairs, too, Johnstone was accustomed to change his allegiance to individuals with bewildering frequency but was consistent in resisting any interference with the company by the government. His knowledge of the subject, which was a dominant theme in Commons debates of the early 1770s, was both considerable and respected. One faithful believer in his promise was his uncle, Lord Elibank, who recommended to his illegitimate son in Bengal, William Young, that he correspond with and cultivate the acquaintance of both Johnstone and General James Murray as reliable men of talent whose friendship would be useful and, though sought by everybody, would be available to Young. It is noticeable that Elibank did not suggest that his son cultivate William Pulteney or John Johnstone, both as closely related to Young as George and very much richer than he. Young evidently did write to Johnstone although not to the general. He was impudent enough to chide his father for not writing to him. Elibank, something of a doting parent, did not reply with anger but explained that, such was the ferocity of East India politics, his letters may have been deliberately waylaid because of his membership in the Johnstone group, which had made him obnoxious to Clive.[42] That Elibank's high regard for Johnstone was general is suggested by the fact that both the Commons and the company recruited him for service on committees dealing with the detailed complexity of the situation in India. The circumstances merit some explanation.

Muckraking writings in Bengal politics in the late 1760s and early 1770s, together with the imminence of financial calamity in the company and the dreaded possibility of the return of the French to India had all aroused public interest and wrath.[43] Company matters clearly required action; yet Lord North, on becoming head of the administration in 1770, could not, for political reasons, intervene strongly to reform them. His heterogeneous cabinet was divided on the mode of reform, while the Opposition would make good use of any chance that might arise to claim that the administration was attempting to extend its power of patronage. North, therefore, hoped that the company itself would devise an acceptable reform plan. Laurence Sulivan, who had been elected once more to the directorate in 1769, did his best but was faced with a very difficult problem. Without alienating the Court of Proprietors his scheme had to be agreeable to a majority of the House of Commons. For such support he needed strong backing from North. He did not get it. Opinion on India was too badly divided. In 1770 and 1771, North's recruiting bills to increase the company's military strength failed to pass through Parliament. A judicature bill of 1772, too, which sought to establish a powerful judiciary in Bengal and to ban internal trading and the acceptance of presents by company servants, faltered when introduced in March and finally collapsed in May.[44]

One of the most effective speeches against this bill was made by Johnstone, whose main objection to it was that it would establish a judicial system in which a Bengali could sue a Briton but not *vice versa*. He claimed, too, that members lacked the information to form a sound judgment on so momentous a topic and vehemently pleaded for an investigation into the company's affairs. The best publicized portion of Johnstone's long speech, however, was a mordant reply to Clive's defense of his own conduct made earlier in the debate. Replete with rhetorical questions and aspersions on Clive's probity, Johnstone's speech attributed all the evils in Bengal to the system established by Clive, which was "a monstrous heap of partial arbitrary inconsistencies."[45] After the governor resumed his seat it was believed that Clive "heartily wished that he had not opened his mouth in his own defence."[46]

Following Johnstone's suggestion and anticipating the failure of the judicature bill, General Burgoyne moved in April 1772 that a select committee of thirty-one M.P.s conduct an enquiry into company affairs and sit through the summer recess while the regular parliamentary session was adjourned. Both the governor and his brother, William Pulteney, were chosen in the ballot for this nonparty body.

The committee toiled without quick result, and North was compelled, against his nature, to take more decisive action with regard to the company when a major financial crisis struck London in June 1772, paralyzing credit and forcing the company to postpone its customary half-yearly dividend. He appointed a small and strong secret committee to gather information which the ministry used to help the company over this crisis and to recommend a scheme to avert a repetition. The same information was subsequently used by Charles Jenkinson for a plan for constitutional reform of the company.[47] Ultimately, firm governmental action and strong parliamentary intervention helped alleviate the imperial problems posed by India, whereas simultaneous application of the same formula to America merely made matters worse.

Nevertheless, the creation of the parliamentary secret committee caused alarm in East India House, and a General Court elected a committee of twenty-five proprietors to ward off damaging encroachments on company privileges and to draft a petition against secret investigation by Parliament. George Johnstone, always to the fore in protection of company rights, was its chairman. His prestige among his fellow proprietors was at its height. When a General Court met on November 13, 1772, he spoke incisively in condemnation of the directors' plan for sending a supervisory commission out to India. He followed by advancing his own ideas for the supervision of the company's affairs. According to one observer, who thought them worthy of publication, they "delighted and astonished the court." When he sat down, the proprietors accorded him "loud and continued peals of applause."[48] The House of Commons was less easily impressed and rejected the petition of Johnstone's committee of twenty-five on December 7, 1772.[49]

During this period of prelude to a parliamentary act designed to solve permanently the problems posed by the company, George Johnstone cashed in on public alarm. With George Dempster as his lieutenant he was, for a while, the captain of proprietary opposition to the schemes of the government and, therefore, of the directorate, which the ministry dominated. The parliamentary Opposition was timorous of espousing his cause for a variety of reasons, one of which was uncertainty as to North's precise intentions and another, which applied particularly to Chatham and Shelburne, was that there was not universal distaste for encroachment on company privileges. One exception was the "radical" duke of Richmond, who joined Johnstone early in 1773—and outranked him. Like the governor he had a gift for passionate oratory, but he had the additional advantages of a peerage, excellent connections with the councillors and aldermen of the City of London, and superior financial resources. Although neither led numerous cohorts in the Houses of Parliament, Richmond in the Lords and Johnstone in the Commons were able to make ministers uncomfortable with their stinging attacks on Indian policy. Their usual battlefield, however, was East India House. Johnstone's house in Old Burlington Street became a headquarters where a variegated opposition planned the tactics of their Indian war.[50]

Support for their cause was sought in all the likely and some unlikely places. Johnstone even approached the duke of Portland whom he had bitterly attacked in connection with the Nullum Tempus bill. "I own I don't understand Mr. Johnstone's politicks," commented Rockingham.[51] More plausibly Richmond's committee persuaded the common council of the City of London to petition against North's Indian legislation, and Johnstone seems to have looked, with limited success, for fellow opponents among the directors of the Bank of England.[52]

A pursuit in which Johnstone excelled when he chose, as in 1773, was in writing cogent, excoriating prose. Obstructionism was Johnstone's forte, and his fervent opposition to any governmental supervision of the company whatever may have been misguided. Reasoned obstruction in a worthy cause, however, may be praiseworthy. In view of subsequent events in Boston harbor that year Johnstone certainly deserves credit for attempting to persuade the chairman of the East India Company to reject the government's scheme to facilitate the sale of company tea in the colonies, a "ruinous mad project" which was one of several financial measures associated with and inseparable from the Regulating bill:

> To give a drawback to encourage the exportation of a commodity, and to impose a duty at the place of consumption 1200 leagues off, is such a solecism in the rules of commerce, that it requires a combination of such heads as now govern this country; first to impose it, then to enforce it, and now to continue it.[53]

He denounced the proposed tea duty some time before it became law, rallying strong company support behind him. The pertinent motion that he submitted on January 7, 1773, to a General Court recommended that the directors "obtain an act of Parliament for them to export their surplus tea to foreign markets clear of all drawbacks and duties as well as to take off the 3d. duty in America." It was carried without dissent.

On May 6, he spoke powerfully in another General Court against North's regulatory bill. He gave a copious description of the baneful effects it was bound to have and urged the court to "steadiness, manliness and unanimity of conduct as the only grounds they had to maintain their rights as proprietors or Englishmen."[54]

Such activities made his name known to Americans as one favorable to their interests, but despite all his efforts he could not thwart the Indian policy of Lord North. The company accepted the tea drawbacks, and the Regulating Act, which became law on June 28, 1773, specified three ways in which the government extended control over the affairs of the East India Company. First, it had the right to receive copies of the company's accounts and of all letters from India on political topics. Secondly, through its majority in Parliament it nominated a governor general and council for Bengal, to which the other English settlements in India were to be, to some extent, subservient. Third, the act limited the size of the General Court of Proprietors by requiring voters to hold £1,000 worth of stock for a year instead of £500 worth for six months, and it established a four-year term of office for each director.[55]

In addition to such formal controls, the period following the passage of the act saw North using John Robinson, his chief "man of business" for Indian affairs, to exert a much more systematic control of the directors and manipulation of votes in the General Court than had been customary.

Passage of the Regulating Act did not cause Richmond and Johnstone to lose interest in it. Judicious and well-organized opposition could modify, hamper, or even negate its enforcement. The duke was the coordinator of an ad hoc group in East India House whose object was to harass the directors into allowing minimal concessions to the government. It included George Dempster, James Adair, and Daniel Wier.[56] Richmond was delighted to secure Johnstone as a recruit to it and enthusiastically wrote that "no man is better able to Judge what is right to be done, more hearty in the Cause or more happy in the method of preparing and conducting Business."[57]

The best way to hobble governmental effectiveness in company affairs was to secure the election of directors who would refuse to cooperate with North. The directorial election of April 1774 would be particularly important in that, for the last time, there would be twenty-four seats at stake at once. In subsequent elections only six directorships a year would fall vacant.

Johnstone decided to seek election and, with Richmond's endorsement, requested the backing of Rockingham.[58] His name, with that of George Dempster and other "new men," duly appeared on the Proprietors' List, which signified the choice of the rebel element in the company, but almost all those elected came from the government-approved House List. Denied a directorship, Johnstone settled down to sniping at and organizing sallies against those more fortunate.

He became a staunch supporter of Warren Hastings, the governor general of Bengal. At a series of General Courts in May 1776, every resource of the North-Robinson organization was strained to influence the proprietors to vote for the removal of Hastings. The Rockinghamites, as Johnstone well knew, had rather detached themselves from Indian affairs after the passage of the Regulating Act and, in any case, were not enamored of Hastings. Fearing the success of the great government effort, the governor begged the earl to support him at East India House and asked him not to prejudge Hastings: "Hear all before you determine."[59] Rockingham responded nobly, appearing in person at the General Court to vote with a heterogeneous collection of dissidents, including the Johnstone group, Sulivanites, and disinterested admirers of the governor general. The result of a secret ballot, a feature of the company constitution unknown at that time to conventional political practice, was to overrule the directors' decision to recall Hastings.[60]

Jubilation ceased when it was discovered later in the year that while the company opposition was championing Hastings, their hero had been negotiating a deal with the ministry through his agent, Lauchlin Macleane. Although he subsequently found reason to renege on the arrangement, Hastings had proffered his resignation, provided that the ministry agreed not to harass him for his conduct in Bengal. Johnstone and

Richmond, who had not been consulted, felt that they had been duped and convened a General Court in order to censure the directors for accepting the governor general's resignation. They found it difficult to persuade anyone else to share their indignation, and their tactic proved totally ineffective. The king was delighted. He suggested that if the fiasco had not persuaded them to abandon public speaking altogether, they should "enter themselves into the famous society of Robinhood."[61] The scornful reference was to a workingmen's debating club which met in London at the Robin Hood Tavern in Butcher Row.[62]

Johnstone did not work closely with the parliamentary Opposition on Indian affairs until 1777. Till then he had worked with any consistency with only one leading Opposition figure in Leadenhall Street. The duke of Richmond was, however, something of a maverick. The leading Opposition group, centering on Rockingham, Charles Fox, and Edmund Burke, had cooperated with Johnstone only intermittently and strictly for party advantage. In 1777 the situation changed when the shocking tale of Lord Pigot reached England from India.

Pigot had been appointed governor of Madras. He arrived there in 1775 and wasted no time in sweeping away several traditional policies. A new broom, he insisted in particular on the restoration of territories taken by the nawab from the raja of Tanjore, an action which would adversely affect the financial position of many company servants in Madras. When his council demurred, Pigot suspended two of them and provoked a coup in which the council deposed and incarcerated him. He died a few months later still in confinement.

Johnstone was a friend of Pigot before his elevation. He had helped him secure his appointment and was close enough to him to refuse an invitation to dine with Rockingham so that he could enjoy a farewell meal with his friend before he sailed off to assume his new position.[63] Unaware of Pigot's death, Johnstone pressed, together with Admiral Pigot, brother of the deposed governor, and the duke of Richmond, at a General Court meeting on May 9, 1777, for the reinstatement of his friend, and when the attempt failed, he raised the question in the House of Commons.[64] In doing so he enjoyed the full support of the parliamentary Opposition. The reason lay not merely in party expediency nor in the intrinsic merits of Pigot's case, but in a personal connection, too. The Opposition had a representative of their interests in the Madras presidency in William Burke, a relative of Edmund Burke and the agent of the raja of Tanjore. If the raja was on the side of right then so was Pigot, and the Madras council and the nawab of Arcot were clearly villains.

Thus both Johnstone and the Rockingham party had a personal interest in working together on Indian affairs. The process of cooperation had been long maturing. Although the governor does not seem to have been a regular diner with Burke, Rockingham, and Fox until 1775, he ultimately attended also the party strategy sessions held near race courses and, less oddly, at Rockingham's home at Wentworth.[65] No doubt close social intimacy was easier after January 26, 1775, when Sir James Lowther and his followers formally crossed the floor of the Commons and began to oppose the North administration.[66]

Subsequently Johnstone attempted to use his influence with his patron to persuade him to support candidates congenial to Lord Rockingham in boroughs where he wielded influence. For example, he wanted Lowther to nominate a radical, William Baker, for Carlisle in 1775, in the knowledge that Rockingham approved of him. In this type of endeavor few men were less malleable than Sir James, although he was at times prepared to respect Johnstone's opinion and did secure seats for Ralph Gowland and James Adair on his recommendation. For Carlisle, however, Sir James preferred Walter Stanhope, who was elected and served his patron loyally. Nevertheless, Johnstone persisted in trying to act as mediator and in June sought to make Burke and Lowther acquainted at his dinner table.[67]

Long before Lowther's conversion, Johnstone, without ever quite adopting its philosophy as his own, had sided with the Rockingham group in denouncing Lord North's American policy. Initially, as his letters as governor of West Florida attested, his attitude toward colonists was patronizing and authoritarian. The only qualms he had evinced in enforcing the Stamp Act had been doubts on legal technicalities, not on the principle involved. Very early in the 1770s, moreover, when opposing Lord North's colonial policies, Johnstone's ground of objection was that they were inexpedient rather than illegal. This stance might be explained simply as sound politics—it is more effective to condemn governmental actions on practical grounds than to proclaim abstract ideals—except that with the passage of time his speeches did become more idealistic. He may even be said to have evolved finally a philosophy of imperialism, which should not obscure the fact that he was more concerned with winning a name for himself and embarrassing the administration than with realizing a vision of empire. His principles were not rigid. Contempt for the policies of North did not prevent his accepting employment from him at a later date, after Johnstone's pleas for concessions to the colonists abruptly changed to demands for their slaughter in 1778.

None of this volte-face could have been foreseen in 1774, when Johnstone made several speeches which, when reproduced in America, must have warmed many rebellious hearts. Although his patron had not formally broken with North at the time, in the general election of October 1774 Johnstone was returned both for Cockermouth, his old constituency, and for another of Lowther's boroughs, Appleby. It was because he preferred to represent Appleby that there existed a vacant seat at Cockermouth for James Adair. The second representative for Cockermouth was

Ralph Gowland, a major in the Durham militia who also appears to have owed his nomination to Johnstone's fervent recommendation; he considered Gowland "the most perfect of human characters without any exception as far as my knowledge of mankind goes. . . ." Whether he had "an elocution capable of enforcing his opinions," as Johnstone claimed, or not is difficult to ascertain, since it seems that during four years as a member of Parliament Gowland never once spoke in debate.[68]

Johnstone, by contrast, did so frequently and at length, particularly on American affairs. In an onslaught several hours long on North's Boston Port Bill he showed, not for the last time, a certain prescience. He claimed that he had warned the chairman of the East India Company against having anything to do with the tax concession the North government had offered the company in connection with tea as being, in the existing circumstances, "criminally absurd." He predicted, moreover, that passage of the Boston Port Bill "must be productive of a General Confederacy to resist the power of this country." He thought it madness to persist with measures that would destroy the immense mutual benefits of Anglo-American trade. His argument against taxation of the colonies was, at this time, pragmatic. Even if there was an undoubted legal right to tax, there was no need to exercise it. Ireland was untaxed; why tax America? In the following month he voted against North's bill for the government of Massachusetts Bay. He imputed "all the misfortunes which have happened in America" to the limitations placed upon the powers of governors. Even after a decade his Floridian wounds still smarted! In June he launched an ironical attack on the Quebec Act. In what was not so much reasoned opposition as a rhetorician's exercise, he criticized not the actual bill but rather the fanciful principles which might be read into the text: "that the Popish religion," for instance, "is better than the Protestant." Temporarily he seemed to have abandoned his pragmatism completely.[69]

His longer speeches tended to be better reasoned. In a debate on the supplies for 1775 he dwelt on the results of a war in America. "Our rivals in Europe cannot be idle spectators in such a scene," he said, and prophesied a French invasion of the British Isles.[70] He referred again to the doctrine of parliamentary supremacy. It was very logical, he argued, but it was possible to be too logical; after all, rotten boroughs were logically absurd, he continued, evidently assuming that nobody in his right mind could question *their* existence. As far as America went, it would be better to forget logic and to adopt "generous, just, pacific measures."[71]

In the year of Lexington, Johnstone spoke many times on colonial themes; time and again he urged the government to abandon the enforcement of legal claims in favor of the practical benefits of conciliation. The colonists had, it seemed, an untiring spokesman who deserved, as much as Wilkes and Barré, to have a settlement named after him. Rockingham, the doyen of the Opposition, repeatedly wrote and met him at this time and no doubt saw in him a hammer to break the power of North.[72] Johnstone seems to have been of a similar opinion. In June, so much had public opinion been outraged by North's American policies, that the governor predicted the imminent fall of the ministry, but if it were foolish enough to cling on to power, he darkly and dottily predicted that "the blood of the advisers must cement the breach between the two countries."[73]

By 1775, Johnstone was arguing the case for the colonists on theoretical as well as pragmatic grounds. The administration was denying them their rights as Englishmen. They were not, he claimed, virtually represented in Parliament in the way that disfranchised inhabitants of the British Isles were. They were also denied the rights of habeas corpus and, in the new Admiralty courts, of trial by jury. Sometimes, too, he found reasons for condemning the government on humanitarian and *realpolitik* grounds. On one occasion he combined the two when he criticized the destruction of the American fishing industry both because of the suffering which would result and also because he foresaw that only the French would benefit from the situation.

Such sentiments, combined with unmitigated condemnation of Governors Hutchinson and Lyttelton and of proposals to raise slave and foreign units to serve in America, must have won him golden opinions among the rebels.[74] Perhaps his most exaggerated speech of the year was one which deplored Burgoyne's recommendation that the Indian be employed against the colonists. "He drinks the blood of his enemies," exclaimed Johnstone, "and his favourite repast is on human flesh."[75]

His extreme fashion of debate provoked even the goodnatured North to remonstrate on occasion. North once asserted that he had not originated the American dispute. Johnstone mocked the statement at such length that North intervened to explain. Johnstone said it was very disorderly to interrupt him in that very abrupt manner. However, he thought the noble lord's explanation or vindication of himself made the matter ten times worse against him.[76]

This type of cheap repartee reads poorly but would have been effective on the floor of the Commons, much more so than his leaden, pseudo-Ciceronian set speeches. Whenever Johnstone crossed swords in debate he usually achieved superiority in invective. On one occasion Richard Rigby reproved him for insisting on details of secret service funds expenditure; such explanations were more appropriate to Leadenhall Street, where, suggested Rigby, corruption abounded. Johnstone's reply was fierce. Rigby's speech was "manifestly scurrilous and indecent"; government interference was the source of anything wrong at East India House, but supposing corruption did exist there, Johnstone knew where to find it. He had seen Rigby "attend regularly at all courts and ballots, to vote with his long train of dependents, clerks and partisans.[77]

By the middle of 1777 Johnstone was saying repeatedly that America was lost beyond hope of recovery and by the end of the year he was talking of peace.[78] The war might be lost but Johnstone's reputation as a House of Commons man was not. In assessing his achievements it is worth noting that on the main subjects of debate in the 1770s, India and America, in knowledge and experience Johnstone was better qualified than most of his fellow members. In his mode of debate he was capable of sustained and cogent reasoning but also of wild exaggerated appeals to emotion, and he chose his style to suit the occasion. His theorizing was often presented in a persuasive way, but his principles were changeable. His pragmatism often disguised a lack of firm principle. And yet, amid the informed self-interest of his Indian speeches and the spurious idealism of his American, an unexpected quality is also discernible, a concern for the individual.

Johnstone once said of Lord Mansfield that he wished his lordship would ride the horse of liberty oftener, "for nobody knew how to ride him better when he mounted him." The words might well have been used of Johnstone himself, for, leaving aside his speeches for American freedom, he was also outspoken in other liberal causes.

In 1775, in a long speech against the employment of Hanoverian forces he digressed to lambaste two features of the English law. He spoke of the manpower within the British Isles prevented from serving in the king's forces: "some millions are lost to defence by the oppressive laws about religion in Ireland"; and again, "5,000 are annually lost in gaol, or as fugitives driven abroad by the severity of your laws respecting private debts." In March of 1777 he supported a bill "for the easy and effectual manning of the Navy" as "the first step to a reformation of an abuse of legal power, or a violation of the laws (take the custom of pressing in either sense)," thus concisely summarizing his objections to the recruitment of sailors by the press-gang. He also made his views clear on the slave trade. It was "a commerce of the most barbarous and cruel kind that ever disgraced the transactions of any civilized people."[79]

Thus publicly and in round terms Johnstone condemned the existing and legal practices of penalizing Irish Catholics, imprisonment for debt, impressment, and the slave trade. Since there was no discernible political advantage to be derived from advocating such views at the time, Johnstone was probably sincere; which means he had a heart.

Most of Johnstone's achievements in Parliament until 1778 were negative; understandably so because his early parliamentary career had been among the Opposition. But he was genuinely good at obstruction and denigration, and his later career when he voted with government would show that he lacked the positive parliamentary virtues of conciliation and persuasion. He was better at destruction than creation. His negativism was apparent even in the one change in parliamentary procedure with which he is credited. On February 2, 1778, disturbances in the gallery of the Commons resulted in an order for the ousting of strangers. By convention such removal was not usually considered to apply to female visitors, but on this occasion Johnstone specifically insisted that the five dozen ladies in the gallery should also be ejected. Thereafter, ladies in the gallery became a rarity and were usually excluded.[80]

Negative attributes can nevertheless afford political advantage, and probably the sharpest weapon in Johnstone's political armory was his ability to embarrass the government. It may have been the prospect of ridding itself of a nuisance which made the North ministry in 1778—a crucial year for Johnstone—so ready to consider favorably the governor's qualifications for employment as a peacemaker in America and to ignore that lack of equanimity which should have precluded his candidacy.

4. "Man of Business"

For the first time in fifteen years Johnstone was offered and accepted an office of profit under the crown when, on All Fools' Day, 1778, he agreed to become one of the commissioners whom George III sent from England with "Powers to Treat, Consult and Agree upon the means of Quieting the Disorders now Subsisting in certain of Our Colonies, Plantations and Provinces in North America."[1]

The peace delegation of which he was a member represented the most serious attempt to negotiate an end to hostilities, but it was not the first. Admiral Lord Howe and General William Howe had been armed with a commission to seek peace in 1776. Even if they had been able diplomats, which they were not, the haughty terms of their commission doomed their efforts. The brothers were ordered to treat with individual colonies and to refuse negotiation with Congress. Moreover, the Howes had been forbidden to discuss independence and had been ordered to insist on colonial recognition of parliamentary supremacy. The terms were framed as might be expected from a British government anticipating decisive victory on the battlefield. They seem unrealistic now, because the verdict of arms was for the Americans, compelling the North government to replace condescension with concession.

The genesis of a new commission lay in Burgoyne's surrender of his army to American besiegers at Saratoga on October 17, 1777. The *Warwick* brought the news in dispatches to the first lord of the Admiralty. Sandwich received it on the evening of December 1, and that night the king was told.[2] On the following day it fell to Lord George Germain to let Parliament know.[3] Lord North, during the course of the ensuing debate, assured the turbulent Commons that "no man from the beginning more firmly wished for peace than he had and . . . no man would do more to obtain it now." There is no need whatever to question the sincerity of North's desire for peace; indeed he might well have expressed himself more warmly. There was every chance that the American coup at Saratoga would persuade France to extend her efforts on behalf of the colonists from informal aid to a formal alliance. The odds against a British triumph would be much lengthened, and many believed, with Johnstone, that "our revolted colonies, aided by a foreign power, must prove an over-match for us."[4] Every diplomatic, strategic, and economic consideration made it urgently desirable that no time should be lost in seeking an accommodation with the Americans before colonial rebellion escalated into a war in which Britain, without benefit of allies, would certainly be engaged on or off four continents. If such a development were to be prevented, it would have to be done swiftly. North knew it and took quick, if not necessarily wise, action.

As early as December 6, a secret agent, Paul Wentworth, received instruction from his superior, William Eden, who was undersecretary for the northern department but who also ran the British secret service on the European continent.[5] Wentworth was to proceed to Paris and attempt to negotiate peace terms with the American commissioners there, Silas Deane and Benjamin Franklin. Wentworth succeeded in seeing Deane several times and tried to persuade him to agree to some type of American dependence on Britain, using as bait British offers of financial assistance to Congress and hints of improvement in Deane's "own dignity and emolument."[6] Using different agents, Germain was simultaneously trying to achieve a similar object.

On December 6, Johnstone's elder brother, William Pulteney, had offered his services to Germain in arranging a rapprochement with the Americans. Pulteney belonged to no major parliamentary group, but his attitude toward American problems was identical to that of his brother George; both shared the Chathamite view that every possible concession except acquiescence in independence should be made to conciliate American opinion. Whatever else was sacrificed, the Anglo-American political link must be maintained. Pulteney wrote again to Germain on December 9, expressing fear of a Franco-American alliance and asserting a conviction that he could persuade Franklin to accept peace terms which fell short of independence.[7] Germain evidently agreed to give Pulteney his head. The upshot was a letter to Franklin's secretary, Edward Bancroft, who was secretly working for the British. Although it was unsigned, it was probably written at Pulteney's dictation by an intermediary trusted by Bancroft and with whose calligraphy he was familiar. It indicated that Parliament, when it returned from the Christmas recess, would be enacting conciliatory legislation designed to placate the Americans, and Bancroft was asked what terms—"a little short of independancy" the author hoped—would suffice to get Congress to agree to peace.[8] A failure to communicate with one another was a chronic malaise of North's colleagues, and Germain had apparently authorized the approach to Bancroft without being aware of Wentworth's similar mission.

Neither of these approaches led anywhere. Seen by the administration as clandestine escape routes, they turned out to be nothing more than blind alleys. They wasted time when time was beyond price, and they had, at best, only the slenderest likelihood of success. Germain and North remained optimistic, however, and three months later Pulteney crossed the Channel as Germain's agent to try to work out an arrangement with Franklin.

The fact of the matter was that Franklin had not been given the authority to conclude a peace treaty with Great Britain, as North's ministers must have known. Presumably they believed that any terms which Franklin agreed to would, thanks to his enormous prestige, be favored by Congress. Franklin astutely encouraged such a belief and did not reject the advances of British agents.[9] A more effective spur to the French to conclude an American alliance than the knowledge that the British were offering Franklin attractive alternatives could not be imagined.

Diplomatic and military crises had not prevented Parliament from taking its usual long recess in December and January. Johnstone must have welcomed the rest from parliamentary activity as he was ill, troubled by giddiness and suffering from the attentions of his physician, who blooded him and put him on a meager diet.[10] The recess gave North, too, a respite from the forensic onslaughts of the Opposition, but he had problems enough without them, including ministerial disunity, which culminated in a threat to the cabinet's very existence when the lord chancellor proffered his resignation,[11] and the necessity of reshaping North American strategy in light of Saratoga. As a prelude to peace talks he had also to construct conciliatory proposals for the Americans which were capable of receiving the approval both of his opinionated royal master and of Parliament.

North asked William Eden and his intimate friend Alexander Wedderburn to draft suitable bills. Edward Thurlow, the attorney general, drafted another to enable the king to appoint peace commissioners. As it finally emerged, North's plan of conciliation contained, in essence, two propositions: that Parliament should renounce the right to tax the colonies, and that commissioners, equipped with wide discretionary powers, should cross the Atlantic to agree on peace with Congress. After the king had urged him to delay no longer, North presented his scheme to the cabinet on the morning of February 11, 1778, and later that day informed the Commons that he would lay a "Plan of Conciliation with America" before the House on the following Tuesday, the seventeenth of February.[12]

George Johnstone seldom had to wait for official announcements in Parliament to know what was afoot, especially where American affairs were concerned. For example, he had referred to General Burgoyne's defeat during the course of a speech which he delivered to the House on November 18, 1777, that is, more than two weeks before Germain admitted the disaster at Saratoga.[13] Similarly he was aware of the plans for negotiating peace with the Americans well before any official announcement was made. On February 5, he wrote from the House of Commons to Robert Morris of Pennsylvania:[14]

My Dear Sir:

I have but a moment to write this letter before the packet is closed. But our correspondence must now necessarily be short.

A reconciliation between Great Britain and the American Colonies upon the footing of the most perfect freedom as fellow-subjects is the object on earth I have most at heart.

Though I am not in the secrets of Government here and have strongly opposed all those measures which are deemed oppressive to

America, and have constantly supported those claims against British taxation and the altering of the charters of government by the mere authority of Parliament, yet I have heard a hint, and I have good reason to think, a proposition will be made to Parliament in four or five days by administration that may be a ground for reunion. I really do not know the particulars, nevertheless, as I have learned, some preliminaries of a treaty have lately gone to France, I think it cannot be deemed unfriendly to either country to give you notice of this intended proposition that you may in prudence do nothing hastily with foreign powers but wait a short time the issue; for I am conscious, from your integrity and patriotism, which I have long admired, that as nothing but necessity forced you to take up arms, so nothing but necessity or honorable engagements will force you to adopt a final separation of interests.[15]

Serving his own interest does not seem to have been Johnstone's motive in writing this letter. Self-seeker that he was, Johnstone, it would be natural for one to suspect, had heard that peace commissioners were to be appointed and, in the expectation of being one of them, was taking early steps to ensure success for their mission. In other respects, however, Johnstone did not act as if he considered himself in the running for an appointment. If he had, he surely would have abated the invective and ridicule which he customarily bestowed on ministers, but in fact his taunting continued as before. On the day after he wrote to Morris, in a debate on the employment of Indians in North America, Johnstone

expressed himself happy that on this day strangers were not admitted into the gallery, as it might have been to be feared, that so great would have been their indignation at the noble lords [North and Germain] and to such a pitch of enthusiasm would they have been worked, that he should have expected those lords would have been torn in pieces by the people in the way to their houses.[16]

There is no need to doubt the sincerity of the views which Johnstone expressed in his letter to Morris. The precipitancy with which he acted may be explained by reference, not to himself, but to his brother William, who, as events were to show, was as likely a candidate for a commissionership and who, perhaps, was responsible for giving George the reliable hint which he mentions.

He needed no inside information to fear the Franco-American alliance to which he obliquely referred. That fear proved all too well founded. On February 6, 1778, the day after Johnstone wrote to Morris, the plenipotentiaries of France and the United States signed two treaties. The first was a Treaty of Amity and Commerce, the second a treaty of "conditional and defensive alliance."[17] Time was short if the French and Americans were not to pool all their resources in a struggle against Great Britain, but three avenues down which the British might yet escape a war with France still lay open.

The first derived from the terms of the defensive alliance; it would take effect only in the event of war between France and Great Britain resulting either from "direct hostilities," or from British interference in French commerce and navigation "in a manner contrary to the Rights of Nations, and the Peace subsisting between the Two Crowns."[18]

The second possibility was that Congress would not ratify the French treaties. The third was the delusory hope, or perhaps prejudice, that, in spite of current differences with Britain, at bottom the Americans would prefer a connection with the English, with whom they had so much in common, to one with the traditional enemy, the alien French. Johnstone was one of those who nourished such a hope.

His letter to Morris adumbrated one method by which he thought American opinion might be swayed away from independence. On as large a scale as possible Johnstone wanted Englishmen to write letters to prominent Americans with whom they were acquainted urging reconciliation between their countries. "Acquaintance," the word used by Thomas Willing to describe the relationship between Johnstone and Morris, was probably more apt than the phrase, "sincere and affectionate friend," with which the Scot ended his letter to the American. It is likely that the two had met in Philadelphia when the governor had been recalled from West Florida, which meant not only that their acquaintance had been very brief but also that it had taken place a full eleven years before. Johnstone must have known how very prominent Morris had become—indeed he was to become chairman of the congressional Finance Committee in 1778—but it is doubtful that he had any conception of how much the American and his colleagues had changed with regard to ties with England. In thinking that he would find his letter persuasive, Johnstone was far too optimistic.

His role, however, during the early years of the American quarrel, had been that of a Cassandra rather than an optimist. It is difficult to believe that Johnstone did not feel a sour satisfaction at the realization of his pessimistic predictions of the course of events in America. Abhorring the notion of American independence, he had yet assured the North administration on October 26, 1775, that for the Americans to declare their independence was "the next step which your conduct necessarily drives them to," although "they wish for nothing more than a constitutional dependance on Great Britain." A year later, on October 31, 1776, after independence, to the governor's disgust, had been declared, he asserted that the administration's mode of waging war on the Americans, in that "we had hired foreign troops to fight against them," had left them with "no other way of putting themselves on a footing with us, than by . . . inviting foreign aid to defend them."[19] Even as he spoke, such aid was attaining sizable proportions. By October 10, 1776, Rodrique Hortalez et Cie., the mock trading company which funnelled Franco-Spanish aid to Congress, had already spent 5.6 million livres, subsidies vital to continuing the war.[20]

Johnstone had long been haunted by the prospect of American collaboration with Britain's traditional enemies, with whom Britain could expect another war regardless of the American quarrel, and on May 3, 1775, he had prophesied that "the present approaching breach with our colonies will be the means of accelerating it." Long before aid in the shape of money and munitions was transformed into the dispatch of soldiers and sailors, Johnstone had anticipated and predicted the consequences. He told the Commons on February 10, 1777, that with the aid of a foreign army the American rebels would be certain to beat the British. By May 9, even without such escalation of the conflict, his pessimism had apparently deepened. "America was lost, he feared, beyond the power of recovery; nay, he might venture to say, irretrievably lost."[21] If this was conviction rather than rhetoric, the military and diplomatic events which occurred later in 1777 and early in 1778 should have hardened his pessimism. Consistency of mood was not, however, one of Johnstone's characteristics, and a change for the better in his personal fortunes was precisely what was necessary to inject some optimism into his gloomy view of events. As one of the severest flails of the administration he could scarcely have counted on selection as a commissioner to represent his country in America, although he may have dimly realized that the easygoing North would enjoy getting a nuisance out of the country for a few months. Horace Walpole, spiteful as ever toward Johnstone, believed that Benjamin Franklin had encouraged the governor to seek a commissionership as a way of ensuring that Americans would not be duped by skillful English diplomacy, but there is no evidence that Franklin communicated with Johnstone, nor that the governor considered himself a candidate for a commissionership.[22] In fact, however, Johnstone was under consideration for such a spot as soon as lists of possible commissioners were compiled.

The first member appointed was its head, twenty-nine-year-old Frederick Howard, earl of Carlisle, who accepted the job on February 22, 1778.[23] For a position requiring the highest diplomatic abilities, Carlisle was an extraordinary choice. During most of his adult life he had been best known as a fop and gambler. His own excesses and the generosity, or lack of judgment, with which he went surety for the gaming debts of his friend, Charles Fox, had caused his withdrawal from the public eye for a year or two. He emerged from obscurity to become treasurer of the household and a privy councillor on June 13, 1777. On February 25, 1778, Walpole wrote that Carlisle "was totally unacquainted with business" and "had but moderate parts and less application."[24] Lafayette knew him as "a fine gentleman, very well powder'd, and a man of bon goust—he began by Ruining his own fortune and wanted to get the Reputation of a man belov'd by the ladies . . . he is a good poet."[25] There is no evidence that William Eden selected him, and he had only one of the qualities which Eden specified as desirable in the commissioners, his peerage.[26] Eden could not reasonably have chosen Carlisle unless he wished the commission to have a weak titular head so that he might the better dominate it. A hint from the king, and as a member of the royal household Carlisle was close to him, or a recommendation to North from Earl Gower, Carlisle's father-in-law and lord president of the council, might more plausibly explain the earl's selection. Manifestly unsuitable, the choice was, according to Walpole, "universally ridiculed, particularly by Burke and Governor Johnstone in the House."[27] Johnstone was unaware, at the time, that he might be a commissioner, but it was unfortunate that the head of the commission was one for whom he could feel little respect, since, under more dominant leadership, Johnstone's subsequent behavior as a commissioner might have been more restrained.

Carlisle was conscious of his own deficiencies. He accepted a place on the commission on condition that it be armed with wide powers and that he "might be joined by men whose characters, rank in life and abilities might restore that importance and weight to the commission that it might lose by my youth and inexperience."[28] Just who should join him was under consideration in various quarters at the time.

Alexander Wedderburn, the solicitor general, sent Eden the names of a score of possible candidates. He did not say on what basis he had chosen them, but they included three bishops, one duke, four lesser peers, and a number of M.P.s, among whom were several opponents of North's American policies, including both William Pulteney and his brother.[29] Johnstone apart, none of Wedderburn's twenty was finally selected.

Simultaneously Eden was concerning himself with the problem. Probably he coveted a place on the commission for himself from the first. Certainly he gave considerable thought to its composition. The qualifications for membership which he devised were precisely descriptive and were suggestive of a larger commission than the body of three men eventually chosen. The commissioners should come from both Houses of Parliament. They ought to be "men of Abilities" conversant with the points in dispute. Whereas one commissioner should be "firm and strong-minded," the rest should be "of conciliatory manners." In any case there should be no "die-hards" and the commissioners should preferably be "men of family." One of them should be a lawyer, one an Opposition moderate, and lastly one only, thought Eden, should be a Scot. Eden included a "short" list of thirty-four names. Johnstone appeared in it as a Scot rather than an Opposition M.P. Again, none of those on the list, with the exception of Johnstone, was to be finally selected. A surprising omission was the name of Richard Jackson, M.P. for Romney and counsel to the Board of Trade, whose suitability Eden would, a few days later, urge on Carlisle.

Jackson's name was, however, one of a dozen suggested in a memorandum by John Hatsell, clerk of the House of Commons, penned about February 23, 1778. His list was as different from Eden's as Eden's was from Wedderburn's, but, as on the others, Johnstone's name also appeared on this third list. His nomination was perhaps surprising in that the only qualification Hatsell spelled out was that the commissioners should be "such men, as, on the whole, cool and dispassionate men in both countries may approve"; surprising, that is, unless such men approve the opposite of what they themselves are.

On the following day, February 24, wrote Eden some months later, "I offer'd to go on the Commission in case Ld. North sh[oul]d not be able to prevail on any other more proper person in Gov[ernmen]t to accept—I at the same time desired to have it understood that my private wish was not to go."[30] On the twenty-fifth, Eden, who undoubtedly pictured himself as the "efficient" commissioner, called on Carlisle, whom he had known since their days at Eton, and said that "it had been proposed to him" that he should be a member of the commission.[31] Carlisle was agreeable. He knew Eden well, had a high opinion of his principles and intelligence, and was prepared to overlook the fact that Eden, too, was relatively young, only thirty-four.[32] Eden soon afterward suggested the name of Richard Jackson, and Carlisle agreed that Jackson's insignificant situation and obscure name were outweighed by his knowledge and experience of American affairs.[33]

Jackson proved a querulous procrastinator who was frightened to act on his own initiative. "I wish," he wrote to Eden, "to be entrusted with no discretion unless it be accurately limited and defined at both ends." On March 29, at a gathering at Lord North's house, where the commissioners met North, Germain, Thurlow, and Wedderburn, Jackson infuriated both Eden and Carlisle by his refusal to be hurried—he protested that he could not be ready in less than a month—and by his pessimism.[34] He would have "driven us mad with doubts and digressions before we got to Portsmouth," concluded Carlisle, and so he was dismissed the following day.[35]

Eden in particular was acutely aware that no time should be lost in finding a replacement for Jackson. He wrote at once to Lord North asking that the vacancy be filled without delay "by some *practicable* Man of *respectable* Character in the Country, & sufficiently *habituated to Business* not to leave me exposed to the Imputation of taking too much to myself. . . . a Man, who should also be *of Some Weight in other Respects*." It is hard to believe that Eden's last opaque phrase meant that he wanted a Scot, but the fact is that all three of the men he suggested for the vacancy, George Johnstone, William Pulteney, and Andrew Stuart were from Scotland, and of the three he was inclined "to think the first would give most weight to Business & I should like Him much as a pleasant Companion."[36]

Wedderburn replied that he preferred Pulteney,[37] but unfortunately he could not "be easily recalled" from Paris.[38] Eden still favored Johnstone: "I foresee He will encourage & not damp the Hopes of the Commission:—but it is necessary to clear the ground towards his acceptance, which I will do to the utmost of my Power before 12 tomorrow."[39]

The solicitor general was still doubtful. Johnstone seemed "a little incompatible" with Carlisle. Wedderburn was not the only one to wince at the thought of the juxtaposition in office of the Castle Howard dandy and the guerrilla of Leadenhall Street; Walpole called the contrasting couple "the monkey" and "the bear."[40] Wedderburn had sounded out Johnstone on the twenty-ninth of March and found that, although he had a strong wish to go, he had, "in compliment to his brother Pulteney," suppressed it.[41] Pulteney, however, was absent; Johnstone was available and "prepared to set out with an expedition that must have been very distressing to his private affairs."[42] Carlisle interviewed him and was impressed. Johnstone had some reservations. He was disturbed by a rumor that Lord North had told John Temple that the commission could not work—only complete independence could end the American war. He also raised some points about meeting merchants and releasing prisoners, the details of which remain obscure. Johnstone's apprehension about the Temple rumor was justified. Temple was an unofficial government agent who was supposed to sail for America at the same time as the commission and to assist it by influencing congressmen in favor of reunion with Britain. Johnstone set great store by the political efficacy of Temple's approaches and no doubt received reassurance from Carlisle that the stale rumor—it was relayed to Wedderburn by Sir James Lowther—was so unlikely as to be incredible. The earl was evidently apprehensive of Johnstone, but the governor, "in great good humour," listened patiently to what Carlisle had to say about his reservations, and the peer thought he merited "every attention" for his behavior.[43] Johnstone could be abrasive or affable as he pleased. His decision to use charm on Carlisle resulted in his appointment as a commissioner. Eden was exultant:

> The change made in the Commission was my own private negotiation, & gives me much better hopes than I had before. Gov[erno]r Johnstone is particularly favourable in his opinion towards me personally—is manly & righteaded on the Points in question—is of much Weight among the most violent Americans, & in his whole Character active, decisive, & bold.[44]

The king, meanwhile, had been kept informed of the progress being made in forming the commission. He seemed concerned less with the suitability of those chosen than with questions of protocol and expense.

Eden was determined that the commissioners should have all the perquisites customary for ambassadors. He applied for an initial grant, the traditional equipage and plate allowance, of £1,600; thereafter a salary of £100 a week should be paid, which, it was estimated, would amount to £4,625.[45] Each commissioner, therefore, would receive for a few months' work £6,225. Although subject to deductions for necessary expenses, it was handsome compensation, quite sufficient on its own to tempt Johnstone, even if he had no other reason for accepting.

George III was caustic and reluctant—but acquiescent:

> The demand of pay made by Mr. Eden seems rather Exorbitant, he seems to think *Éclat* a part of the character of a Commissioner, I think *business* their sole occupation; but I shall certainly consent on that head to whatever You may think reasonable, always trusting that the expence is not in the end to fall on my Civil List, for it is as much a part of the American Contest as the Victualling Ships.

The king did reject Eden's request that the commissioners hold rank as privy councillors. It was planned to add the commanders of the land and sea forces in America to the commission, and since he was not a privy councillor and could not come to England to kiss hands, Sir Henry Clinton would be relegated to junior membership, a possibility which sat ill with the king, who believed that the commander-in-chief of the army should be second only to the head of the commission.[46]

The king seems to have entertained a grudging respect for both Eden and Johnstone. When Jackson was dropped from the commission he wrote: "I am very clear that he ought not to be allowed to go, and that Johnstone if made palatable to Lord Carlisle which I think Eden might easily manage would not be an improper person."[47]

North, writing on the same day, foresaw political advantage to himself in the change: Johnstone's "friends will . . . be better inclined to side with administration." It seems clear, however, that this would be a happy by-product; it was not the reason for Johnstone's appointment.

Between the day of the governor's acceptance, April 1, and the day of his departure aboard the *Trident* on the sixteenth, Johnstone was busy. Among other activities he may be presumed to have sounded out his brother William Pulteney on American reaction to his peace overtures.

Pulteney had at last been sent to Paris at the end of March to discuss peace terms with the American commissioners. The king was reconciled to the effective loss of the thirteen colonies, provided that some semblance of dependence was preserved, and was now mainly concerned that successful rebellion should not spread. He would allow no mention, in any treaty that Pulteney might negotiate, of Canada, Nova Scotia, or the Floridas. "The more they are kept unlike the other colonies the better, for it is by them we are to keep a certain awe over the abandoned colonies."[48]

On March 29 and 30, Pulteney saw Franklin, to whom he revealed a scheme which conceded the substance of "Home Rule" together with the offer of American M.P.s at Westminster. George Johnstone left for America under the impression that Franklin had agreed to the Pulteney scheme. The truth was otherwise.

On March 30, Franklin, in a letter addressed but never sent to Pulteney, wrote:

> The [British] ministers cannot yet divest themselves of the idea, that the powers of Parliament over us is constitutionally absolute and unlimited; and that the limitations they may be willing now to put to it are so many favours, or so many benefits, for which we are to make compensation. As our opinions in America are totally different, a treaty on the terms proposed appears to me utterly impracticable, either here [Paris], or there [America].

It was a confirmation of what he had already said to him in person.[49]

It is hard to believe that Pulteney would not have communicated to his brother details of his proposals and of their rebuff by Franklin, but it is even harder to believe that Johnstone decided to act as though Franklin had accepted the scheme when he knew that he had not. Even if the commission had been able to act instantly on its arrival in America and to persuade Congress to accept in principle the English treaty, there was simply not enough time for all the concomitant formalities to be completed before the arrival of Franklin's report of how and why he had rejected the Pulteney proposals. The probability is that the means by which Pulteney communicated information of the Paris negotiations to his brother was faulty. What is sure is that Johnstone genuinely believed that Franklin had been receptive to Pulteney's suggestions of a constitutional scheme for America which stopped short of complete independence.

It was with optimism that he viewed the prospect of reunion with America and with eagerness that he sought to discuss methods of achieving it with members of the government. To his fury he found the ministers so evasive that he soon became convinced that they wanted the efforts for peace to fail. In a splenetic letter to Eden on April 5, the governor complained of his treatment. He had wanted to discuss John Temple's role in negotiation with John Robinson, the secretary to the treasury, and, to be sure of seeing him, had sent word to Robinson that he would be at home from three to eleven. Robinson arrived at Johnstone's house in Old Burlington Street by chaise. But, even though Johnstone's servant told Robinson's coachman that his master was at home, the secretary gave the order, mixed with expletives, to drive on. Commotion among his horses made it impossible for the driver to obey instantly, which gave Johnstone's lad the chance to run up to the vehicle and tell Robinson in person that the governor was at home. The secretary ignored him and again shouted "Go on!" to his driver so that, by the time Johnstone himself reached his front door, Robinson was out of sight.

Although the governor saw wider implications, Robinson's lack of cooperation at least indicates that he did not share Johnstone's enthusiasm for Temple. It is hard to understand why Robinson, unless directly ordered to by North or his sovereign, should have bothered to call at the governor's house at all, since, with admirable judgment, he had clearly determined to waste no time whatever in staying to talk about Temple.

Robinson was a canny man. As his work for North had already shown and similar activity for the younger Pitt would even more clearly demonstrate, he was more of a "man of business" than Johnstone would ever be. Perhaps his good sense told him what Johnstone's letter of April 5 tells us, that the governor completely misjudged the game in America. "Next to Franklin," he wrote, "I regard Temple as the greatest card in the Pack for our Purposes."[50] Benjamin Franklin, Johnstone's ace, to continue his metaphor, was not even in the British hand, while John Temple, far from being a king of trumps was, as Robinson probably perceived, nothing but a knave. It would be entirely understandable if the secretary simply could not bear to listen to a man in Johnstone's position endorsing Temple's extremely high valuation of himself.

Temple was a Bostonian who had worked as a customs official on both sides of the Atlantic. He was in England during the earlier stages of the American war, at which time he consistently denied connection with the celebrated affair in which Benjamin Franklin had acquired and publicized damaging confidential letters written by Governor Hutchinson of Massachusetts. Later, when it was safe to do so, he admitted involvement in the business. A resolute opponent of independence while in exile, Temple held views on American affairs which seemed similar to those of Johnstone. In 1778 he offered to assist the peace commissioners going to America and was taken astonishingly seriously.[51]

The terms of his engagement still exist. He was to be paid £4,000, half immediately and the other half when he had taken action found satisfactory by the commissioners. In addition he was to be honored with a baronetcy and, "independent of the success of the commission," an annual pension of £2,000. All rewards, apart from the initial £2,000, were subject to his conduct's meeting with the commissioners' approval. Even so, Temple was being treated with inexplicable liberality—to such an extent that Lord North felt compelled to restrict one part of the agreement. Temple should not expect his pension if the commission should fail completely, glossed North in defiance of the wording of the man's engagement, but only if the commission were to fall short of complete success.[52] It may be that Robinson, who was responsible for disbursing secret service funds, resented having to place much money on as poor a card as Temple seemed and as, in the event, he was to prove.

Johnstone, however, was clearly enthusiastic about the possibilities inherent in Temple's method—unofficial approaches to Congress—and for what reasons it is impossible to say, he thought that Temple would carry weight with its members. He himself did what he could during his last days in England to sway congressional sentiment in favor of reunion with the mother country by seeking out men who had friendships from prewar days with congressmen. Offering to act as a mailman, he persuaded fifteen of them to write to their American acquaintances to urge the benefits of reconciliation.[53]

More formal steps in the same direction had already been taken in other quarters. North's conciliatory propositions of February 17 had been dispatched across the Atlantic in the *Andromeda* to acquaint the Americans with the official abandonment of former British pretensions, such as the right to tax them. Once these proposals became statute law, Admiral Gambier sailed on March 13 with copies of the acts to let it be known that Parliament approved of the new policy.[54]

At this busy time Johnstone himself found it worthwhile to pen a long letter on April 10 to General Joseph Reed, although he must have known that it could scarcely reach America before he did. Johnstone established acquaintance by name-dropping; he wrote that he had a letter for him from his brother-in-law, Dennis de Berdt, and that General James Robertson had been most complimentary about him; he then defined his own position on the quarrel with America.[55] The policy of the British government had been misguided. He himself had resisted it. So, quite justifiably, had the Americans, and to such good effect that Britain was at last "convinced of her folly and her faults." What Johnstone wanted was "that every subject of the empire might live equally free and secure in the enjoyment of the blessings of life;—not one part dependent on the will of another with opposite interests, but a general union, on terms of perfect security and mutual advantage." The purpose of the Carlisle commission was to settle "in a manner consistent with that Union of force on which the safety of both parties depends" all differences between Britain and America. His qualifications for membership of the commission were his zeal and his integrity. It was Johnstone's hope that the colonists preferred "freedom, in conjunction with Great Britain, to an union with the ancient enemy of both." He hoped, too, that they would forget "recent injuries" and remember "former benefits." Finally, he hinted at possible reward for cooperation with the commission.

> The man who can be instrumental in bringing us all to act once more in harmony, and unite together the various powers which this contest has drawn forth, will deserve more from the king and people, from patriotism, humanity, friendship, and all the tender ties that are affected by the quarrel and reconcilation, than ever yet was bestowed on mankind.[56]

   This letter is important in that it contains the fullest extant exposition of
Johnstone's ideas on imperial relations. It also shows his continued conviction that Americans fundamentally preferred Britain to France and how
the "man of business" hoped to make leading Americans amenable to the
commission's proposals.

   On the day that he wrote to Reed, Johnstone spoke in the Commons
against a motion for declaring America independent. Charles Fox voted
the other way but still found it possible to praise Johnstone. The commission, he said, should not be deluded into thinking that Americans were
disunited in their support of independence. The Conciliatory Acts were
totally inadequate for their purpose and if any good came of them he would
attribute it solely to the influence of Johnstone. The latter replied that he
would not prophesy success for the commission, which was merely "an
experiment to be tried." Chances of success would be improved by the
repeal of the Quebec Act and of the Declaratory Act, "which was downright
nonsense as it now stood in our statute books." Such action would unite
Britons in the conviction that they were fighting a just war but would
increase the disunity of the Americans who were already divided on
independence—the "people of the old settled interest and property"
dreaded it. He thought Parliament legally incapable of declaring America
independent, although he would have voted against the independence motion in any case. To independence Johnstone preferred "an union of two
unequal parts," and he hoped, once he had shown the Americans that
France was dragging them into misery, that they would too.[57]

   Johnstone's assumptions about American views of independence may
have been widespread; certainly his brother shared them.[58] The hopes they
inspired proved to have little foundation, but the government could
scarcely send commissioners like Richard Jackson, who had not the least
degree of optimism. Eden was too much of a realist to be very hopeful. In
the hectic days prior to embarkation, he declared himself "mad vex'd" by
the exclusion of Sir Henry Clinton's name from the commission and considered "the Business as more than half damn'd by it." He was by now
disturbed by Johnstone's quarrelsome nature—perhaps the result of closer
acquaintance. He asked Wedderburn "to give him a kind Lecture adverted
to make us go on well together—If we do not it will be a bad story."
Wedderburn was able to right the first concern and reassure him about the
other. By May 4 on his way across the Atlantic, Eden was in a proper state
of equanimity: "I am in neither extreme either of Confidence or Despon-
dency."[59]

   The royal instructions for the commissioners were issued on April 12,
only four days before embarkation. They were to go to America and to
make contact with either Congress or George Washington, whom they
should address in any style necessary to get talks under way. They were
not to let the Americans use the necessity of referring back to Parliament

as a reason for not negotiating, and while the talks were actually in progress they should admit, as a temporary expedient, any claim to independence that the Americans might make. As inducements to American cooperation, they were to be promised that their trade would enjoy the protection of the Royal Navy as soon as peace was established, that no British troops would be kept in America in peacetime, and that no alterations would be made in their governments or charters without their consent. They were to arrange a cease-fire but, if possible, maneuver the Americans into making the request for one.

Even if the commissioners' scheme had not been offered at the wrong time and occasion, which was its main defect, it would probably have been doomed by the government's continued determination to raise money in America; nevertheless, the instruction on that subject was ingenious. American contributions were to be voluntary and geared to some yardstick, like population or exports, so that as the country grew, so too would its contribution. If this notion was rejected, the commissioners would be allowed to abandon it, while making it clear that the Americans would have to raise and pay their own defense forces, although—and there was no provision for backing down from this lethal determination—the king would appoint the officers for those forces.

Also unpalatable would be the stipulation that Americans would not be allowed to use paper to settle private debts, although the British would assist in contracting the amount of paper in circulation, and without paying for the war, help the Americans pay their debts. Many of the traditional controls exercised over Americans would be relaxed. Americans would be governors, initially selected by the commission but subsequently through election. All customs officers would be put under the authority of the states and some of them would be appointed by state assemblies. Any crown offices thought unnecessary by the Americans would be suppressed. The powers of the Admiralty courts would be restricted and the Navigation Acts, as they related to the thirteen colonies, would be relaxed. The new states would be responsible for duties on foreign imports. The commissioners were cautioned not to be too liberal in promising export bounties; any new trade regulations for America would have to secure parliamentary approval. Without being empowered to promise that Americans might elect M.P.s to Westminster, they were allowed to promise that a system for the representation of American views would be created before the passage of any trade act for America. Nevertheless if the question of American M.P.s was raised, the commissioners were not to reject the idea but rather to refer it back to Parliament. Similarly, if the Americans wanted Congress to continue as an institution, the commissioners were to welcome the idea as long as they made it clear that its powers might not infringe British sovereignty. Presumably in the hope that events would turn it into a dead letter, the commissioners were not to demand the repeal of the Declaration of Independence.

Several instructions related to the judicial process. Judges would be independent, and a speedier system of appeals from court decisions was to be created, while all treason cases arising from the war would be tried in local courts. For those guilty merely of rebellion, a general pardon was promised.

The crown was concessive in forgiving all arrears of quitrents but determined to resume its authority over coinage, forts, and warships and generous in promising compensation for those who had suffered losses in the war, among whom there was particular concern for the clergy.

The notion shared by Johnstone that Congress did not represent the will of the whole people was firmly embedded in the instructions. The commissioners were advised to try to have the state assemblies summoned before breaking off negotiations, although no hint was given as to how they could do it, and if Congress proved recalcitrant, the commissioners were authorized to negotiate separately with other bodies, individual colonies, or even likely individual men. Finally, the commission was given the discretionary power to do almost anything rather than to allow negotiations to break down.[60]

The new type of imperial relationship envisaged in these instructions was not ludicrous. It might have been accepted in the spring of 1776, or even later if it had followed a substantial British military victory. Undoubtedly more concessive than it would have been if the Franco-American alliance had not been nearing completion, it was not, nevertheless, a panic measure to secure peace at any price. It embodied, rather, a type of imperial connection advocated by some of the most acute students of empire of the day. The essentials of the commissioners' instructions may be found in Chatham's proposals of 1775 and in the thinking of Shelburne who, in 1782, thought that a reconciliation between Britain and the United States might follow the conclusion of a peace treaty. When demanding a new constitutional arrangement between England and Ireland in the early 1780s, Irish leaders, too, like Grattan, would make constant reference to the offers made to the Americans in 1778.[61]

George Johnstone must be numbered with Chatham and Shelburne as one of the few imperial theorists of the eighteenth century who argued in vain against the powerful coalition of conservatives and vested interests in advocating a federal system in the British empire.[62]

> The supremacy of the legislative authority of Great Britain! This I call unintelligible jargon. Instead of running the different privileges belonging to the various parts of the empire into a common mass of power, gentlemen should consider that the very first principles of good government in this wide-extended dominion, consist in subdividing

the empire into many parts, and giving to each individual an immediate interest, that the community to which he belongs should be well-regulated.[63]

Johnstone, then, could wholeheartedly agree with the principles underlying the instructions; Carlisle, entrusted with the first important assignment of his career, and the ambitious Eden had every reason to carry them out if they could.

By April 16, all three were aboard the *Trident,* together with the secretary to the commission, Adam Ferguson, who apparently had been chosen by Johnstone. Another contender for the position had been Jeremy Bentham, whose early work, *A Fragment on Government,* was so much enjoyed by Johnstone, possibly for its cynical humor, that he carried a copy in his pocket and bored his friends by reading aloud from it.[64] Bentham asked a friend of Johnstone's, John Lind, to intercede for him, but the post had already gone to Ferguson, a professor of moral philosophy at Edinburgh University whose work also was much admired by the Scottish commissioner.[65] Accompanying them were the pregnant Mrs. Eden, Anthony Storer, M.P. for Carlisle and yet another old Etonian who "went as an idle man *pour s'amuser,"* and three private secretaries, twenty footmen, two female servants and an important fellow passenger, Lord Cornwallis.[66] In demonstration of coincidence or, perhaps, the smallness of the eighteenth-century establishment, the captain of the *Trident* was that same John Elliot who had vainly sought election with Johnstone for Storer's constituency a decade previously.

On the day of departure, Johnstone wrote with an odd mixture of happiness and pessimism to his brother. He found Cornwallis captivating, Carlisle pleasant, Ferguson "Philosophy itself," while the Edens were "the most obliging beings on earth." At the same time as he anticipated an agreeable voyage, however, he nourished no hope of keeping France and Spain out of the American war. "The storm must come," he wrote, and asked his brother to do what he could to initiate a preemptive strike on the twenty ships of the line which, he asserted, were completely manned and victualled and waiting at Cadiz for Spanish participation in the war.[67]

On April 21, just an hour before the *Trident* sailed, it was discovered that its rigging had been skillfully sabotaged, an incident which, in the light of subsequent discoveries by the commissioners, might be considered symbolic.[68]

5. A Philadelphia Story

The commissioners spent forty-four days crossing the Atlantic, arriving in the Delaware on June 4. The voyage was made without any remarkable occurrence despite some considerable discomfort. Including the crew and troop reinforcements, 600 human beings were crammed into a 64-gun ship, and the Edens were sick much of the time. On May 6, Johnstone had submitted to the consideration of his fellow commissioners a list of proposals which his brother William Pulteney had put to Franklin.

The first was that existing state governments should continue. Carlisle, evidently a believer in "divide and rule," penned a comment, the only one of any significance written in the margin, against this suggestion: "If they be content with their present Governments, little objection occurs to this article, as the constitutions of those governments are essentially different; any union injurious to Great Britain seems to threaten less by leaving them their ancient forms."[1] But whereas Pulteney had proposed that the king should name one governor in three he also specified that all judges and civil officers should be nominated by the state governments and that Britain would have no veto over legislation of the state assemblies, except for laws affecting the trade with Britain. Even then, if a state decided to prohibit the importation of blacks it might do so. The much hated Admiralty courts would continue to exist but only to deal with prizes. Appeals to the privy council, except from such courts in time of war, would cease. Congress was to continue to exist, but its powers would have to be defined and the king would choose its president.

To right two of the Americans' chief grievances, Pulteney suggested that Britain would raise no taxes and station no troops in America without the consent of the state assemblies, although army officers would still be commissioned by the king. Nevertheless, the assemblies would be empowered to remove them. The states were to assume responsibility for ungranted lands and for quitrents, both of which the crown was prepared to abandon in return for compensation.

Pulteney's sweeping proposal to end trade disputes was that the states should have free trade to and from all places, and that there should be no office of customs in America. The only reservations were that grants to existing companies might not be impaired and that those aspects of the mercantile system which had benefited the Americans—bounties, and prohibitions which favored them—would be discontinued.

It was proposed that the states should take responsibility for the expenses of both their defense forces and also of civil government. In addition they were to make a contribution to the British government, settled in such a way as to grow as the states did, presumably to help pay for the protection provided by the Royal Navy.

The Americans, it was also proposed, were to have their own members of Parliament at Westminster but were expected to allow a surprising amount of power to the king, who was to be the only supreme governor of the states with authority to make war, peace, and alliances. As before the war, all judicial proceedings, acts of government, and grants would run in his name. All hostile resolutions, by which was meant preeminently the Declaration of Independence, were to be annulled.

None of the above systems could operate until hostilities by land and sea had ended, which would be the first step in a pacification which would include mutual amnesty, mutual restitution of territory, and mutual compensation for wanton war damage.[2]

Pulteney's proposals were similar in principle to the instructions given to Carlisle, but they contained differences, such as definite rather than provisional agreement to American M.P.s, and they raised the thorny questions of unsettled land and the claims of the land companies, as the instructions did not. In tenor and in some details the Pulteney scheme was more generous; it proposed, for instance, that officers appointed by the king be removable. Because the earl was told by Johnstone that Franklin had agreed to them, although he had in reality done no such thing, optimism must have lightened the hardships of the voyage. Despite predictions to the contrary, he and Eden got on with Johnstone, who was similarly buoyed up with delusory hopes. "The Gov[erno]r has hitherto gone on well with us," wrote Eden as late as June 18, "& I believe is well satisfied as far as we are concerned."[3]

There is an odor of apartheid about Eden's comment. As a commissioner, Johnstone was equal to, but unmistakably separate from, the Etonian clique. He belonged to an entirely different species of political animal from Carlisle and Eden. He had not obtained such political celebrity as he enjoyed from birth, wealth, or services to the administration but rather, and almost solely, from his effectiveness, both rhetorical and organizational, in opposing the government and the directorate of the East India Company.

Johnstone's record as a conciliator was less than impressive, but the commissioners' instructions provided that if Congress and Washington refused to negotiate, and the realistic Eden must have anticipated that possibility, the commission might deal directly with any province that wanted "to revert to the ancient form of government" under a governor appointed by the commissioners. Any three of the commission might "enter into any Correspondence or Treaty with particular Colonies, Bodies, or Individual Persons, to answer the purpose of the Commission."[4] Johnstone had some experience in organizing malcontents, which might prove relevant should the occasion arise, but even if it did not, a man was needed who could guide members of Congress and leading figures in American society to agreement with Britain. Eden had underlined the necessity for such a commissioner when Jackson was dropped, and though Eden himself had some experience in persuading Americans to work for

Britain, he preferred someone else to do it in this instance. A commissioner was wanted, it may be recalled, "sufficiently *habituated to Business* not to leave me exposed to the Imputation of taking too much to myself."[5] By experience, if not by personality, Johnstone was the best commissioner for the role. To be sure, Eden's brother Robert had been governor of Maryland, but former governor George Johnstone had American contacts and, unlike the other commissioners, had lived in America and enjoyed popularity there for his condemnation of North's colonial policies.[6]

It was probably anticipated from the beginning that material inducements would be used to win over Americans to cooperation with the commissioners, who were empowered by their instructions to appoint governors, but who also, there is some evidence to suppose, expected to use money for the same purpose. When Eden had first assessed the expenses of the commission he had written: "Some arrangement should be settled as to the power of drawing for secret service money, which should be vested in the three civil commissioners upon the unique agreement according to the circumstances which may arise."[7] Carlisle showed a similar inclination when writing to his wife from the *Trident:*

> When I lay aboard the galley . . . what do you think my bed was supported by?—a twelve-pounder on one side, and a box containing ten thousand new guineas on the other. . . . I believe, if the Commission was suffered to act to the extent that these two powerful agents could carry them, there would be no doubt of succeeding.[8]

Ultimately Johnstone was to be accused of attempting to bribe prominent Americans to attain the ends of the commission but, although he bore the full opprobrium for the offense, it would seem that the notion was not alien to his fellow commissioners. It would seem, too, that the same Congress which was outraged by Johnstone's alleged attempts at bribery was not immune to the lure of gold. Its president wrote to Governor Houston of Georgia on August 27, 1778, of the "scenes of venality, peculation, and fraud which I have uncovered [in Congress]."[9] If this situation was promising for the commission, a favorable military situation would have been more so.

It was axiomatic, even to the diplomatic tyro Carlisle, that a powerful and threatening military force in a strategic position would enormously enhance the commission's prospects. As far as the passengers aboard the *Trident* were aware, Sir William Howe's army was in the enemy capital, relegating the Continental Congress to makeshift quarters in York and the Continental Army to the rigors of life in Valley Forge. The occupation was the mainstay of the commission's bargaining position. To evacuate Philadelphia was to saw the stay at least halfway through. As Johnstone, quoting Montrose and Bacon, was later to comment, "Nothing is more contemptible than a retreating army or a supplicating prince . . . and . . .

no body of men ever thanked you for clemancy who were not first sensible of your power."[10]

However, unknown to the commission, and because of the near certainty of hostilities with France, the North administration had decided not to wait for the outcome of the peace attempt but immediately to redeploy British forces in America to cope with the new enemy. Even before the news of the Franco-American treaties became public, Germain had taken action which made evacuation of Philadelphia a distinct possibility, in that he had adopted a defensive strategy for mainland America. Available troops were to be used for small raids on the New England coast and consolidation of the British hold on Canada, Nova Scotia, Newfoundland, and the Floridas; when the offensive was resumed in the fall of 1778 it was to be in the southern colonies, not in Pennsylvania.[11] Once the Franco-American alliance was made public on March 13, the need for a defensive posture in mainland America was intensified, since a descent on the French West Indies with troops from the mainland was at once planned. "It is a joke," wrote the king in consequence, "to think of keeping Pennsylvania."[12] He wrote new instructions on the twenty-first, ordering the evacuation of Philadelphia, the end of offensive operations on the American mainland, and the dispatch of an expedition for the conquest of the island of St. Lucia.[13]

Not a syllable of these new orders had been imparted to the members of the commission before its departure. The need for military secrecy does less to explain this unpardonable failure than does North's inability to coordinate policies. Germain, who was responsible for military operations, had been all but completely excluded from the planning of the peace commission. He seemed unconcerned at the effects of military schemes on the commission's prospects, and his gesture of begging Clinton to try to hold at least New York "to give Dignity and Effect to the Commissioners' Negotiations" lacks the ring of conviction.[14] Carlisle had seen Germain just before the commission embarked and had asked him why its specified destination was New York rather than Philadelphia. With nice ellipsis Germain replied, "Perhaps that city may not by your arrival be in our hands."[15] Carlisle did not press him to expand on his answer and certainly did not guess its true implications.

Lord North meanwhile had made it difficult for commissioners to ask him questions—"Lord North . . . had rather . . . meet the Devil sooner than a Commissioner"—and even when cornered left conversations inconclusive, "very much in the stile of a common acquaintance who is stepping from your Room to the water Closet, and means to return in five minutes."[16]

Nothing that occurred during the voyage of the *Trident* dispelled the commissioners' delusions. On May 27, about seventy leagues from the American shore, the brig *Stanley* was sighted; Captain Whitworth told them that General Clinton and Lord Howe were both at Philadelphia.[17] The importance of a meeting of all the commissioners as soon as possible was obvious, and Carlisle, Eden, and Johnstone agreed that the *Trident* should go straight to Philadelphia rather than New York.[18]

The civil commissioners finally reached the city on June 6. The news which greeted them was calculated to induce despair. The British troops were poised for evacuation, and Congress had shown not the least inclination to take British peace approaches seriously. On April 22, the day after the *Trident* had left England, and before reports of Franklin's diplomatic triumph in securing the Franco-American alliance had reached America on May 2, Congress had totally rejected North's conciliatory propositions unless, as a preliminary, Britain withdrew all its fleets and armies or expressly acknowledged American independence, in which case Congress would deign to talk with the commissioners.[19]

Clinton refused a request to hold up the retreat from Philadelphia until the commissioners had had a chance to present their proposals to Congress. He would not have been inclined to do so, even if his orders had not forbidden delay, since the terms being offered were far too liberal for his taste.[20] He did not, however, refuse his place on the commission, although his considerable military responsibilities preoccupied him and he was not an active participant.

The other commissioners, meanwhile, acutely aware that the normal slow pace of diplomatic procedure was inappropriate in their circumstances, wrote to Congress on June 9, displaying their entire stock of bait, such as it was. A copy of their commission, to prove their right to treat, and copies of the parliamentary Conciliatory Acts, to show the alleged new temper of Britain toward America, accompanied offers of a ceasefire, the restoration of trade, the abrogation of the right to keep troops in America, help with American debts, and finally, seats for American M.P.s in Parliament (to be reciprocated by seats for Britons in state assemblies). All of these were to ensure "under our common sovereign . . . the irrevocable enjoyment of every privilege that is short of a total separation of interest, or consists with that union of force, on which the safety of our common religion and liberty depends." The wording here is reminiscent of Johnstone. He had used the distinctive phrase "union of force" in his letter to Joseph Reed in April. He may, therefore, also have been responsible for the sentence immediately following, in which was noticed "the insidious interposition of a power, which has, from the first settlement of these colonies been actuated with enmity to us both." The sentiment accords with Johnstone's known prejudices, although were the language not so mild it might have been written by Carlisle.[21] (In any event, the actual words used gave great offense to Congress). Surely, the commissioners' letter concluded, the Americans "will prefer a firm, a free, and perpetual coalition with the parent-state, to an insecure and unnatural foreign alliance."[22]

Professor Adam Ferguson, the secretary to the commission, was chosen to carry this message to Congress, but Washington would not grant him a passport through the American lines, so the letter went by ordinary military post, reaching York on June 13. Congress broke off debate to hear it read, but its presentation was interrupted by protesting congressmen after the first derogatory reference to France; it was not read in full until after a committee had considered it, on June 16. The following day a tart reply, containing a reference to "His Most Christian Majesty, the good and great ally of the States," and condemning the commissioners' plan as "founded on the idea of dependence," was returned, offering a conference with the commissioners only if there were "an explicit acknowledgement of the independence of these States" or the withdrawal of the British fleets and armies.[23]

The notion long nursed by Johnstone that there was a strong anti-French feeling which could be appealed to was shown to have little basis in Congress. Open diplomacy had failed—the congressional letter could not have been more intransigent. Johnstone decided to work by more covert methods. The ten days the commission stayed in Philadelphia were, therefore, busy ones for him.

He seems initially to have been borne along by optimism and enthusiasm and expressed an "intention of selling what he has in England" and settling in America. He scandalized the leading loyalist, Joseph Galloway, who thought his talk of a "Federal Union" absurd and impracticable, and he shocked Ambrose Serle, Lord Howe's secretary, by carrying amiable letters to Thomas Willing, an inveterate revolutionary but one who, as the governor surely knew, had joined Robert Morris in absenting himself from Congress on July 4, 1776, and had discussed peace terms with General William Howe in 1777.[24] Actually Johnstone was less concerned to conciliate loyalists than to woo rebels.

His first step was to establish credit with them by presenting letters of introduction from people in England who had highly placed American friends. Having scraped acquaintance, he evidently hoped to influence his new friends by argument, charm, and ultimately by dangling before them the prospect of rewards for cooperation. Not for the last time, he talked much and indiscriminately. His lack of diplomatic reserve made his plans common knowledge on both sides of the Atlantic. A junior officer in Clinton's army was able to write to a Hampshire friend on June 20:

> I saw Gov[ernor] Johnstone in Philadelphia a few days before I left it, and had some conversation with him. Thro' the means of the commander in chief and Mr. Galloway, he sent several private introductory letters of himself to some American gentlemen in power; one to Mr.

Morris, a leading member of the Congress, from a Quaker house in London; and also three others to Gen[eral] Washington, Mr. Johnson, the Governor of Maryland, and to a Mr. Carmichael, lately secretary to the Commissioners at Paris: these last were given to him by a Maryland gentleman, who lives at B——, and visited the Commissioners on board the *Trident* before she left Spithead. These letters were laid before Gen[eral] Clinton; and he appointed Mr. Brown, with a flag of truce, to carry them. I understand they were merely introductory to Gov[ernor] Johnstone, and conveyed the hopes and wishes of their writers, that such introduction might lead to personal conversation, and tend to produce an accommodation on honourable terms to both countries.[25]

Johnstone's campaign to increase his influence depended on personal impact. "He thinks his powers of argument sufficient to bring back the Americans to their duty," wrote one English observer.[26] Wraxall, in a more general assessment, said that he possessed "a species of ardent, impetuous, half-savage eloquence, restrained by no delicacy of language, yet capable of powerfully affecting his hearers by the display of information, by his energetic appeals to their passions, and even his gesticulations."[27] For the success of Johnstone's plans the goodwill of Washington would be all but indispensable, but the American took his time about replying to initial overtures. Pending permission to visit behind enemy lines, since time was short, Johnstone began what the *Annual Register* called "his insinuating scheme of conciliation" by writing more letters—which was unfortunate for whatever chance of success he may have had, since he was less impressive on paper than in person.[28]

On June 10 he wrote two letters from Philadelphia to Henry Laurens, the president of Congress. One was simply a covering note for letters he had brought to Laurens from friends in England. The other letter had more substance and ended with a request:

> If you should follow the example of Britain in the hour of her insolence and send us back without a hearing, I shall hope, from private friendship, that I may be permitted to see the country, and the worthy characters she has exhibited to the world, upon making the request in any way you may point out.[29]

Laurens replied in a long and courteous letter which conceded nothing. Congress would not treat with the commissioners until British fleets and armies were withdrawn. Johnstone was welcome to see America, but only after independence had been acknowledged.[30]

On the same day that Johnstone wrote to Laurens, he also wrote to Congressman Francis Dana. Because he knew Dana well, "it will be presumed," wrote Johnstone, "we will lose no opportunity, from false punctilio, of meeting to discuss our differences fairly."[31] He assured Dana that "Franklin, on the 29th of March last, in discussing the several articles we wish to make the basis of our treaty, was perfectly satisfied they were beneficial to North America and such as she should accept." He went on to argue that the French treaty was generous only because France had been compelled to outbid Britain, and he ended his letter, not with a request such as he had made to Laurens, but a demand: "If you follow the example of Britain in the hour of her pride, insolence, and madness, and refuse to hear us, I still expect, since I am here, to have the privilege of coming among you and seeing the country."[32]

Both Johnstone's letters indicate a desire to meet American politicians face to face, preferably, one suspects, on the backstairs rather than in the halls of power, but there is no hint in them of rewards for cooperation. Six days later, on the eve of the British evacuation, the case was different.

On June 16, Johnstone wrote a private letter to Robert Morris which began by expressing the desirability of Anglo-American reconciliation. He passed on to discussion of the French treaties, which he clearly thought he could persuade American leaders not to honor. Then, having claimed to believe "the men who have conducted the affairs of America incapable of being influenced by improper motives," Johnstone went on to reflect that in such transactions as he was proposing, "there is risk, and I think, that whoever ventures should be secured, at the same time that honour and emolument should naturally follow the fortune of those who have steered the vessel in the storm, and brought her safely to port." He wrote specifically of favors for Washington and Laurens and ended with a threat of what might happen if there were ministerial changes in England. "It is the same blunderers who produced the war who have conducted it. When the sense of the nation is roused, believe me she can make struggles that few have received, but which I should be sorry to see executed."[33]

In these letters Johnstone showed neither wisdom nor prudence. His talk of "Britain in the hour of her pride, insolence, and madness" can surely have impressed his reader little, while it did him much harm among Britons when made public.[34] On the day that he wrote to Morris, the sixteenth, Johnstone had an interview which led, perhaps, to a more blatant bribery attempt.

It took place in the house of Charles Stedman, Johnstone's residence in Philadelphia. Stedman was a Pennsylvanian officer of twenty-five years who donned a scarlet tunic when war broke out. He served under Lord Percy at Lexington and General Howe in Pennsylvania and New Jersey. Also staying at his house was a friend of Eliza Stedman, Mrs. Elizabeth Ferguson, who merits some consideration here because her unsupported testimony would demolish Johnstone's reputation among Americans and kill any chance he might have had to win them over to his views.

She was born in 1739 in Pennsylvania. As the daughter of Dr. Thomas Graeme of Graeme Park, and the granddaughter, through her mother, of Sir William Keith, Governor of Pennsylvania, she enjoyed a good position in the colony's society. In her teens she had developed a close relationship with Benjamin Franklin's son William, who was destined to be the last royal governor of New Jersey. Their understanding never flowered, being blighted, most probably, by separation. While he was in England in 1758 William was crestfallen to receive a letter from Elizabeth terminating their friendship. Elizabeth herself visited England six years later but, in spite of affectionate correspondence with a Liverpudlian suitor, returned to Pennsylvania and married a Scotsman eleven years her junior, Henry Hugh Ferguson. Her temperament seems to have been literary rather than political—she even wrote an epic poem, *Telemachus*[35]—but her proclaimed sympathies lay with the revolutionaries in the 1770s, despite her many loyalist associates. Chief of these was her husband, who returned to Scotland without her in 1775 but who voluntarily came back to Philadelphia after its occupation by the British, where he accepted employment as Howe's commissary of prisoners.

In 1777, before her husband had accepted British pay, Washington had allowed Elizabeth Ferguson to pass through the lines to visit Ferguson in Philadelphia. She carried with her, on her return, a letter to Washington from the Reverend Jacob Duché, a clergyman whom both British and Americans had reason to consider a turncoat. Duché's message to the general was an appeal, largely on snobbish grounds, to forsake the cause he had joined and to do what he could to revoke the Declaration of Independence, using, if necessary, the Continental Army against Congress. Washington thought it his duty to publicize Duché's letter—with unfortunate results for the cleric's future.[36]

His postwoman, however, was not so discredited that she was refused permission in the following year to return to Philadelphia. She had much to distress her when she met Johnstone there. Not only had her husband decided to retire to New York when the British forces evacuated Philadelphia, but she was to be left to combat the consequences of his loyalism on her own. An American court was to try him for high treason. Because he would not be present, he could not be physically punished if he were found guilty, but Elizabeth Ferguson stood to see the court order the confiscation of her property which, legally, marriage had made her husband's.

She told the governor of her hopes and fears. Her intention was to pass through the American lines yet again in order to submit a memorandum asserting her Scottish husband's innocence of treason to the Pennsylvania supreme executive at Lancaster.[37] Johnstone listened to her tale with interest, because General Joseph Reed, who as a figure of influence in both Congress and the Continental Army was one of those with whom he most hoped to conduct unofficial negotiations, was reputed to be at Lancaster.

During their third conversation, according to Mrs. Ferguson, Johnstone, supposing that she would see Reed, told her that if the general "after well considering the nature of the dispute can, conformable to his conscience and view of things, exert his influence to settle the contest, he may command ten thousand guineas and the best post in government," and he wanted to tell him so. The lady asked if he did not think that bribery. "By no means, Madam," he is supposed to have replied. "This method of proceeding is customary in all negotiations; and one may very honourably make it a man's interest to step forth in a cause."[38] When she relayed the conversation to Reed three days after the British evacuated Philadelphia, he replied, according to Mrs. Ferguson, that "my influence is small, but was it as great as Governor Johnstone would insinuate, the king of Great Britain had nothing in his gift that would tempt me."

On June 17, before the Scot could have known the disastrous outcome of his vicarious overtures to Reed, he wrote yet another letter seeking support for peace by negotiation. It was addressed to General Charles Lee. If Johnstone had supposed that Robert Morris would be open to his arguments because of his initial disapproval of the independence declaration then he probably thought that Lee's history would make him even more amenable to persuasion. He had three reasons for hope. The first was that after being made a prisoner of war in December 1776, Lee had presented the British commander-in-chief, Sir William Howe, with a detailed plan of how best to defeat the Americans. The second was Lee's well-known and deep differences with Washington. The third was that Lee had written to Johnstone, after his arrival in America, a friendly letter which apparently touched on the desirability of Anglo-American conciliation.

Johnstone's reply was affable. It offered no bribe other than a vague and unexceptionable reference to "the many and mutual advantages both [countries] would derive from an agreement."[39] The governor probably expected no great result from this letter: he must have known that Lee was a controversial rather than an influential figure among the Americans. Indeed his court-martial condemnation in July 1778 was soon to put a complete end to Lee's participation in the Revolution. Actually it is doubtful that Lee even received Johnstone's letter because on the very day that it was written, June 17, Congress resolved that "because many letters, addressed to individuals of these United States, have been lately received from England, thro' the conveyance of the enemy, and some . . . contain ideas insidiously calculated to divide and delude," the individual states should be recommended "to take the most effectual measures to put a stop to so dangerous and criminal a correspondence."[40] Nor was Washington softened by Johnstone's paper carronades, and on the following day, the eighteenth, he spiked them. To attempt to send their secretary, Professor Ferguson, to Washington's camp at Valley Forge had been one of the first actions of the peace commission after their arrival in Philadelphia. He had set off on June 8, in a phaeton escorted by a dragoon and a trumpeter, but as we have seen, Ferguson was stopped before entering American lines and his correspondence was carried initially to Washington.[41] It included a letter from Johnstone in which he introduced Ferguson and sought a meeting with the general on his own behalf. Washington's original, fairly prompt, reply to this letter was drafted on June 12 and read:

> The sentiments you are pleased to entertain of me, cannot but be extremely flattering, separated as we are, by the circumstances of our political stations; and have a just claim to my warmest acknowledgements. If in the course of events, an opportunity should be afforded me, you may be assured I shall take pleasure in shewing Dr. Ferguson every civility, it may be in my power to render.
>
> I shall ever be happy to relieve the anxiety of departed friends, and where letters are calculated, either to this end, or to effect matters of mere private concern, they will have the earliest conveyance.

The final version of Washington's reply, on June 18, was a good deal more severe:[42]

> I am thankful to you, Sir, for your very indulging opinion of me, and much obliged to my friend for his intention to bring us acquainted. I am sorry that pleasure must be denied me until the termination of your intended negotiation with Congress; for, situated as I am, were it ever so much my wish to see you, my occupations, and duty to the cause I am engaged in, are essential barriers for the present.
>
> You will find, Sir, when you become more acquainted with this country, that the voice of Congress is the general voice of the People,[43] and that they are deservedly held up as the guardians of the United States. I shall always be happy to render you any services, and for the present I have the honor etc.[44]

Washington had evidently been intensely annoyed by Johnstone's attempts to make contact with other Americans, and to Henry Laurens, on the same day that he answered Johnstone, he wrote:

> I shall take every measure in my power to prevent an intercourse between the Army and the Enemy, and also between the Inhabitants and the Latter. You may rest assured, that whatever Letters come from their lines shall be, as they ever have been, minutely inspected; and wherever they import any thing of an insidious cast, they shall be suppressed.[45]

The sequel to this censorship policy came in the following two months. On July 9, Congress resolved that "all letters received by members of Congress, or their agents, from any subject of the King of Great Britain, of a public nature," be laid before Congress.[46] The resolution never became mandatory, but enough of Johnstone's letters were surrendered to damage him. He was not totally discredited, however, until the story of his conversation with Elizabeth Ferguson was made public in the *Pennsylvania Packet* of July 21, 1778. On August 11 Congress cited his letters to Reed and Morris and the Ferguson testimony as reason to resolve that it was "incompatible with the honour of Congress to hold any manner of correspondence or intercourse with the said George Johnstone, Esq., especially to negotiate with him upon affairs in which the cause of liberty and virtue is interested."[47]

Clearly the incident which irredeemably damned Johnstone was the Ferguson conversation. Nobody seems to have questioned the lady's veracity except Johnstone, who flatly denied it. It would not have been out of character for Johnstone to have been led away by his feelings into speaking openly of rewarding Reed with 10,000 guineas, but he had been careful not to mention money rewards in otherwise indiscreet letters. There were no witnesses to say that Mrs. Ferguson embroidered the truth, but her version of her exchanges with Johnstone reads more like stage dialogue than a real conversation. She had strong personal reasons for persuading American officials that she was a true patriot. It might have been highly prejudicial to her life and property and those of her husband had she been seen as simply an emissary of the Carlisle commission. That she should have been so viewed was likely because she had been Duché's messenger in 1777. Moreover, her testimony suggested that the meeting with Johnstone was purely fortuitous, yet Johnstone had sufficiently anticipated it as to bring her from England Washington's picture in the lid of a snuff-box.[48] The fact that her husband was related to the secretary of the Carlisle commission further complicates a story of which the intricacies will never be fully revealed. Nevertheless, the evidence, fragmentary as it is, does indicate that Elizabeth Ferguson had the strongest possible motives to curry favor with the American authorities, and suggests that she did so by putting into Johnstone's mouth words which he may have thought and hinted at but did not actually utter.

The poetess ruined Johnstone's reputation without persuading her countrymen that her own was stainless. In spite of her efforts the property of both Fergusons was confiscated in 1778. Only through the intervention of a friend in government was she allowed to live on at Graeme Park.[49] In his satirical poem, *M'Fingal,* John Trumbull suggested what may have been the common American opinion—that she was no more than Johnstone's accomplice:

Behold, at Britain's utmost shifts
Comes Johnstone, loaded with like gifts,
To venture through the Whiggish tribe

> To cuddle, wheedle, coax, and bribe . . .
> And call, to aid his desp'rate mission
> His petticoated politician;
> While Venus, join'd to act the farce
> Strolls forth embassadress to Mars. . . .[50]

If Johnstone's individual overtures failed, the commission as a body did very little better. It left Philadelphia on June 16 aboard the galley *Ferret*, which took it to the *Trident* the next day. Thanks to unfavorable winds, the *Trident* did not reach New York until June 30, and not until July 2 did the commission receive Congress' reply to its letter of June 9, to which it sent a despairing answer dated July 11.[51] The commissioners claimed that they could not withdraw their fleets and armies because of the presence of the French, and truly, even as they wrote, d'Estaing's ships rode at anchor off Sandy Hook. With regard to the other preliminary to negotiation, the commissioners contended that independence was "fully acknowledged," by which they meant conditionally acknowledged, since they defined independence as the "privilege of the people of North America to dispose of their property, and to govern themselves without any reference to Great Britain, beyond what is necessary to preserve that union of force, in which our mutual safety and advantage consist."[52]

Congress made short shrift of this feeble attempt to keep negotiations open, declaring that neither of the necessary preliminaries originally specified by them had been complied with; it resolved, on July 18, that no answer should be returned to the commissioners.[53]

When it became clear that Congress was intransigent, the commission decided that nothing was to be lost by broaching an unpleasant subject. On August 7 they sent a remonstrance against the failure to fulfill that clause of the Saratoga Convention by which General Gates had agreed, as a condition of British surrender in 1777, "that a free passage be granted to the army under L[ieutenan]t-Gen[eral] Burgoyne to G[reat] Britain, upon condition of not serving again in North America during the present contest; and the port of Boston is assigned for the entry of transports whenever Gen[eral] Howe shall so order."[54] The commission demanded that Congress reply.

Instead, the next communication was that declaration of August 11 by which Congress resolved to have no more dealings with Johnstone. This gave him the opportunity, when he answered Congress, as he did on August 16, of impugning the motives and characters of his accusers instead of rebutting the charges against him. The congressional resolution which condemned him was "calculated as an excuse to a deluded people for not sending an explicit answer to a plain requisition." It was also the pretext for thwarting the object of the commission "which the real friends of America had so long requested . . . and which so many of the inhabitants of this continent now desire." A once admirable Congress had sullied its principles by alliance with "the ancient enemy." Johnstone was "not anxious about the good opinion of such a body." He reserved the right to publish a justification of his conduct before he left America.[55]

Johnstone gave his letter of justification, such as it was, to Adam Ferguson when he left America on September 24. It appeared in the *New York Royal Gazette* of September 28, 1778, and turned out to be the rind, not the pith, of the matter. Nothing he had done or said, he claimed, could be construed as an attempt to corrupt Reed's integrity. He possessed complete and undisputed evidence of his innocence. Only "a regard to the faith of private communication, and an attention to the peace and safety of innocent individuals, under the horrid cruelties that are daily exercised to maintain the present system of government by congress and committees" restrained him from making that evidence public and refuting the unwarranted aspersions on his character.

The coda to this flourish was an assurance that his return to England owed nothing to congressional action—he had always intended to go back to London for the new session of Parliament "to give my voice and opinion against yielding to the claim of independency."[56]

To leave made good sense; if Carlisle and Eden were to have any chance of negotiation with Congress, Johnstone would have to return to England. Long before he did so, however, and even before Congress proscribed him, Johnstone had contemplated departure. Carlisle had written to his wife on July 6 that if a number of troops sufficient to maintain offensive operations were not left in New York, "from what I can gather from Governor Johnstone, he will stay no longer."[57] Johnstone had been in a rage with Germain ever since his arrival in America, both for concealing his military plans from the commission and because of their nature. The letter of protest sent by the other commissioners he evidently considered too mild; in a personal postscript, he described the evacuation of Philadelphia as "a fatal ill Conceived, & Ill advised Retreat, highly dishonourable to his Maj[esty's] Army & most prejudicial to the interest of his dominions."[58] He also condemned the local military commanders for their inactivity; they attracted as much of his anger as was not vented on Germain and Congress. The abundance of lightning rods saved Eden and Carlisle from being scorched. London gossip had it, according to Walpole, that Johnstone and Carlisle had quarrelled.[59] It seems not to have been true.

With Eden there was, to be sure, at least one occasion of disagreement. Writing to Carlisle in opposition to a madcap scheme, not dissimilar to the Temple venture, whereby an American in British pay, John Berkenhout,[60] was to be sent to Philadelphia to negotiate secretly with Congress, Eden wrote that he knew Johnstone would say that his view was narrow, the result of inexperience in "business." It pained him to be thus roughly addressed "but after a moment's recollection I can always smile at such insinuations, and will not dispute."[61] There is no hint of resentment of Johnstone in Carlisle's letters to his wife, and there is at least an appearance of belief in his integrity to the extent that, in a phrase of a draft of a letter to Germain (omitted in the final version), he described Mrs. Ferguson's allegations as "an incoherent tale unsupported by any evidence whatsoever, and which we have every reason to believe is not founded in truth." In September Eden was able to write that Johnstone would be sailing on the following day "in perfect Good-Humour & Friendship with the other Commissioners," although less well disposed toward Lord Howe.[62] Johnstone left America assuring Carlisle, in his fulsome way, that he would "consider the opportunity I have had of knowing your Lordship's great worth and honour as the happiest circumstance of my life."[63]

The commissioners had little of importance to do in New York, although their position guaranteed them an active, if arid, social life. Eleanor Eden was a niece of Andrew Elliot, Sir Gilbert's brother, who was superintendent of the port, and through him the Edens became friendly with William Smith, the last chief justice of New York under British rule.[64]

Johnstone had a low opinion of the naval and military commanders at New York. His feeling was reciprocated, according to Charles Stuart, a statement backed by Major Bowater, who wrote of Johnstone as a black rascal. Stuart himself considered Johnstone's performance in America "low, cunning," and "disgraceful" as well as one which had gained the contempt of both enemies and friends of Britain in the colonies.[65]

The governor understandably looked for friends outside the hierarchy of British officialdom and he made the acquaintance of a wealthy young American lawyer, Robert Williams, whose chief interest in the war seems to have been the preservation of his estate in South Carolina. Williams' coolness toward the Declaration of Independence endeared him to Johnstone, who arranged passage under flag of truce to South Carolina for him and two friends, Richard Beresford, another lawyer-planter, and a Charleston merchant, John Hopton.[66] In a conversation on or about September 19, Johnstone told Williams of an imminent British descent on Charleston to secure South Carolina and Georgia, specifying details of the ships which, he alleged, would escort or carry 10,000 troops detached from the New York garrison.

The Charleston expedition did not in fact sail for more than a year, but what Johnstone had imparted was the main strategic idea contained in Germain's "most secret" instructions to Clinton of March 8, 1778,[67] and information of an impending tactical redeployment of the utmost importance and interest to the American military authorities, who expected no such move.

Williams was not the loyalist that Johnstone evidently took him for. Although probably more of a trimmer than a patriot, he wasted no time in using Beresford to relay Johnstone's revelations to Henry Laurens, the

South Carolinian president of Congress. Laurens promptly informed General Washington and Patrick Henry, the governor of Virginia.[68] Laurens knew that any such British initiative would be singularly dangerous to the American cause, although he thought it possible that Johnstone had been making sport of Williams, so incredible was it that the commissioner should talk casually of such affairs to an American. He underestimated Johnstone's penchant for gossipy indiscretion.

At that time Washington was using every means in his power "to come at Clinton's designs,"[69] since his normal line of communication with New York City had broken.[70] Initially he was skeptical of the intelligence forwarded by Laurens and almost completely convinced that it was a "deception." Nothing could be more implausible than that the British would detach large numbers of troops from New York. Both they and those left behind would be too vulnerable, as would the fragmented naval forces necessary for such an expedition. It would be "an act of insanity." Moreover, argued Washington, the British were not interested in occupying territory. They realized that destroying the American army was the only way to win the war. "Nevertheless," he concluded, "I may be mistaken."[71]

He was indeed much mistaken. Strategically, Germain had reverted to supporting a winter offensive in the southern colonies, and on August 5, he instructed Clinton to pursue the countermanded orders of March 8 as far as circumstances would allow. In the same month advisers urged Germain to make Charleston the starting point for such operations.[72] The essential content of Clinton's new orders combined with others of March 21 commanding an expedition to the Caribbean were what Johnstone had told Williams in September.[73] Act of insanity or not, a powerful detachment from the New York garrison, close in total strength to the number given by Johnstone, was precisely what was afoot. In November, 5,000 troops and thirty-two vessels were to leave New York for St. Lucia, and in December a further 3,500 soldiers were to embark under Archibald Campbell for Savannah, in the first stage of the conquest of Georgia.

But whereas Washington refused to take action based on Johnstone's indiscretions, it was otherwise with Congress and its South Carolinian president. Beresford made his report to Laurens on the evening of September 22; on September 23 Laurens told Congress, which appointed a committee of five to consider the intelligence. The committee recommended action, and as a result, on September 25 Congress requested the state of Virginia to march 1,000 men and North Carolina 3,000 men into South Carolina. Congress undertook to pay them and appointed Major General Benjamin Lincoln to take command in the South and "to repair immediately to Charleston."[74] Laurens may have wondered if he and Congress had been stampeded into unnecessarily drastic action when he received a letter a few days later in which his son expressed amusement at the way in which his friend Beresford had been "bamboosled" by Johnstone.[75]

Nevertheless the die was cast. Lincoln fortified Charleston to such good effect that when finally, in 1780, he was faced by a sizable British army, he was loath to abandon it. According to one American historian, "It would have been better for the American cause had the city been less well prepared for defense," for the port and its garrison of 6,000 fell intact to the British.[76] Thus, quite fortuitously, there is a link between Johnstone's gossip and the greatest British victory of the Revolution.

The question of whence Johnstone derived his information remains unanswered. Germain's orders to resume offensive operations in the South were on the high seas when Johnstone held his conversation with Williams. No poltroon, Clinton was yet not known for his offensive spirit; he was, in fact, using every artifice to hoard his garrison at New York. For example, when reporting the strength of his forces to Whitehall, instead of stating, as was customary, the total number of effectives, he cited only the rank and file fit for duty. Johnstone, therefore, is unlikely to have passed to Williams any formal plans for attack conceived by Clinton. Nevertheless it was probably from Clinton that he derived his story. In September the general had not been told to resume offensive operations in the South but was under orders to send men to St. Lucia and to do what he could to strengthen the defenses of the Floridas, both of which meant detachments from New York. The prospect threw him into a fit of pessimism, and a few days before the Johnstone-Williams conversation the ministry received a letter from Clinton which prophesied that, as a result, he would probably have to evacuate New York and retire to Halifax.[77] Without necessarily imparting details Clinton probably communicated to his fellow commissioners something of his distress at having to reduce the forces at New York.[78] Johnstone might have guessed that Charleston would be the most likely objective, since he could well have heard Clinton quite separately and informally advocate its conquest. It was a strategic objective about which he was enthusiastic and which he thought feasible if enough men were available. He certainly told Carlisle and Eden so, though it is uncertain exactly when.[79]

Once Johnstone left America, the commission lost its most active member. The diminished cast was left to play out one final act in the form of a manifesto and proclamation which bore both the mark of despair and, perhaps, of Johnstone's influence. Part of a letter exists which Johnstone had written some time in July, advocating ruthless policies and the use of "Fire and Sword" on a military expedition in an attempt "to Engage the inhabitants of the Province [New York?] to declare in our favour and give them every substantial encouragement."[80] The other commissioners were convinced by mid-September that a "war of ravage and destruction" was the only means to achieve success in America, a notion scorned by the more intelligent of the English officers in New York.[81]

Both the notions implicit in Johnstone's letter, a war of devastation and the division of the Americans by appeals to individual groups, reappeared in the Manifesto and Proclamation of October 3, 1778. Even Carlisle considered them "a sort of last dying speech . . . from which I expect little success."[82] In that they tried to turn Americans of various sorts—members of state assemblies, soldiers, and ministers of religion—against Congress, the only body with whom peace could be negotiated, issuing them was an act of despair.[83] As Carlisle had predicted, their effect was negligible.

The earl had one final formality to attend to before leaving America. The dashing Marquis de Lafayette wrote to him demanding either that he retract the derogatory reflections on France in the commissioners' letter to Congress of June 9 or that he meet him on the dueling ground. Lafayette no doubt considered his challenge chivalrous: Carlisle treated it as juvenile. He confessed, he wrote to the Frenchman, that he found it difficult to return a serious answer to it. The alleged insult was in a public document. "As you ought to have known," he admonished, a royal commissioner was not responsible for his public conduct to any private individual. The dispute between their countries, he concluded, would be best decided by the meeting of the fleets of Byron and d'Estaing—a sensible footnote to an increasingly senseless essay.[84]

The commission had been a complete failure, but few had ever expected it to succeed. "The Commissioners have kissed hands and why not? For God knows it is all nonsense, as it has been for a long time," wrote Townshend before the commission had even left England.[85] Later, Lord Pembroke reported that "the Commissioners have been received ludicrously, & their Papers burnt by the American hangman. How could it be expected otherwise?"[86] In the following month Germain remarked of the negotiations, "I cannot say I expected much good from that quarter."[87] North never wrote as frankly, but his actions indicate a certain hopelessness. The commissioners he chose were far from Britain's ablest diplomats. He armed them with instructions drafted by underlings which embodied principles contrary to any he had ever professed. He made it difficult for the commissioners to see him before they left, and when they returned empty-handed, he rewarded them.

If North never looked for success, the commission can only be explained as an attempt at mollification and diversion. Sending the commissioners would appease the Opposition at a time when the ministry was in danger of disintegration. It might delude the French into thinking that a negotiated peace most interested the British when a descent on French possessions was in fact planned. Lastly it may have been hoped that, since planned withdrawals would render the British army vulnerable, the Americans might hesitate to take positive military action while peace talks were in progress.

Johnstone talked much and with passion about the American situation when he returned to Britain. His ideas had not undergone a radical transformation. Appointment to the commission had not turned him into a partisan of the king's ministers. He still blamed them, especially Germain, for criminal incompetence: "As their Wickedness began, their Blunders will compleat the Loss of America." The failure of the commission could be directly—and conveniently—laid at their door. He harbored no resentment against his fellow commissioners, but it was reported that he "foams at the mouth, and swears that he will impeach Lord Howe and Sir William for not reducing America."[88] Clinton, who was both commissioner and commander, escaped either eulogy or damnation, being dismissed as "a very able executive officer." Johnstone continued to oppose independence for America with Chathamesque fervor. Where his views appeared to have changed as a result of his American tour was with regard to the best method for preserving the union with Britain:

> Instead of taking away the Troops, they could be . . . employed in Plundering and ravaging, laying waste, and burning all the accessible parts of America of Consequence to the Northward and Southward . . . he has not a doubt but the Americans would sue for the terms you have offered.[89]

Johnstone's experiences in 1778 had not changed the course of the American Revolution; no amount of blundering could damage the prospects of a hopeless diplomatic mission. He, too, was left unaltered except in one respect: he had been converted from a dove to a hawk.

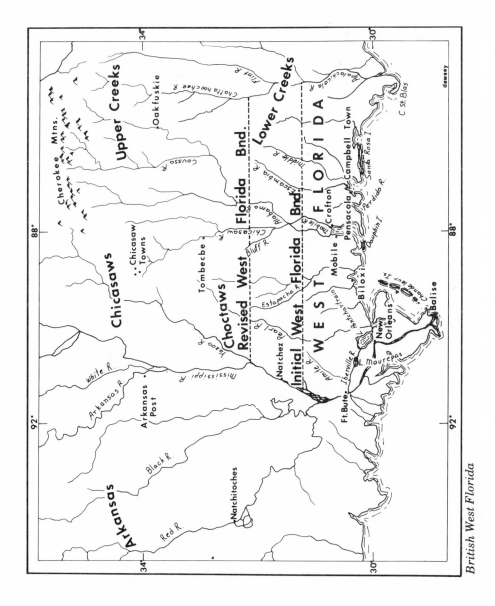

British West Florida

East India House, Leadenhall Street, London (Reproduced by Permission of the Director of the India Office Library and Records)

The Right Honorable William Eden

The Right Honorable Charles Jenkinson

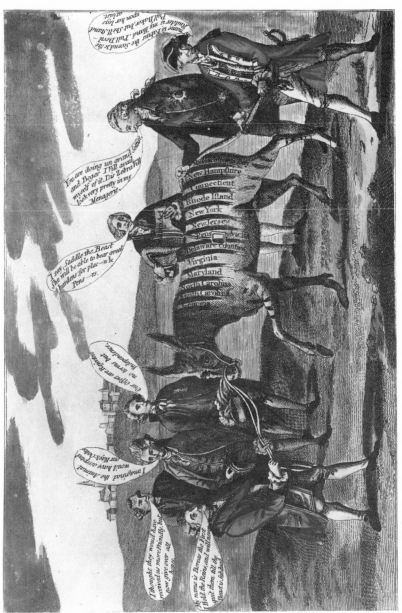

The Curious Zebra

Sailors Taking On Water at Porto Praya

Charlotte Johnstone and Son

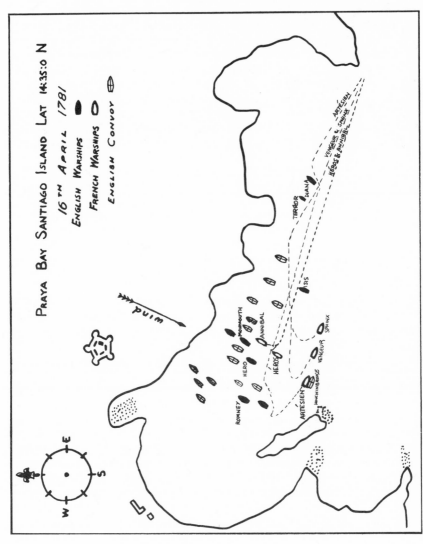

Praya Bay, Santiago Island

6. Gunpowder and Port

Ebullient and self-righteous as ever, Johnstone landed in England toward the end of October 1778, his estimate of himself undimmed by the complete failure of his dubious diplomatic methods. To a surprising extent this opinion was shared by others.

His fellow commissioners in America wrote that only Johnstone's "Strict Sense of Honour" had caused him to leave them, and they bemoaned his departure. If the diplomatic horizon brightened, they did not know how they would cope without "the Advantage of Mr. Johnstone's Abilities and the Authority of His Name."[1] They consoled themselves with the reflection, and no irony appears intended, that the ministry would have the benefit of his expertise.[2]

Reporting to Germain on debarkation Johnstone found that he was not in disgrace with the administration either. Instead of berating him, the American secretary seemed relieved that Johnstone was "seemingly in good humour with the Ministry."[3] To the public he claimed, and was evidently believed, that he had done more to secure victory than any use of force had achieved, by sowing the seeds of enmity to Congress among the American populace.[4] The English public had already been treated to another version of the commissioner's work. An anonymous ode had charged that the earl of Bute dominated the peace delegation, that Eden alone of its members was in his confidence and that the one-time favorite, with byzantine cunning and for his own ends, had intended that Johnstone and Eden should fall out and that the commission should fail.

> Eden was charg'd with all B-te's Store
> of Secrets—Colleagues were no more
> Than Cyphers in the Case.[5]

Any readers prepared to accept this farfetched analysis of the commission, which, incidentally, accepted as fact the unfounded rumor of Eden's quarrel with Johnstone, would presumably also be ready to exonerate Johnstone as a mere dupe.

Shortly after the governor's arrival, the young marquess of Granby, a noble Opposition sprig, wrote to him, assuring him of undiminished "attachment and sincere friendship."[6] Immediately before the peace commission had been mooted, Johnstone had tried to tie Granby into a political combination with Chatham, Shelburne, and Rockingham.[7] By October of 1778 that alliance was impossible, but it did not seem to have occurred to Granby that Johnstone might have veered away from Opposition.

For some time, indeed, Johnstone's political stance was to remain ambiguous. On November 26, he delivered a long apologia for the work of the peace commission in the House of Commons. Quite characteristically he defended by attacking and blamed the failure of negotiations on three culprits. The first was Congress, which had conducted itself "with the low Cunning of an election jobber" at a time when two-thirds of the people it was supposed to represent, or so Johnstone alleged, wanted to resume the connection with England. The Howe brothers were also culpable, he said, because they were responsible for the sad military situation which had weakened the commission's prospects. Finally, the North administration had contributed to that situation by its extraordinary dilatoriness in maintaining British naval strength on the North American station. As for himself, said Johnstone, he had tried to bribe nobody, although, he added obscurely, "I do not mean to disavow I have had transactions where other means than persuasion have been used. It was necessary: in my situation it can be no reproach."[8]

The Opposition was divided in its opinion of the commission. John Wilkes condemned the other commissioners, but Johnstone, he said, "possessed a superior understanding, an happy temper, and thorough knowledge of business. If success had been attainable, I am persuaded, to his wisdom, prudence, and temperate conduct, England had been indebted for the restoration of the blessings of peace." Carlisle, by contrast, he derided as a playboy who had taken with him "a group of little laughing loves," while he characterized Eden as "distinguished by a set of principles wonderfully adapted to the spirit of coercion and cruelty."[9]

This last charge was ironical in view of a speech made by the "temperate" Johnstone a few days later, in which the savage proclamation issued by the commissioners on October 3 was discussed. It certainly did mean a war of desolation, said Johnstone. It could mean nothing else; and if he had been on the spot he would have signed it. He was not saying so as a convert to administration policy, since, he declared, he was of no party.[10] Nor, for the moment, was he. As though to prove it, ten days later, on December 14, he made a bellicose speech in the Commons which drew criticism from Fox and Burke but which roundly accused Germain of the major failure of the war which was, alleged Johnstone, the expedition to Philadelphia, since it had caused the Saratoga disaster.[11]

During the Christmas recess the governor seems to have revised his views on the administration. In the second week of January he and Eden met at Lord North's for conversations with their host, Germain, and Amherst, presumably on America. It may be that he found North unexpectedly cordial.[12] At all events, by the end of January he was contemplating joining his administration. Lord George Gordon got wind of the news and wrote Lord Rockingham a slightly apprehensive letter very hostile to Johnstone. He had not seen the governor since his return from America and had small inclination to meet him privately. He had heard that Johnstone spoke violently against Congress and believed that granting independence to the thirteen colonies would not now be sufficient to end the American war, and that his confidence in the Opposition was shaken.

Johnstone was boasting of the offers that the government had made him since his return from America, and rumor had it that both Johnstone and his brother William were about to accept "very high" office, although the governor had not severed all connection with his Opposition friends, having recently gone to visit the duke of Richmond at Brighton.[13]

Gordon was right. Johnstone had indeed been negotiating for entry in the administration, making hard conditions and tall claims. Germain and Sandwich would have to go, while the Howe brothers were to be denied entry. His patron, Sir James Lowther, would have to be found minor office. If these conditions were met, he himself was prepared to come in, perhaps to head the Admiralty. He thought, astonishingly, that he could bring in Charles Fox and suggested suitable appointments for Grafton and Grenville, who, he believed, would be prepared to join a ministry with himself and Fox in it.[14] No mention was made of Richmond; evidently the Brighton interview had not been satisfactory. Nothing came of these ambitious negotiations, but thereafter he was markedly more lenient with the administration in his speeches, and particularly with Germain.

On February 17, for instance, he told the Commons that the Philadelphia expedition was not after all, as he had previously alleged, the work of Germain, but rather of the Howe brothers. His speech evoked the sorrowful condemnation of Fox. In fighting America, said his former ally, Britain was fighting justice, "a force never to be subdued." There had been a time when Johnstone had thought so too, but now his honorable friend had found the secret of winning the ministry's esteem, which was "to blacken the characters of our commanders."[15]

At the time, Johnstone evidently felt confident of the prospect of participation in the rewards for the peace commissioners, which could be ruined by resumption of his criticism of North. A disgruntled Eden was pressing hard for them and insisting that Johnstone should have his share.[16] A few days later, on February 24, Johnstone spoke openly of his reluctant but definite allegiance to the North government: there was no man who had a more sovereign contempt for the present administration than he had; but he had still rather give them his support, while they seemed determined to prosecute the war, than those who, if they were in office, would abandon it.

And so Johnstone left his customary seat under the gallery on the Opposition side of the House and sat on the treasury bench, the only one there of any "weight and consequence" according to Isaac Barré, who exercised his wit on the governor for the company he had chosen to keep. Johnstone found Barré's humor labored and told the colonel that he was making a scaramouch of himself, an unparliamentary expression which caused the Speaker to cut short their repartee.[17]

Johnstone did not become a slavish disciple of North. While his employment was under discussion he clearly felt it would be judicious to restrict his arc of fire. The result was that the few remaining targets which he allowed himself, preeminently the Howe brothers, received concentrated blasts. In a speech on March 22, 1779, the main object of which was to prove that Admiral Howe had lost an opportunity to destroy the French naval forces off North America, Johnstone, in turn, made a scaramouch of himself by using a method of reasoning so ridiculous that it was remembered with contempt by naval writers decades later.[18] In essence his argument was that what mattered when facing the enemy at sea was not so much the number of men-of-war that could be pitted against him, but the number of guns. If Howe had employed frigates, of which he had many, together with his men-of-war, in which he was inferior to the French, against d'Estaing off Rhode Island, he would have won a victory, particularly as the French crews were sickly. Howe, who was present, was outraged, and trying to pull rank said, "I can assure the gentleman, that Admiral Howe will not apply to Captain Johnstone to instruct him in the elements of his profession." The governor was not cowed by that kind of pomposity and replied that although he was no more than Captain Johnstone, he would not give up his experience to Admiral Howe; he had seen as much service as the noble lord, and had been in more battles. In this speech, he openly offered his services as a naval officer to the administration, alleging that he would accept even the command of a bumboat. Actually he was a great deal more ambitious and discriminating; a man-of-war was too small for the governor who had turned his coat.[19]

It must not be taken for granted that only anticipation of material reward explains Johnstone's apostasy. To be numbered among the Opposition meant, more and more, to be in favor of complete independence for America, a position which Johnstone never could bring himself to adopt. Even before going to America with the peace commission, in March of 1778, he had said of independence that he was extremely sorry to see the idea adopted by gentlemen with whom he had acted; that if he found he had been acting with gentlemen who were ready to give up the supremacy of this country over America he would sooner cross the floor and join those whose measures he had always disapproved.[20]

Thus Johnstone could assert that he was merely acting out an old promise when he began to support North's American policy in February 1779, although it was obviously no harder to fulfill because doing so would bring employment. The Admiralty offered him several attractive seagoing appointments. The king interested himself in the matter, and Sandwich wrote to his sovereign to say that not only was the *Alexander,* a 74-gun ship of the line, being kept vacant in case Johnstone should accept its command, but also that the governor might "have the command of some frigates on the Lisbon station, himself in a 50 gun ship with a broad Pendant and a Captain under him."[21] Another, vaguer possibility was an independent commodoreship embracing the Georgia and East Florida coast and the

Gulf of Mexico. It was Johnstone himself who had suggested in memorials to the Admiralty the creation of such a command. He had not anticipated that he would be offered it and was dubious about accepting it, because it would not be viable without full Admiralty support; he suspected that he would get only halfhearted backing from Sandwich, the first lord, and from the latter's ally, Lord Mulgrave, who was also a member of the Admiralty board.[22]

Johnstone would probably have preferred a place on the board to a seagoing appointment, since it would be better for his health, which had been poor, and he would be nearer the center of political power. A vacancy on the board would occur if Sir Hugh Palliser were successfully tried.

Palliser was a rear admiral who had played a subordinate role in an indecisive engagement against the French fleet off Ushant in July 1778, in which the commander of the British ships was Viscount Keppel. Stung by subsequent newspaper reports that it was his own backwardness which had caused victory to elude the British fleet, Palliser had rashly initiated court-martial proceedings against his superior, but not only did the court exonerate Keppel, it also found Palliser's charges malicious and ill-founded. To exculpate himself, Palliser had no choice but to submit himself to trial, the ethically necessary prelude to which was resignation from all his various offices, including his seat on the Admiralty board. That Johnstone should fill it was relished by Sandwich almost as little as his own replacement by the governor, a possibility seriously considered in the spring of 1779. He was probably delighted to be able to tell the king that Lord Mulgrave, whose service on the board was valued by George III, refused to sit on it with Johnstone. It was "absolutely necessary," insisted Mulgrave, that any vacancy that might occur should be filled by a flag officer.[23]

While the door to an administrative appointment remained ajar, the governor had delayed committing himself to another appointment, to the annoyance of the king who wrote that "the true test whether . . . the gentleman is serious in wishing to be employed" was his answer to the offer of the Lisbon commodoreship. Once the administrative door was closed, Johnstone, as Charles Jenkinson informed the king on April 8, declared that he would take the Portuguese post, although his appointment was not officially made until May 6.[24] Thereafter that year he refrained from long or even frequent speeches in Parliament, and when he did join in debate it was in support of the administration's determination to fight on in America.

In this connection Eden asked him to submit a paper to Germain on the measures necessary for the conquest of New Orleans. The resulting plan was over-optimistic but not altogether unsound. Johnstone thought an attack up the Mississippi too difficult. Instead he advocated neutralizing the Indians with gifts and securing several islands as bases, followed by an advance via Lake Pontchartrain. The enemy were to be distracted by a feigned attack up the Mississippi. Where he was too hopeful was in imagining that 1,500 men would be sufficient for the task. Admittedly, to these would be added the garrison of West Florida, but as subsequent events were to demonstrate, they would have strengthened the inadequate force but little. He also imagined, unrealistically, that the population of New Orleans was so discontented with Spanish rule that it would welcome British liberation.[25]

Even while these dreams of overseas conquest were discussed, the homeland was threatened with invasion. Thirty French ships of the line were waiting off Corunna; when joined, though tardily, by a Spanish fleet of thirty-six, the combined armada outnumbered any force the Royal Navy could possibly collect to oppose them. The allies' object was to command the English Channel for sufficient time for an army of 30,000 to cross from Normandy, seize the Isle of Wight and Gosport, destroy the naval base at Portsmouth and, with luck, create such panic that the British credit system would be wrecked.[26]

It was all possible, and in the circumstances it was natural that Johnstone and his new command should be ordered to join Sir Charles Hardy, who had just been appointed after twenty years of shore duty to command the Channel fleet. Johnstone himself had not commanded a vessel for seventeen years but had retained a keen memory of inconveniences suffered in time past, and on June 10, 1779, wrote to the secretary of the Admiralty asking that, when his new flagship, the 50-gun *Romney*, returned to Plymouth Sound for refitting, certain alterations which he had found "very beneficial to the easy working of ships of war" be incorporated in her. They included such minutiae as outsized lower studding sail boom irons, red-and-white checkered flags, and a leaden pump in the head and indicate not merely that he had retained his eye for technical detail but also a certain and perhaps surprising enthusiasm for his new appointment.

The *Romney* was not initially to serve with Hardy's main force but rather to support frigates and privateers operating from Jersey, whose task it was to seek out the assembly points of enemy transports on the French coast. A London periodical reported almost with jubilation that Johnstone had a roving commission allowing him to "take, sink, burn, and destroy" all French ships wherever he might find them, as though confident that the bellicose Scot would exercise his right to the full.[27] On June 29, 1779, Johnstone left London for Plymouth, where the alterations he had requested for the *Romney* had been carried out. From there he sailed for the Channel Islands, carrying on board a number of supernumeraries allowed for his future command in Portuguese waters and accompanied by a flotilla also intended for service off Lisbon: the *Crescent,* the *Cormorant,* and the *Rattlesnake.* By July 10, he was south of Guernsey. Before putting in to Jersey, his intended destination, he took the liberty of opening correspondence from General Conway, commander of the military forces in the Channel Islands, to Sir Charles Hardy. As a result of what he learned, he decided to head without delay for St. Malo.[28] The function of his little command was to watch the motions of the enemy and relay intelligence of their designs back to the Admiralty, to thwart as far as possible the collection of troops and landing craft along the coasts of Brittany and Normandy, and to protect Jersey and Guernsey from enemy attack. The ridiculous gossip in London was that Johnstone had been assigned not merely to hinder but to destroy the French embarkation force.[29] In fact Johnstone was not hopeful of even damaging the French invasion forces, because he thought that they would be kept inaccessible until a decisive action at sea was fought, the outcome of which, he rightly predicted, could "determine our existence as a maritime power."[30]

It was with energy rather than optimism, therefore, that Johnstone cruised off St. Malo and Cancale Bay in Normandy. The press, desperate for news to offset invasion fears, wrote of the little he achieved as favorably as it could. Two lugger privateers which he had sent into St. Malo harbor discovered seven frigates stationed there. *London Magazine* gloated over the fact that Johnstone had kept his little squadron sailing so close to the port that the French had spent thousands of shots and shells during three days and nights without doing any damage.[31] Subsequently Conway rebuked him for pressing Jersey islanders, who were protected by tradition from all except voluntary service; this was hard on Johnstone, whose orders were to press without limitation, but Conway would not be panicked by an invasion scare into forfeiting the islanders' goodwill.[32] As time passed, Johnstone's flotilla was augmented by the sloop *Wasp,* and by three privateers, the *Minerva,* the *Beezley,* and the *Hawk.*[33] However, although he went at least twice to Cancale Bay in July, he achieved nothing material: he did, nevertheless, acquire useful intelligence. On the last day of July he reported that he had authoritative information that the French and Spanish fleets were about to unite. He anticipated, correctly, that a good week would be consumed, once the junction was made, in issuing orders and settling signals, and estimated that the Franco-Spanish armada would be in the Channel on the fourth or fifth of August.[34]

There was jubilation and no fear at the prospect of battle in the letter which Johnstone wrote to his brother William at the time, in spite of the size of the enemy armada. The Spanish fleet alone, according to his intelligence, amounted to fifty sails, including thirty ships of the line. Always optimistic about what his brother might achieve, he urged William to do what he could to ensure that every exertion, domestic or diplomatic, be made to strengthen Britain at sea. Whether the transports at St. Malo and Havre sailed depended on the "great Battle for the Dominion of the Seas & God grant I may be present." Determined to take part in the fight, he left

Guernsey in the *Romney* accompanied by the sloop *Cormorant* and joined Hardy's Channel fleet on August 4.[35] He wagered and lost ten guineas with a Captain Stewart that they would see action within a week. Sir Charles, acutely conscious of the disparity in numbers between his own forty ships and the enemy's sixty-six, and afraid that d'Orvilliers might aim for Ireland rather than the Channel ports, kept well to the west and, much to the chagrin of the king and Johnstone, did not seek him out.

Hardy was not aware that the enemy had entered the Channel until August 17; when he received the information, whether he wanted to engage or no, he could do nothing about it, driven as he was by strong easterly winds which carried his fleet, by August 25, a hundred miles west of Land's End. The same winds also blew d'Orvilliers out of the Channel. A week of maneuvering followed. D'Orvilliers tried to close with the British fleet; he wanted to use his numerical superiority to render it incapable of hindering the passage of the invasion transports, but he could not catch it. His numbers and the copper bottoms of the British made the chase futile. Some British observers thought the French effort halfhearted, and Johnstone's brother, Captain Gideon Johnstone, in defiance of his own admiral's intentions, several times tried to lure the enemy into engaging his vessel but without success. Hardy used Fabian tactics. He tried, successfully, to work his way into a position where he could use the British lee shore to his advantage to draw the enemy up the Channel and to replenish his stocks of water and beer at Spithead. These maneuvers were unglamorous and unpopular but, as it turned out, precisely correct. D'Orvilliers was at the end of his tether. Hasty preparations and weeks of waiting had brought formidable epidemics to his fleet, and sea burials by the dozen were daily occurrences. On the very day that Hardy finally cast anchor at Spithead, d'Orvilliers was ordered to return to Brest.[36]

On September 5, Lord Sandwich was in nearby Portsmouth to urge Hardy to put to sea again as soon as possible and to sound out the morale and opinions of the naval officers. Johnstone, with whom he had a "long and very close conversation" was eager for action but "violent" against Hardy's replacement, either by Howe or Keppel.[37] Or so the first lord believed.

He was only half right. It was true that Johnstone thought that calling in Howe or Keppel would have a disruptive effect. But he made it clear in a letter to his brother, written on the *Romney* at Spithead and containing the telltale final instruction to burn it—nearly always indicative of indiscretion and often of sincerity—that he did want Hardy recalled. In his place aboard the flagship *Victory* he envisaged either Kempenfelt or himself! Personal ambition did not, however, dominate Johnstone's letter. William was asked to show it to Lord North, to Chancellor Thurlow, and to Alexander Wedderburn, the solicitor general, before destroying it. Johnstone's overriding idea was to end delay and engage the enemy at once. He suggested that any captain who protested that he could not sail within four days should be superseded. Of course his alarm was misplaced. The effect of Hardy's postponement of battle was not that Britain was undone, as Johnstone prophesied, but rather that d'Orvilliers sailed back to port having inflicted no damage except to the crews of his own fleet.[38]

When Johnstone had left Jersey he had not intended to remain long with the Channel fleet.[39] In fact, however, he was away for more than six weeks and when he returned to the Channel Islands it was temporarily; he was resummoned to the Channel fleet by Hardy, who cautiously believed that the French admiral's retirement from the Channel did not preclude his return, and he refused to turn Johnstone loose. When he found himself still in Portsmouth in the last week of September, Johnstone applied for leave, using as his excuse that the great property loss his family had sustained by the enemy capture of Grenada required his presence in London.[40] His real reason was to "view the Political Hemisphere & to settle my own Situation in future on some firm Basis."[41] In November, after repeated fruitless conversations with Hardy, Johnstone was still with the admiral who, he believed, would never "detach any part of the force while the matter is left discretional with him."[42] Finally, in exasperation, the Scot went over Hardy's head and appealed, successfully, to Sandwich.

He had kept the first lord directly supplied with what he called "the main-spring in war," good intelligence. On September 23, he told Sandwich that d'Estaing had sailed for North America: it was true—d'Estaing had left the West Indies for the mainland colonies, not Jamaica as many imagined, at the end of August. In October Johnstone wrote again with fresh information about d'Estaing, who had twenty-five sail of the line and eleven frigates and who would, by Johnstone's calculations, have reached New York on August 23.[43] This news was only partially correct. D'Estaing had twenty sail of the line, but his objective was not New York but rather a surprise attack on Georgia. Johnstone's letters to Sandwich, were not, it may be worth noting, deferential. He gave advice on strategy to his superior and did not scruple to denigrate senior naval officers (Admiral Byron, for example) whose conduct he deplored.

Portugal, for which Sandwich authorized Johnstone to sail on November 6, had altered a great deal since he had last been there. Under the premiership of the marques de Pombal, who had fallen only in 1777, much in Lisbon had been reformed and much rebuilt, although earthquake ruins still abounded. A Scottish visitor in 1775 wondered where all the capital's dirt and filth, of which she had read, might be found. She considered the Lisbon streets as safe as any in Europe, but in other respects—lighting, theater, and the role assigned to women—she found it inferior.[44]

Thanks to Pombal too, the dominance of the English commercial community was less than it had been twenty years before. Nevertheless, the English factories still did a great deal of business and provided a ready-made social life for visiting Britons, of which there were many, particularly as it was a fad among eighteenth-century English physicians to recommend the Portuguese climate to recover the consumptive or rather, as the crowded British cemetery in Lisbon proves, to prolong the lives of the dying.

Here, on authority given him on November 9, Johnstone flew the broad pendant of a commodore, an appointment rather than a rank. Once the duty which entitled him to the commodoreship was over he would revert to being a simple captain unless, as proved to be the case, he was transferred to a job of similar responsibility. There were eight vessels in the new commodore's squadron. They included the *Aeolus* and *Cerberus,* each of 32 guns, the *Brilliant, Tartar,* and *Crescent,* each with 28, and the small *Cormorant* and the *Rattlesnake* with 16 and 14 guns respectively.[45] He himself went in the flagship *Romney* of 50 guns, which had a new captain, Rodham Home, and a new third lieutenant, who was the commodore's natural son John.[46]

As "Commodore and Commander-in-Chief of His Majesty's Ships and Vessels employed and to be employed from Cape Finisterre to Cape St. Vincent and along the Southern Coast of Portugal," Johnstone stood to enjoy not merely good society but also considerable prize money. He was entitled to one-eighth of the value of any merchantmen taken by his captains, whether he was present or not. Those hostile to him were quick to comment on this aspect of his new job: "Governor Johnstone," write Horace Walpole, ". . . has made his bargain, and is turned into a commodore of a cruizing squadron. It is judicious enough . . . to convert such men, as go upon the highway of fortune, into privateers. . . ."[47] Lord Pembroke was scandalized that "ease, never before heard of in the service is added to lucre, for he [Johnstone] is to live on shore . . . with Envoy's pay," but more so because Johnstone's position was a reward for political subservience rather than naval prowess. "I wish I was a Laplander, or anything, but a Briton," he wrote disgustedly.[48]

These strictures were not completely fair. For one thing, Johnstone did go to sea when he could; for another, Pembroke's claim that he was paid as an envoy was a canard; and finally, unknown to the likes of Walpole and Pembroke, he had responsibilities impossible for a seagoing commodore to perform.[49] From Lisbon Johnstone was running an intelligence network, collecting and collating information about enemy ships, personally dispatching agents to Spain and interviewing them upon their return. Absence and delay were inadmissible in such work. Furthermore he engaged himself, whether officially or not, in a task which was even more important, one quite impossible to conduct except on land—an attempt to take Spain out of the war.

Soon after his arrival in Lisbon Johnstone talked with Luis Cantofer, a Portuguese merchant acquainted with Floridablanca, the Spanish foreign minister. Johnstone told Cantofer that he and Lord North had conferred several times before he left England. North and George III were both anxious for friendship with Spain. Britain was prepared to pay for Spanish neutrality with Gibraltar; for an alliance the price would include Florida and the Newfoundland fisheries as well.

Although the commodore's gasconades were implausible, a little reminiscent of earlier claims to inside knowledge of the Charleston expedition, they were not impossible. As an agent Johnstone was rather less bizarre than others assuredly employed by North, who included a shady Irish priest, Thomas Hussey, and Richard Cumberland, a dreamy playwright civil servant.[50]

North was perfectly capable of using Johnstone as one of several unofficial diplomatic representatives. The commodore's claim that George III was prepared to cede Gibraltar is, however, incredible. It seems to be a case of wishful thinking, for Johnstone himself did not prize the rock. Once, in an official letter to Sandwich, the commodore digressed from purely naval subjects:

> The pride of the King of Spain has been wrought upon by the hopes of gaining Gibraltar . . . Gibraltar is the key upon which any true Spaniard can be brought to vindicate this war. They hate the French, they detest the Americans, they condemn the grounds of war. . . . If Gibraltar could be ceded I am persuaded Spain might be brought to assist in reducing the American colonies, guaranteeing each others' dominions, and commanding France to desist and restore her conquests. . . . what advantage the retaining Gibraltar can produce equal to those . . . I cannot conceive. We had a cry at the loss of Calais; we had a cry at giving up Tangier; we had a cry at ceding Louisburg; but England flourished after all these cessions.[51]

Cantofer sent a letter to Floridablanca describing Johnstone's proposals. The Spanish minister demonstrated loyalty to his French ally by passing it on to Vergennes with a copy of his letter of rejection to Cantofer in which he commented on the lack "in the Commodore of any signs of authority to treat on subjects of such importance."[52] Nevertheless, Floridablanca, without informing the French that he was doing so, encouraged the continuance of the conversations between Johnstone and Cantofer even as late as May 1780, which was curious because in February Germain had told Father Hussey, the liaison agent between Madrid and London, that Johnstone's proposals were completely unauthorized, a disavowal swiftly relayed to Floridablanca. Part of the reason for the continued interest of the Spanish minister was undoubtedly that Spain would have very much liked peace. If Britain were prepared to give her, as the price of that peace, what she had hoped to gain by war, it was pointless to persist in fighting simply to secure American independence, the realization of which would provide, in Spanish eyes, a lamentable example for Spain's own colonies. Another reason for Floridablanca's continued interest in Johnstone was that he found it difficult to believe, if Johnstone's persistent diplomatic activity remained unpunished, as it was, that he lacked at least some vestige of authority. He could not know, of course, what a singularly difficult man to discipline the commodore was. Finally, the Spaniard continued to listen to Johnstone's proposals because they were so much more congenial than those conveyed by Hussey or, later, by Richard Cumberland, an accredited agent of North.

Having got nowhere with his approaches to the Spanish court in November 1779, Johnstone had formulated new proposals in February 1780, which envisaged not a separate peace with Spain alone, which was what the British ministry sought, but rather a scheme which would enable Spain to make peace without having to violate her treaty with France. His plan suggested that the American colonies should have the autonomous status just short of independence offered by the Carlisle commission in 1778; that Britain, France, and Spain should restore all conquests throughout the world and guarantee each others' American possessions; that Spain should receive Gibraltar in exchange for payment; that Spain should enjoy the same fishing privileges as France in Newfoundland Bay; and that all discussions should be based on the Paris Treaty of 1763.

Richard Cumberland's instructions envisioned no such expansive scheme. He arrived in Portugal on May 17, 1780, but was under orders not to proceed to Spain for negotiations unless it was understood that the cession of Gibraltar was not to be discussed. Floridablanca nevertheless managed to lure him to Aranjuez in June and, evidently persuaded by reports originating from Johnstone that, under pressure, Cumberland would agree to give up Gibraltar, tried to open the negotiations on the basis of Johnstone's proposals.[53] Cumberland replied that one of the duties he was charged with was "to disavow those overtures in the most direct terms; they neither originated with the Cabinet, nor were ever before it. . . ."[54] Floridablanca would not accept the repudiation. Eventually, he was sure, Cumberland would become more flexible on Gibraltar; but he was wrong. After many interviews and conversations which achieved nothing, Cumberland returned to Lisbon in March of 1781, no doubt bitter with Johnstone for having muddied the diplomatic water. In fact, however, the desires of Floridablanca and Cumberland's instructions were too far apart for accommodation to be feasible.

Another of Johnstone's diplomatic ventures had failed, but unlike the American fiasco, the chief blame for failure could not plausibly be laid on the commodore's shoulders. That he should have acted without authority is certainly puzzling, yet it should be remembered that Johnstone committed nothing (that has survived at any rate) to paper. All we know about what he claimed and suggested in these negotiations is at third hand. The

Scotsman's normal mode of communication with the Spanish court was through Cantofer and an intermediary called Fernan Nuñez to Floridablanca. What the Spanish minister wrote of Johnstone probably suffered from distortion. Even so, what Johnstone seems to have suggested was eminently more sensible than the offerings of the North ministry.

Spain was inordinately eager to possess Gibraltar. Its cession could, without much doubt, have secured Spanish neutrality in 1779 or 1780, a boon pregnant with incalculable possibilities for which Britain should have been prepared to pay a very high price. Gibraltar would have been a comparatively cheap one. There was no Suez Canal to protect, Britain's Mediterranean trade was unimpressive, and, in any case, in 1780 there was still a usable, if strategically inferior, British naval base in the western Mediterranean. Minorca was held by his uncle, James Murray, and would, under Johnstone's plan, have remained in the British empire. Royal and public opinion vehemently opposed the surrender of Gibraltar, but there were many in high places who shared the commodore's disdain for the place. Sandwich himself had revealed such an attitude in 1770 when he had refused to have his insouciance ruffled by rumors of a planned Spanish attack on the rock: "there might be such a plan; and what then? Gibraltar . . . was open to the sea, and we could retake it if we pleased;" though, upon the whole, he did not think it of much importance.[55] There is evidence too that the American secretary, Germain, and the secretaries for the northern and southern departments, Stormont and Hillsborough, were all prepared to part with Gibraltar. Johnstone would have known their dispositions and possibly counted on their support if he managed to get promising negotiations under way. The negative result of four successive cabinet meetings to discuss the cession of Gibraltar while he was in Portugal could not have been anticipated by the commodore.[56]

Evidence is wanting for an answer to the question of whether Johnstone was acting on his own or not in his Spanish overtures. It is possible that, affected by the proximity to power which he had achieved in 1779, he had carried with him to Portugal delusions of grandeur which moved him to attempt, completely without authority, a diplomatic *coup de main*. It is more likely, however, although impossible to prove, that he did have permission to sound out unofficially the possibility of peace with Spain. All such approaches had to be unofficial; otherwise France would know without doubt that Spain was considering the violation of her alliance. Father Hussey and Richard Cumberland were both unofficial envoys. In addition, by a curious coincidence, an Englishman, Sir John Dalrymple, happened to be traveling through Spain in 1780 and presented a peace memorandum to Floridablanca in April. Like Johnstone, he claimed intimacy with North's views and advocated a settlement not unlike Johnstone's second proposals.[57] It looks very much as though North started several hares, intending to chase only the most promising and to ignore the rest.[58] Finally it should

be noted that Floridablanca had expected, reasonably, that an unwarranted assumption of diplomatic authority by Johnstone would have been
punished. But when Johnstone returned to England he was not disciplined
but, instead, given a much more desirable naval appointment than the
Lisbon commodoreship. The likelihood is that he had not exceeded the
limits of activity set by North, despite the minister's description of
Johnstone's diplomatic proposals as "undigested and crude."[59]

Diplomatic overtures apart, Johnstone had been very busy ever since his
arrival at Lisbon in November 1779. His first task was to use his squadron
to convoy a fleet of thirty-seven ships carrying barrels of wine from Oporto.
The merchants there were impatient, but Johnstone prudently delayed the
operation because he had captured intelligence of superior Spanish naval
forces in the area. There were, for example, according to a report of
November 25, four 74s and two enemy frigates at Corunna.[60] Johnstone
prepared a dummy letter to deceive the Spanish which read as though he
wanted the convoy to wait indefinitely, whereas in fact he was making
preparations, including secret signals, to have it sail home under the
protection of false Dutch colors and his own squadron. He was infuriated to
find that despite his letters dating from November 12, advising them to
hold themselves ready to come out over Oporto's harbor bar, when he
arrived on December 6 some of the merchantmen were unprepared. Those
that did come out then were sent on to England, escorted by Johnstone's
entire force except for the *Romney* and a cutter. Severe weather forced
Johnstone to return to Lisbon. He gave instructions that the remaining
merchantmen should, when possible, leave Oporto and head for Lisbon
where he would provide protection for the voyage to England.[61]

Johnstone repeatedly demanded more vessels from the Admiralty, but
seldom in the history of the Royal Navy were there fewer to spare. In
February 1780 his small command was scattered; the *Crescent*, the *Cormorant*, and the *Rattlesnake* off Oporto, the *Romney* and the *Brilliant* off
Cape St. Vincent. He took no prizes at that time, but "my own ill luck is
amply compensated by the good fortune attendant on Sir George Rodney,"
he wrote, alluding to his friend's successes in the West Indies, where
Rodney's capture of sixteen transports and six frigates on January 8 was
followed eight days later by victory over six Spanish ships of the line.

Johnstone collected information about enemy naval activity in various
ways. He interviewed the masters of Portuguese fishing smacks and the
officers and communicative passengers of other neutral vessels, as well as
receiving reports from English privateers and the commanders of his own
squadron. He also had contacts in Madrid and sent knowledgeable spies to
Cadiz to view the shipping there. From these and other sources the commodore was able to report accurately on the movements of Admiral
Guichen's fleet in February; he surmised correctly that an expedition to
the West Indies rather than a renewed invasion attempt on Britain was

planned.[62] The Admiralty received corroboration from other, less conventional sources.[63] In April Johnstone tried to repeat an exploit of nearly twenty years before. He learned that on April 20, a squadron of Spanish warships with numerous land forces had left Cadiz. It was the West Indies expedition of Don José Solano. Johnstone informed the Admiralty and, fearing that Captain John Ford of the *Brilliant* had been distracted and was unable to speed with the news to Rodney, sent Captain John M'Laurin in the *Rattlesnake* to the admiral.[64] He need not have bothered; Ford had been able to carry out his orders. In addition, Captain Man of the *Cerberus* knew of Ford's orders, and when he, independently, saw Solano's fleet, he too sailed for the West Indies. The result was that Rodney received the same news from three different ships of Johnstone's command.[65]

In spite of this early warning, Rodney failed in his attempt to meet and destroy Solano's squadron before it could join Guichen, but Sandwich took notice of the commodore's prompt action—"nothing could be more judicious."[66]

In response to Johnstone's report on June 9, 1780, that two enemy squadrons were out to intercept the outward and homeward bound trade convoys, the Admiralty detached Admiral Geary from the Channel fleet to deal with the enemy—another example of the administration's respect for information from Johnstone.[67]

In fact Johnstone's intelligence reports were good. They were as precise as he could make them, and he was careful to indicate when he could write with certainty and when not. Nevertheless, accurate intelligence had to be acted on to be of use. The septuagenarian Geary put to sea, found nothing, and returned too soon to England, with the result that a convoy bound for the East and West Indies was met by the enemy off Cape St. Vincent on August 9. Without protection, all but three of the sixty-four ships were captured, together with 3,000 hands and troops, a stunning loss which killed any hopes of success that Richard Cumberland might have had in his negotiations with the Spanish court.[68]

Johnstone, well aware of the enemy strength in the area, asserted that he would have posted a frigate off Cape St. Vincent to give warning of a threat to the convoy had he not assumed, reasonably, that Geary would take such a precaution. The commodore meanwhile was organizing the whole force under his command to escort another wine convoy from Oporto to England.[69] He himself, in the *Romney*, together with the *Brilliant* and the *Crescent*, accompanied the convoy as far as Cape Finisterre, leaving the *Cerberus, Tartar,* and *Cormorant* to take the forty merchantmen the rest of the way.

In the latter part of the year, another, less routine expedition was being discussed in London, and Johnstone was required to command it. But, on one pretext or another, he would have returned in the autumn to England in any case. A general election was imminent, and Sir James Lowther had not made him a first-string candidate for any of his boroughs. Alexander Wedderburn, now Lord Loughborough, wrote to John Robinson, North's political manager, suggesting that a government borough be given to Johnstone: "It would be idle to enlarge upon the advantages of bringing in so powerful and active a friend, who you know does nothing feebly. . . . "[70] Clearly, even as late as the time of this letter, Johnstone's adherence to the North administration was still in question, though not after December 1, when he was elected to the pocket borough of Lostwithiel in Cornwell. He did not campaign, but if he had, he might well have done so as a war-hero candidate.

His tour in Lisbon proved that he had not lost his competence as a naval officer. Apart from sending useful intelligence to the Admiralty, he had successfully convoyed two valuable merchant fleets in exceptionally dangerous waters, and despite the small size of his squadron, which he had preserved intact, he had acquired several valuable prizes. On his initial voyage to Lisbon he had taken a Spanish frigate, the *Santa Margarita*. Then, in 1780, the *Romney* under the command of Captain Rodham Home had, on July 1 and 6, captured two French frigates. The *Pearle* of 18 guns and 138 men, taken off Vigo after a five-hour chase, was a fine catch, but the second, the *Artois,* was finer. Equipped with 40 guns and a crew of 460, she was larger in dimensions than the *Romney,* full of a "superabundance of all kinds of stores," and brand-new.

Johnstone returned to London from Portugal on September 29, 1780, to be followed four days later by his trophies. On October 6, he had one of the few audiences of his career with the king.[71] What they talked of is unknown, but it is more than likely that his sovereign sized up Johnstone's suitability for the command of a secret expedition which had been much discussed in cabinet meetings since August.

Its origin was an offer by two Scotsmen, William Fullarton and Thomas Humberston, to raise the troops and buy the privateers for a predatory raid on the Spanish colonies in the South seas.[72] By August the East India Company had agreed to support the scheme with ships and troops if the expedition would go via India, conquer islands belonging to Holland (soon expected to join Britain's enemies) before attacking Spanish colonies in the Western hemisphere. By November another or alternative objective—the only evidence does not clearly specify which—was the River Plate. This expedition, referred to in a cabinet minute of November 2 as "the second Project suggested by Commodore Johnston[e]," would have to employ East India Company forces, and was decided on by the cabinet on the twenty-fifth. In December the directors of the company declared that the recent entry of the Dutch into the war made it impossible for them to cooperate in any way with ventures in the Western hemisphere. The result was that on December 29 the cabinet changed the objective yet again. The expedition now would attempt the conquest of the Dutch base at the Cape of Good

Hope.[73] Johnstone had probably dreamed of Spanish treasure ships, and according to *Political Magazine* of March 1781 was to grumble "that he had lost £10,000 by a change in his orders."[74]

Thanks to the delays which seemed inescapable between the formulation of any naval plan and its execution in the eighteenth century, Johnstone had six months on shore between his return from Portugal and his sailing for the Cape, during which time he spoke seldom in Parliament. Possibly contributing to this uncommon taciturnity was a bereavement resulting from the enormously destructive hurricane in the Leeward Islands in November 1780. The hurricane, wrote Admiral Rodney to his wife, had deprived their friend the governor of a very valuable young man. Captain Johnstone had been on his ship anchored in Gros Islet Bay, St. Lucia, when it struck, and been heard of no more. Rodney scarcely knew how to break the news to his friend.[75] The missing officer was Johnstone's natural son John, who had been his father's third lieutenant on the *Romney*. Admiral Rodney also helped the professional advancement of George's brother Gideon, who served under him in the *Adamant*,[76] but had shown particular favor to John, making him a post-captain in command of the *Yarmouth* on November 3, 1780, only a few days before the hurricane. "Fortune," wrote the governor, "had whisked [him] to a giddy height with all her gaudy plumes and guilded Prospects, to make his fall the more affecting." And the governor was badly affected, too distracted, he alleged, to be capable of looking into the affairs of others.[77]

On February 1, 1781, Johnstone made his first long speech of the parliamentary session. His subject was Sir Hugh Palliser's appointment as governor of Greenwich Hospital, a belated consolation prize to an administration supporter whose legal jousting with the Opposition hero Keppel had ruined his seafaring career. Johnstone's performance was extraordinary.

He began by praising the first lord of the Admiralty in a fulsome and ridiculous way. Perhaps, giving him the benefit of the doubt, we may imagine an ironic smile on his face as he said, "Admiralty preferments [have] scarcely ever been bestowed with so much fairness, as since the earl of Sandwich [has] been at the head of Admiralty." For others he could find no good word. As he recalled Keppel's performance against the French fleet in July 1778 (when he personally was in America), he hid his face in his hands and repeated "Oh, God!" Commenting on Palliser he called his political conduct "rash, resentful and blameworthy." "Politics and party," he continued hypocritically "were the bane of all service." Toward the end of his speech he blamed Keppel for his unpatriotic words in calling the American war unjust—quite as though Johnstone himself had not publicly said the same a dozen times—and accused certain other opponents of the war, especially "by unavoidable implication, Fox," of being paid by Britain's enemies to traduce and subvert her greatness. Thomas Townshend, worried about the mischief that might ensue—perhaps he was remembering how he had once seconded Germain in a duel as a result of Johnstone's language—intervened to shut him up. Other members shouted, "Go on!" but Johnstone subsided.[78] To the disgust of Walpole he voted with the government, despite his caustic words on the ministerial hero Palliser.[79] If his harangue gave only mixed pleasure to the ministry, it completely outraged the leaders of the Opposition. Edmund Burke replied to it by declaring before the entire House of Commons that he considered his former friendship with Johnstone at an end, while Charles Fox, on whom Burke, years later, would heap a similar public humiliation, vowed privately never to speak to the governor again.[80]

By turns fawning, splenetic, histrionic, and slanderous, Johnstone's speech did not reflect the powers of judgment to be hoped for in a commodore entrusted with an important mission, even if, as is possible, he was drunk.[81]

7. The Broad Pendant Wavers

Johnstone had been highly favored. Given command of an important naval expedition and thus the chance of prestige and prizes, he had also been granted freedom from one of the usual disadvantages of such a responsibility. He was not under Admiralty orders but answerable only to the earl of Hillsborough, the secretary of state for the southern department. His mission was twofold: first he was to attempt the conquest of the Dutch settlement at the Cape of Good Hope; then, whether successful or not in that object, he was to convoy troops to reinforce the East India Company settlements in Bengal and on the Coromandel coast, but he seems to have been given considerable discretionary power in executing his orders.

The genesis of the expedition has been called political by G. Rutherford. It is certainly true that without his political support for the North administration, particularly in attacking Howe and Keppel, Johnstone would not have been appointed to its command. It is perhaps a little unfair to call Johnstone, as Rutherford does, "inexperienced," and it is worth remembering that prior to the emergence of Hughes and Rodney in its final stages, the war produced no British naval heroes.[1] Johnstone, when recalled to the colors in 1779 had shown competence and even a certain fire and initiative, both in the Channel Islands and on the Portuguese station. That these qualities, if given great scope, could achieve great results was the legitimate gamble which North and Hillsborough took.

It was a misjudgment. Johnstone proved incapable of abandoning the habit, which his years as a politician had reinforced, of making the pursuit of prizes his prime object. Strategic considerations suffered. At no point in his conduct of the expedition did Johnstone seem to realize the magnificent strategic coup possible if only he would concentrate his time and effort on the important tasks—the capture of the Cape and the destruction of the French squadron opposing him. Both were possible and had he done either, the French empire in the East, Île de France (Mauritius) and Réunion, would have passed into British hands to be followed in all probability by the Dutch East Indies.

The story of Johnstone's failure, which he called victory, has been told several times.[2] Even if the French had not been informed of the commodore's "secret" expedition through their intelligence system, the British press supplied a running and detailed commentary on it. *Scots Magazine* of March 1781, for example, reported that

on the 13th sailed . . . from Portsmouth, under the command of Com. Johnstone, a fleet, consisting of one ship of 74 guns, one of 64, three of 50, three of 32, one of 28, two of 16, one of 14, one bomb vessel, one fire-ship, and seven armed ships; having under their convoy the *Hastings, Queen, Chapman, Valentine, Osterley, Lord North, Latham,*

Essex, Asia, Hinchenbrook, Locke, Fortitude, and *Southampton,* East India men, and a fleet of transports.

This information was correct, although incomplete; the total number of vessels under Johnstone's command was actually forty-seven.[3] The commodore did not fly his broad pendant from the 74-gun *Hero* or any of the several ships in his command which were large or new. Instead he took up quarters aboard the fourth-rate 50-gun *Romney*, the flagship of his Lisbon days, which had been launched in 1762. If his ships of war were called on to fight a comparable French squadron they could be expected to outmaneuver the enemy, since they were all copper-sheathed, as the French were unlikely to be,[4] although the customary superior design of French ships in other respects might offset the advantage.

If ships of war had been his sole responsibility, Johnstone would have been able to sail more promptly, and the outcome of his expedition might have been quite different from its actual fate, even though they were so ill-prepared when he received them that he wrote Hillsborough a letter of complaint which he asked should be placed before the king.[5] As it was, a series of misfortunes, all but one involving armed transports, delayed departure.

On February 17 the *Raikes* and Captain James Cook's former ship *Resolution* collided while anchored in the Downs and had to be sent to Sheerness for repairs. Two days later there was trouble aboard the *San Carlos,* as a result of which Captain Boyle had to put two soldiers in irons. The ship was seriously undermanned. For the same reason the East Indiaman *Pondicherry* had not joined the convoy by February 23. The commodore suggested that the soldiers it carried should be used to work the ship.[6]

Up to the very time of his sailing Johnstone had, significantly, to deal with dissension. On March 12, the crew of the *Porpoise* refused to weigh anchor, and on March 13 those of the *Raikes* and the *Resolution* followed suit, complaining that they had received no pay for five years. Although he could not allow his expedition to be delayed because of this grievance, the commodore was sympathetic, reserving his anger for officers like Lieutenant Thoresby of the *Royal Charlotte,* who was reluctant to part with any of his crew to make good deficiencies on other vessels.[7] Finally at three o'clock on the afternoon of March 13, the expedition was able to set sail.

Between Johnstone's squadron as it set off down the Channel and Admiral Darby's fleet, which preceded it by a day, was a convoy bound for the West Indies. The commodore was anxious to escape the crowd; although he would have enjoyed the safety of numbers if he had stayed with Darby as far as Gibraltar, the chances of his being observed would be less and his speed greater if he moved independently. This he did and, wisely giving Ushant and Cape Finisterre a wide berth, kept westward, passing two hundred miles clear of Cape St. Vincent as he worked toward the Cape

Verde Islands. Despite a delay caused by the ill-fated *San Carlos'* running into the *Hero* on April 6, this leg of the voyage took just over a month—fast going for a squadron encumbered by storeships, troopships, and victuallers (some of which, particularly the ordnance ship *Prudence* and the victualler *Jupiter*, were rotten), and miserable sailers.[8]

During the voyage, very necessary military instruction was given to the recruits intended for the attempt on the Cape. The troops on the expedition numbered some 2,500 and consisted of two corps newly raised by Fullarton and Humberston, a battalion of the Black Watch, and four companies to fill gaps in the depleted Eighth, Ninth, Twentieth, and Twenty-seventh regiments already in India, in addition to a small artillery detachment. All were under the command of Major General William Medows, the hero of St. Lucia and a man of considerable military experience; but many of his men were tyros, "a set of poor undisciplined wretches," who tried, on the voyage, to learn the elements of musketry.[9]

Johnstone also exercised his squadron at this time in sea maneuvers. He appears to have been one of those awkward commanders from whom those under him never knew what to expect save that, when things went wrong, he could be relied on not to blame himself. On March 27 he tried to get his squadron into "line of battle abreast." "Such conduct I never saw," wrote Captain Pasley of the *Jupiter*,"—constant signals thrown out that such and such ships were out of Line with the *Romney*. I can only say that in my opinion he acted throughout this day both unlike a Seaman and an Officer." If such was the opinion of Pasley, who was well disposed to Johnstone, much less would the commodore have enjoyed the confidence of his other captains. He, for his part, seemed "dissatisfied with every Officer under his Command" except, thought Pasley, with himself.[10]

He was also on poor terms with those commanding the ships of the convoy. During this same leg of the voyage the captain of the East Indiaman *Hinchingbrook* signalled him to bring the *Romney* near, so that he might speak to the commodore. As Johnstone approached, through his telescope he observed many feminine onlookers aboard the *Hinchingbrook*, whose captain reported that he had just quelled a mutiny and asked that Johnstone take off the ringleaders. The commodore agreed but could not resist shouting through his speaking trumpet that it was the result of carrying so much beauty. "They are enough to cause the stones of Rome to rise and mutiny!" There were those who thought that a mutinous riot in which one man was killed and ten wounded was no occasion for a "low indecent joke."[11]

The mutual lack of confidence between Johnstone and the captains had dire results. Even before reaching the Cape Verde Islands, however, he showed an equally ominous readiness to divide his force. On March 29 the sloop *Porto* and the cutter *Lark* were detached to take on wine at Madeira; on April 1 the 50-gun *Jupiter* and the frigate *Active* sailed to look for prizes, while on April 4, the sloop *Shark* was sent to Brazil.[12] It was not the possible loss of these vessels which boded ill for the future—although the pursuing French squadron was unlucky not to catch any of them—so much as the indication that Johnstone was still dreaming of Spanish gold and prizes when he should have been singleminded in his determination to get to the Cape of Good Hope as quickly as possible. On April 10, a further detachment was made to Mayo in the Cape Verde Islands. The 64-gun *Monmouth,* the 50-gun *Isis,* the frigate *Diana,* the fireship *Infernal,* the bomb-ketch *Terror,* two East Indiamen, and ten ancillary ships were left to load water and food while Johnstone took the rest of his command to La Praya in the island of Santiago. The commodore was justified in this division. The facilities at La Praya were likely to be overloaded, and Pasley, who had been there in 1780, told him that good water was available at Mayo. Moreover, splitting his force for watering and provisioning would save time.[13] Such dispersal would have been unjustifiable had Johnstone known that a French squadron was behind him, but at the time he did not.

The Cape Verde Islands belonged to neutral Portugal, and La Praya proved so amply equipped to supply Johnstone's ships that he summoned there the ships diverted to Mayo, where water supplies proved disappointing. They sailed to La Praya on the morning of April 14.[14]

A French privateer, the *Serapis,* had lain at La Praya in the latter part of March. Johnstone, "man of business" that he was, did not scruple to use bribes to obtain letters left there by her captain. They contained what should have been galvanizing information: twenty French sail under the command of Commodore Pierre de Suffren might be expected to stop in the middle of April at La Praya for water and provisions.[15]

With a battle squadron of six and a small convoy of fourteen, Suffren had left France only nine days after Johnstone and was hard on the Scotsman's heels. The letters in which the intelligence was contained have not survived, but for whatever reason, Johnstone evidently took it lightly, appears to have confided it only to Pasley, and did nothing to speed revictualling or to interrupt the leisurely round of social activity. For example, an *al fresco* dinner was held on the fourteenth and a dance aboard the *Southampton* on the fifteenth.[16] Because the late arrivals from Mayo anchored where they could find space as they entered the harbor, a dangerous situation developed, which Johnstone did almost nothing to correct: the ships in La Praya were not in an ordered defensive position. Johnstone did not even post a frigate outside the harbor mouth to warn of an enemy approach. Even if he thought the French intelligence dubious, his lack of caution was inexcusable and inexplicable.[17] When Suffren appeared to do battle on the morning of April 16, he achieved complete surprise. Half of the complements of the British ships were ashore when the cannon began to fire.

Had the French squadron been commanded by any officer other than Suffren, Johnstone's vessels would almost certainly have remained unmolested. The orthodox tactical and strategic doctrine of the eighteenth-century French navy was defensive; the underlying principle was "preserve your ships!" In action the French line always sought to get to leeward, because it was easier to disengage thus than from the windward position. In gunnery the French always aimed high, firing on the upward roll, destroying the masts and rigging of the enemy to hinder him from pursuit. The orthodox French commander, in Suffren's position, would have left Johnstone alone and incurred no blame for doing so. After all, his chances of reaching the Cape of Good Hope before the Englishman would have been excellent. The mere fact that the French squadron, which had left the Channel nine days after the English, had caught up with them, proved superior speed. Encumbered by a much larger convoy, the English were unlikely to outstrip their opponents on the journey to the Cape. On the face of it, small benefit could derive from attacking Johnstone's squadron in harbor. The Royal Navy vessels were more numerous than the ships of their enemy and were supplemented by fourteen East Indiamen, each with 24 guns, which, though negligible for offensive purposes, might be of use in defense. Even if the anchored ships were deployed only half efficiently, they were likely to inflict far more damage than they received, and there was a strong possibility of crippled French vessels slowing the hitherto excellent progress to the Cape. Reason, therefore, would have dictated to the orthodox French commander that hurrying on to the Cape in undamaged ships with a full press of sail was the thing to do.

Pierre de Suffren was an unorthodox French commander.[18] Incurably pugnacious, he was a sailor of great experience who had suffered much in his time from the caution of superiors like d'Estaing, whom he had freely criticized.[19] The ubiquitous William Hickey interviewed Suffren early in 1783 and wrote a graphic description of the Frenchman, who, if Raeburn's portrait of Johnstone is any guide, looked remarkably like the English commodore although perhaps less brawny:

> He looked much more like a little fat, vulgar English butcher than a Frenchman of consequence; in height he was about five feet five inches, very corpulent, scarce any hair upon the crown of his head, the sides and back tolerably thick. Although quite grey he wore neither powder nor pomatum, nor any curl, having a short cue of three or four inches tied with a piece of old spun-yarn. He was in slippers, or, rather, a pair of old shoes, the straps being cut off, blue cloth breeches unbuttoned at the knees, cotton or thread stockings (none of the cleanest) hanging about his legs.

He talked freely and, it seems, frankly with Hickey about the action at La Praya. His hurried departure from France had caused him to sail without enough water. It was this shortage, rather than the preconceived plan suggested by the *Serapis* letters, which caused him to put in to the same harbor as Johnstone. He was "astonished and vexed" to find it already occupied; vexed because he thought Johnstone might interfere with his attempt to get to the Cape. But then he noticed the negligent way in which the British ships of war were positioned, leaving the convoy liable to be partially cut off or destroyed. According to this account it was not nice calculations either tactical or strategic that caused his decision to attack but instead the mouth-watering sight of "a forest of masts of merchantmen laying unprotected and exposed towards the mouth of the harbour."[20] The trigger for his offensive spirit was, in short, less cerebral than predatory. In this he compares rather than contrasts with Johnstone.[21]

In attacking, Suffren was taking a great risk. He had the advantage of surprise, but his captains were not briefed for an attack and their ships were not physically prepared for one. Before he could lift prizes he would have to neutralize a squadron which was superior to his own both in numbers and in weight of metal and, though not anchored to best advantage, yet capable of returning fire. The odds were that he would retard his voyage to the Cape, receiving more damage than he inflicted.

Having made his decision, Suffren did not wait for his laggards (the *Vengeur* and the *Sphinx*) after hoisting the signal for "line of battle ahead" but led the way into the harbor aboard his flagship, the 74-gun *Héros*. As the wind was from the northeast, and the harbor faced south, he was able to sail in smoothly on the starboard tack. Ignoring smaller ships he headed for the most accessible man-of-war. According to Johnstone's account of the battle Suffren luffed up and dropped anchor with the intention of engaging the 64-gun *Monmouth*. The spring of his ship's cable did not hold, however, with the result that the *Héros* drifted back and stopped abreast of a similarly named English 74, the *Hero*.[22] Resourcefully the commander of the 74-gun *Annibal*, the second ship to enter the bay, overtook the *Héros* and anchored ahead of her, within range of the *Monmouth*, but whereas the *Héros* was ready for action, firing at opportune targets even before anchoring, Captain Trémigon of the *Annibal* had not anticipated the possibility of attack. Her decks were cluttered with casks, livestock, and sick men, while the gunports of her lower battery were closed when she anchored. The result was that for a time the ship received fire without being able to return it, and suffered terribly. Trémigon was killed, his second in command was badly wounded, 200 of the crew became casualties, ammunition blew up, starting a fire, and the vessel was all but dismasted.[23]

The third French vessel to enter the bay, the 64-gun *Artésien*, had better luck than her predecessor by ignoring the British fighting ships and concentrating on the East Indiamen. According to Benjamin Slacke, the *Artésien* cast her anchor behind the *Héros*, but it would not hold; she then closed with the East Indiaman *Fortitude*, but several Frenchmen were shot out of her shrouds by the muskets of a company of the Ninety-eighth Regiment under Captain Jenkinson, who further depleted the boarding party before the *Artésien* drifted away from the *Fortitude*. A more successful boarding attempt secured the East Indiaman *Hinchingbrook*, which the *Artésien* carried out to sea.[24] The reason for the failure to take the *Fortitude*, according to Suffren, was that the captain of the French vessel, M. de Cardaillac, was killed by a musket ball just as he was about to anchor, and because his second in command had to be summoned from the lower battery, the *Artésien* drifted, leaving eight of her boarders as prisoners on the *Fortitude*.

The last of Suffren's ships to enter La Praya were the 64s *Vengeur* and *Sphinx*. Like the *Artésien,* the *Vengeur* failed to anchor. Raoul Castex, a French author who wrote an entire book about this battle, claimed that her captain gave the order, but his voice could not be heard above the din of battle.[25] For whatever reason, the *Vengeur* spent but a short time in the bay, although her passing fire on some of the smaller vessels wrought considerable damage. The little *Terror*, an 8-gun bomb-ketch suffered badly, as did the fireship *Infernal,* which cut its cable and drifted out to sea. It seems from Slacke's account that the *Vengeur* was a heavy sailer; she attempted to weather the frigate *Diana* but was unable to sail close enough to the wind and had to pass under her stern, so closely as to tear her ensign. She was trying, according to the same source, to close with the 50-gun *Romney* but had to bear away repeatedly and nearly ran onto the rocks at the west end of the harbor, not, however, without firing on both vessels.[26]

Of the French ships engaged, the *Sphinx* did least of all, though she did maintain "a very hot fire" as she passed through the anchored British fleet on her way from one end of the bay to the other. Suffren's corvette, the *Fortune*, never managed to enter the harbor at all.

When Suffren realized that the *Heros* and the *Annibal* were the only two of his ships to succeed in anchoring and, at the same time, that the *Annibal* was in danger of being turned into a hulk, he decided to end the action. He ordered the *Heros* to cut its cable. Some fifteen minutes later the *Annibal* followed suit, subsequently drifting from the harbor under heavy fire; of her masts, only twenty feet of the foremast remained.

Suffren had hoped to pick up some of the dozen or so British vessels that had sought safety outside the harbor once battle began. The necessity of protecting the *Annibal* and taking it in tow, however, preoccupied his squadron, with the result that, apart from the *Hinchingbrook*, only the fireship *Infernal* was captured by the French, although they should have taken the *Terror* too. The bomb-ketch could scarcely have been worse prepared for action. Situated outside the protection of other vessels the *Terror*, having sprung a bowsprit, was under repair when the enemy appeared and received early attention from the *Vengeur*. The consequent misfortune of catching fire proved lucky. The French hesitated to board her, so Captain Wood ordered the cable cut and his vessel drifted beyond the bay where the foremast as well as the unsound bowsprit went overboard. Enemy ships approached, but, seeing signs of British pursuit preparations, Wood refused to strike his colors and instead contrived to hoist stay-sails, which enabled him to escape capture and eventually to regain the safety of the La Praya roads.[27] Johnstone, therefore, had not suffered as much, perhaps, as he deserved, mainly because his unreadiness for defense had been matched by Suffren's lack of offensive preparation. It is appropriate now to consider the battle from the defenders' viewpoint.

At 9:30 on the morning of April 16, when Captain Sutton of the *Isis* signalled the presence of strange ships to the northeast, the commodore was in a rowing boat among the convoy, ordering the relocation of a storeship which was being driven onto an East Indiaman. He at once went aboard the *Romney* and flew the signals for all ashore to return to their ships and prepare for battle, reinforcing his summons with gunfire; he also sent a boat ashore for stragglers. He then went to the *Isis* and assessed the approaching ships, from their signals, as French.[28] As he returned to the *Romney* he was infuriated to discover that on some ships his signals had been ignored. As he passed the East Indiaman *Valentine* he saw that her crew were washing the ship's sides with a pump engine. Instead of directly reproving the captain, Johnstone did so obliquely, telling him that he wanted to speak to John Macpherson, a passenger and East India Company acquaintance of the commodore, who was awakened and, his head poking out of the stern gallery and still in his nightshirt, received the commodore's tirade:

Good God, Mr. Macpherson! Could I have expected this shameful conduct from you, whom I chose for my elephant in the hour of danger, and placed next myself in the line of battle, to be scratching your sides like a Highlander and pissing with this engine, when my signals for battle have been flying this half hour, and the enemy are actually off the point? Do you mean to engage them with this stream? A man ought to be crucified alive who can be guilty of this neglect.[29]

Once back in his flagship Johnstone realized from the positions being adopted by the French that the *Romney*'s guns were partly masked, so he transferred his flag and himself to the *Hero* in the probable heart of the action.

There is uncertainty about the precise hours when events occurred. Not everybody present had a timepiece, and nobody had one of unquestionable accuracy. It seems, however, that the *Isis* signalled Suffren's approach at 9:30 A.M., that the *Héros* cast anchor at 11:00 and that the *Annibal* cut its cable at noon. There was, therefore, enough time for a high proportion of the 1,500 Britons ashore to reembark and to clear their decks before firing began, although not time for Johnstone to redeploy his vessels.

The descriptions of Suffren's attack made separately by Captains Douglas and Metcalfe of the East Indiamen *Queen* and *Locko* are of particular interest because their commentaries are detached. They were not partisans of the French, but they had no stake in favoring or denigrating Johnstone either. Douglas complained of the unmethodical disposition of the vessels in the anchorage at La Praya which had resulted in the warships being sited within, rather than protectively outside, the company ships. He mentioned, as Johnstone in his official report did not, that in addition to the commodore's signals for all ashore to return to their ships he flew another ordering all vessels to fly French colors. It was not a fatuous order, in that it could have deterred or at least delayed a Spanish or Dutch force, which might have taken the British squadron for Suffren's. Unfortunately for Johnstone, the visitors were French and Suffren knew that his was the only sizable French force in the area.

Douglas saw the capture of the *Hinchingbrook* and the attempted seizure of the *Fortitude* and thought the taking of East Indiamen rather than the destruction of Johnstone's warships the enemy's object. His own vessel, the *Queen*, seemed to be threatened. Her exposed position had made it possible for her to fire on the first three French vessels entering the bay, but as the *Annibal* sought to cast anchor in a place which suggested a boarding attempt on the *Queen*, Douglas cut in an attempt to run but, for fear of going aground, had to reanchor less than a cable's length (i.e., according to the convention of the time, less than 240 yards) astern of her former berth. In her new position Douglas found that his vessel was exposed to fire both from the anchored *Annibal* and also, only a pistol shot away, from one of the other French ships—his account makes it impossible to decide which one—that was sailing slowly, cannon blazing, through the British fleet. In defiance of the rules of war but not of common sense, Douglas struck the *Queen*'s colors until the marauder had passed. He then rehoisted them and began firing again.[30]

Captain Metcalfe of the *Locko*, too, thought that *Annibal*'s intention was to board the *Queen*. He praised the bravery of the French crew and their seamanlike handling of the *Annibal* as, with all her ropes cut and her canvas shredded, she zigzagged out of the harbor after her ordeal by fire. It was her supreme misfortune, he thought, that in doing so she had to present her stern to a heavy and well-directed broadside from the *Isis*, which carried off all her masts except for the already-lost mizzen. Metcalfe approved of Douglas' deception in feigning surrender. The result had been to keep down casualties on the *Queen*: ten men had been wounded and only three, a cadet, a sailor, and a soldier, had been killed. The ruse was justified, he considered, because the French had violated Portuguese neutrality.[31] As the company captains rightly estimated, Suffren's attack had weakened his own squadron much more than his enemy's. Castex thought that the French had 97 killed and 215 wounded, compared with 9 dead and

47 wounded on the British side.[32] Suffren's withdrawal should have been, in the circumstances, the cue for a strong counterattack.

Nothing in Johnstone's previous career gave grounds for supposing that he would shrink from initiating an offensive. Even Sir William Burnaby, son of an old friend of the commodore and one of his most violent critics, acknowledged his courage. Burnaby intended to spit in his face when the expedition was over: "I'll make the scoundrel fight me, for want of personal courage is not one of his faults."[33] Johnstone summoned a council of war on the *Romney* immediately after Suffren's retirement and began by calling for damage reports. "Shall we," he then asked, "Cutt and follow our Blow by giving them Battle again before they recover from their drubbing?" The loyal Pasley, who is the sole authority for these bellicose words, had foreshadowed what followed. Two days before the battle, he had written that "the Commodore is Brave, and I hope will be properly seconded, tho' I have my doubts of some." Now, wrote Pasley, the malcontents raised "numerous difficulties," testimony corroborated by another witness who specified General Medows as chief of the objectors.[34] Johnstone's determination to pursue Suffren prevailed but only after lengthy argument, for it was not until 2:30 in the afternoon, according to Slacke, or 2:40 by Pasley's reckoning, that the *Romney* slipped its cable.[35] Pasley's *Jupiter* followed at once and the *Hero* shortly after, but the *Monmouth* did not get under way until half an hour after the *Romney*, and the *Isis* was later still, failing to slip its cable until perhaps as much as an hour after the flagship.

Captain Evelyn Sutton of the *Isis* had reason for his delay. The *Isis* had been the outermost of all the vessels in the harbor of La Praya and as such had been a convenient target for every French ship which entered. Sutton's vessel was shot up worse than any other in Johnstone's command, far more so than the commodore was prepared to admit. Because every one of her boats had been damaged by French shot, Sutton had been unable to attend the council of war with the other officers and arrived late in a boat borrowed from the *Rattlesnake* for a private briefing by the commodore, who evidently made light of his subordinate's assertion that his vessel was badly damaged.[36] The details of Sutton's case will be considered at greater length elsewhere. For the moment it will suffice to say that he did obey Johnstone's order to slip his cable but that the commodore determined either that his captain was a malingerer or, more probably, that he would make a useful scapegoat. Subsequently, and wrongly, Johnstone charged Sutton with the full blame for all the delay in pursuing Suffren.

Once outside the harbor Sutton ran the *Isis* under the *Romney*'s stern and told Johnstone that he needed to make further repairs to the masts and rigging. Johnstone told him that the damage was "nothing at all." Nevertheless, as soon as the English ships maneuvered to form "line of battle abreast," the foretopmast of the *Isis* fell off and the squadron was delayed for another forty minutes.[37]

The result of the various delays was that, even though the French were encumbered by a ship in tow, it was 5:30 or 6:00 before Johnstone had closed sufficiently with them to signal his ships to form "line of battle ahead" preparatory to engagement. The French were two miles away. The sun was setting, but Sutton thought that another fifteen minutes on their existing course would have brought the squadrons within cannon range of one another.[38] It was then that Johnstone decided to end his attempt to reengage Suffren and instead to return to port.

The decision caused Johnstone, or so he alleged, an anguish such as he had never before experienced. He made his decision "after maturely weighing the subject in all its consequences with those persons on whose judgment I have most confidence." In summary his argument was that the waves were rising and he could not fight in the dark. If he pursued Suffren through the night he would expose his convoy to danger and would himself be so far to leeward of the Cape Verde Islands as to be in the grip of the prevailing northeast winds and southwest currents, which would make regaining La Praya difficult. He discounted Suffren's chances of getting to the Cape swiftly, because he thought he would go first to Brazil for food and water. If the Frenchman did head for the Cape in spite of thirst and hunger, Johnstone calculated that he would have to detach two of his disabled ships to the West Indies for repairs, which would enable him to attack Suffren in Table Bay with a great numerical advantage.[39] On this reasoning, therefore, the commodore returned to La Praya and stayed there for two weeks making repairs and completing provisioning before sailing for the Cape on May 2.

The comments of the commander of an East Indiaman on Johnstone's conduct are interesting. The commodore, wrote Metcalfe, was brave and well intentioned, and if Sutton had needlessly delayed the pursuit of the French the captain should be shot. Nevertheless, Johnstone had no business stopping at La Praya, since every ship in his command carried enough water to last all the way to the Cape. Furthermore he had let slip an unprecedentedly fine chance of destroying a French fleet, and if asked in the future why he had let the chance go by, wrote Metcalfe, "I shall follow the example he set in the House of Commons . . . and hide my eyes with both my hands."[40] As the captain of one ship in the convoy in whose interests Johnstone had broken off his pursuit of Suffren, Metcalfe was, it seems, singularly unappreciative.

Johnstone's solicitude for his convoy indeed made small sense. The only danger it faced was Suffren's squadron. If that were destroyed or captured, no damage could have resulted from leaving the convoy, even, if necessary, for weeks. That the French should have sent to the Cape Verde Islands another force as strong as Suffren's was incredible. That a smaller reinforcement had been sent was possible, if unlikely; but even if such a force had existed and had attacked the ships at La Praya, success would have been uncertain. Between them the vessels left there mounted over 200 guns. Johnstone would have been eminently justified in ignoring the risk of the existence of such a force.

Nor were Johnstone's other excuses more convincing. It was true that fighting at night was difficult. Even the impetuous Rodney after beating the French fleet in April 1782 off the Saints, would decline pursuit because his tired men and crippled ships were likely in a night action to damage one another more than their opponents.[41] Nevertheless the same commander had engaged a Spanish fleet on the night of January 16, 1780, and despite wild seas and cloudy skies had sunk one and captured six of the enemy, as Johnstone would have known well.[42] After the action at La Praya the Scottish commodore had damaged ships but none that was crippled. Suffren had both, and the *Annibal* would have been lucky to survive the night if attacked. No account mentions poor weather, so visibility would have been acceptably good, especially as the French ships carried lights.[43]

His gravest miscalculation, however, concerned Suffren. The Frenchman's problems were similar to Johnstone's, but unlike him, Suffren refused to let difficulties deflect him from his main purpose. Despite protestations in a council of war from some of his captains—dastardly poltroons, Suffren called them—that his plan to abandon his convoy and press on with all speed to the Cape was "impracticable and unjustifiably wild and chimerical," the French commodore was firm. Far from going to Brazil for water, Suffren evenly divided what water remained in his squadron among his ships, rationing every sailor to a quart a day. Instead of detaching the *Annibal* and a towing ship to the West Indies, he drafted every carpenter in his command to refit her at sea; in eight days she was "as completely new masted and rigged as if in Brest."[44]

In his written explanation Johnstone did not mention two additional reasons for not pursuing Suffren. One was that his health was poor. His brother William described the symptoms as a hard swelling in one of the glands of the throat, accompanied by great pain which disturbed thought and prevented sleep. The malady was intermittent, and Pulteney noted that it abated on Johnstone's voyage "*from* the Cape of Good Hope."[45] By implication the commodore was suffering on his way to the Cape; that is, while he was at La Praya, and if so, it would help to account for the poor judgment which he showed in his encounter with Suffren. His official silence on his illness is understandable. Mentioning it would be to admit unfitness to command. Similarly understandable, in that it, too, would have reflected on his powers of leadership, was his failure to mention another and perhaps more important reason for not pursuing Suffren. In Pasley's opinion, it was "above all the *lukewarm* conduct of part of his squadron determined him to return."[46] The mutual lack of confidence between the commodore and his officers was apparent, as has been noted, even before the affair at La Praya. It was part of the pattern of Johnstone's life that he could and did attract adherents but always, and at the same time, alienated others with whom he had to work. His gift was for faction—not for creating unity of purpose. The anonymous author of the *Monmouth Letter* claimed to have had exceptional qualifications to assess Johnstone from having served under him for five months in the same ship. He admitted that he was popular with the other ranks "from entering into the low humour of the seamen, and seldom punishing them for the most vicious enormities," but added that he was "more detested than beloved by the officers" except for those on the *Romney*, the *Jupiter*, and the *Active*.[47] If he had decided to attack Suffren at sea and received from his captains the same type of pusillanimous support that Suffren had from his when going into the harbor at La Praya, his chance of a triumph would have been small.

Once back in Santiago, Johnstone put Sutton under arrest and busied himself with the details of repair work—too much so, thought Pasley, who wrote that he should have given more time to preparing dispatches.[48] Reporting his actions would indeed require artful use of words if Johnstone were to escape censure. By delaying his report—the fair copy was not complete until April 30—the commodore was at least able to write that both British ships carried away by Suffren had been retrieved.

Pasley's ship, the *Jupiter*, picked up the East Indiaman *Hinchingbrook* on the seventeenth of April.[49] The fireship *Infernal* had been deprived of her captain, Henry Darby, most of her crew, and numerous soldiers, all of whom became French prisoners, but thanks to enemy mismanagement she had not been equipped with a prize crew. The French had hastily abandoned her when they saw that British warships were about to pursue them. And so, shorthanded and damaged, under the command of Lieutenant Hamilton, the *Infernal* limped back to Santiago on April 26.

One of the reasons for Johnstone's incredibly long delay in Porto Praya may have been that he was tempted to alter the object of his expedition. "So many schemes enter his head that they confound and confuse him," wrote Pasley. One such scheme was to revert, now that Suffren had a good chance of beating him to the Cape, to an expedition against Spanish America.[50] On June 7, five weeks after the squadron and its convoy finally left La Praya, Colonel Fullarton presented Johnstone with a paper arguing that the attempt on the Cape of Good Hope was now futile, but one on Buenos Aires might be profitable. Johnstone agreed, thought Pasley, but General Medows would not, because, again according to Pasley, John Macpherson had dazzled most of the army officers with his descriptions of the riches to be won in the Dutch colonies in the East, particularly Ceylon.[51] Johnstone was far from immune to the lure of Spanish gold and might, if subjected to unanimous pressure from the soldiers, have been prepared to head for the Western hemisphere, although he knew, as Pasley perhaps did not, that by agreement with the East India Company, if he failed to take the Cape he was supposed to send some of the troops he was escorting to India, and the remainder to the Leeward Islands. So, at any rate, wrote the author of an early history of the American war, Charles Stedman, who appears, unlike any modern historian, to have read Johnstone's instructions.[52] Nevertheless, although he may have been strongly tempted to divert his whole expedition westward, Johnstone must have been aware from his involvement in East India Company business that the company had given considerable help to his expedition because its primary intended sphere was India and the East Indies. The company wanted no part of Spanish America, partly because it thought that such a conquest would be indefensible and partly because that area fell within the jurisdiction of the South Sea Company. These views had been made plain to the government.[53] The commodore had probably been allowed a certain latitude in implementing his instructions. What he lacked when Fullarton made his proposal was sufficient information on which to base a sensible decision. He therefore took steps to acquire intelligence, dispatching a brace of frigates and two cutters on June 12 to scout off the southern coast of Africa.

On July 1 the detached flotilla took a prize which proved rich in every sense of the word. It was the *Held Woltemaade,* a Dutch East Indiaman of 1,200 tons, loaded with stores, provisions, and £40,000 in bullion.[54] She provided the certain intelligence that the French had landed in False Bay at the Cape of Good Hope on June 21. If he had nourished any guilt for lingering in Santiago, this news must have made Johnstone feel better. It meant that even if he had left La Praya on the day of the battle there, the French would have reached the Cape before him unless he had abandoned his convoy—which he could scarcely have done, since it bore the troops needed to overcome the Dutch defenders of Capetown.

Further intelligence from the *Held Woltemaade* helped the commodore determine his next course of action. He learned that the British military situation in India had become critical. Hyder Ali had invaded the Carnatic and a strong force of British troops under Baillie had been cut off and was under siege. He decided that the circumstances demanded the abandonment of any military detachment to the West Indies and the dispatch of all the soldiers who accompanied him to India except, if he were lucky, for a garrison at the Cape of Good Hope.[55]

So far, the intelligence yielded by the East Indiaman had been severe, but the officer placed in command of the prize, Lieutenant d'Auvergne, made himself agreeable enough to her passengers to extract information that was more promising. Forty-eight miles north of Capetown, in Saldanha Bay, from which the *Held Woltemaade* had come, were hidden six more Dutch East Indiamen, five of them fully loaded with cargoes from China and Bengal, and all originally bound for Europe. Their capture would be extremely difficult, since all preparations had been made to burn them in the event of an attempted attack.

Johnstone determined to try, and the incident showed the commodore at his best. To capture prizes intact could evoke his resolution and ensure support from all his officers as nothing else could. To achieve surprise he determined to approach by night. Darkness and the fog which succeeded it on the morning of July 21 certainly helped to keep the Dutch in ignorance of the attack but added to the perils of an enterprise already made hazardous by the wind. With a following wind the British could have sailed directly toward their targets. Instead the wind was from the northeast, compelling them to tack their way into a bay which, to the commodore at least, was completely unknown. He personally supervised the pilotage of the entry, periodically using the lead to assess depth and distance in the gloom.

Initially he had promised the honor of leading the attack to Pasley, who was chagrined when the commodore changed his mind and instead offered the position to d'Auvergne of the cutter *Lark*. Perhaps it was to reduce hard feelings that Johnstone changed his mind again and himself led the attack in the *Romney*.[56]

Firing began at 11:00 A.M., as soon as the British were in range of the Dutch vessels, all of which had struck their colors by noon, after being set on fire. Thanks to extremely deft work by the men sent in armed ship's boats to board the Dutchmen, five of the six fires were dowsed before doing much damage. The sixth and biggest of the East Indiamen, however, was wreathed in towering flames. Johnstone ordered his officers to extinguish the fire, particularly as the blazing *Middelburg* broke loose from her anchor when her masts fell and threatened to drive aboard the other prizes and consume them. Failing to get instant obedience, the commodore himself went in his own barge, taking a fire engine from the *Jupiter* and cursing those he saw holding back. When he found that the fire was indeed beyond control he braved almost intolerable heat and took his boat in close enough to the *Middelburg* to throw a grapnel into her stern. Then, with the assistance of other boats, he towed her to the lee shore of the bay, where she exploded ten minutes later.

A similar exploit over thirty years before had saved Johnstone from court-martial condemnation. This time his reward was the unity of his subordinates. Even the prim author of the *Monmouth Letter,* whose purpose in citing the Saldanha incident was to draw attention to the commodore's coarse language, had to admit that, whereas before Saldanha Bay Johnstone was "not a favourite with the captains and officers," afterward he was "considered as a species of divinity."[57]

Johnstone also acquired an unusual amount of acclaim in England for his coup. The country was famished for good news of the war at sea. Graves and Hood had met with de Grasse at the mouth of the Chesapeake and had failed to win a victory. Rodney, too, had "a little overgilt his statue," wrote Walpole; he had lost much of the popularity achieved by his capture of the

Dutch island of St. Eustatius by wholesale confiscation of the contents of the warehouses there, much of it the property of British merchants. The news from Saldanha, therefore, made Johnstone "the hero of the day" and evoked a laudatory biographical sketch of "the intrepid commodore" in *Town and Country Magazine,* in which his expedition was described as "a very glorious as well as fortunate enterprise."[58]

The public might consider that the capture of the Dutch ships made up for Johnstone's failure to destroy Suffren, but the Scottish commodore was probably uneasily aware that, at the very least, his conduct was open to criticism. It was not so very long, after all, since Admiral Byng had been shot on his own quarterdeck for backwardness in engaging a French fleet. Byng had been the victim in a peculiar political situation such as did not exist in 1781, and Johnstone had small reason to expect a similar fate; nevertheless universal applause for his exploits was unlikely, and he could scarcely have expected his former allies in the Opposition to let him off unscathed. And indeed, on the very day that Suffren reached the Cape, Charles Fox was belittling Johnstone's "paltry" success at La Praya in the House of Commons. He did not forget that although the commodore had been very ready to criticize others for fighting too defensively, he himself had not taken one enemy ship, not even the almost defenseless *Annibal.*

Lord North creditably hastened to speak up for the absent officer, lauding his skill and zeal for Britain's honor. The House had received many proofs of his uncommon talents; the public esteemed his ability and integrity. At La Praya, he concluded, the commodore's achievements had been threefold: he had repelled the enemy with great loss to them; he had preserved his squadron intact; and he had protected the Indiamen in his care.

Perhaps inspired by North's repeated use of the word "commodore," Fox switched his assault to another flank. He contrasted the first lord's praise of Johnstone with the other's hostile speeches against him and suggested that North had promoted his assailant above the heads of more eminent naval officers to secure a respite from his attacks.

North replied that if Johnstone's admitted eloquence had been a factor in his employment, the administration would have found him an appointment in England so that he could have used his tongue on the Opposition. The first lord's defense was reinforced by Johnstone's old East India House ally, George Dempster, who said that his friend had won honor for himself and his country in La Praya bay. The only thing preventing a more perfect success had been a lack of obedience among his subordinates. Other defenders were John Courtenay and Francis Eyre, who denied that the British could have boarded the *Annibal.* The current in the bay, Eyre correctly declared, with uncommon knowledge, was so strong that the boarding party would have probably been swept out to sea.[59]

Even if Johnstone could have been aware that he had pleased some backbenchers—North's compliments may have been political—he was wise enough to seek something more tangible and permanent than his Saldanha prizes to placate Hillsborough and the Admiralty, who were unlikely to be so easily satisfied. The capture of the Cape of Good Hope would have served admirably, but all the surviving evidence suggests that both Johnstone and the army officers considered any such enterprise a forlorn hope. On July 25 the commodore summoned all commanders to a council of war and formally assured General Medows that he could land him and his troops in Table Bay or False Bay, but he would not guarantee to maintain communication with him if Suffren should use his squadron for an attack. Medows did not use the guarded nature of Johnstone's assurance to excuse his own caution. He said instead that the prior arrival at the Cape of the French made any attempt on it "the height of Rashness," and that the 1,900 troops fit to land were such "as he did not choose to Risk his Reputation on." In the circumstance he would as soon think of attacking Paris as the Cape.[60]

Thereafter Johnstone divided his command. On July 25, he sent several of the smaller vessels on to St. Helena to await him; on the twenty-seventh he sent the bulk of the convoy with all the soldiers aboard on to India under the protection of the *Monmouth,* the *Hero,* and the *Isis.* He stayed near the Cape until August 6 aboard the *Romney,* accompanied by the *Jupiter* and the *Lark,* which were commanded by his favorite officers, Pasley and d'Auvergne. He was disappointed in his hope of picking up stragglers from the French convoy and, since he never seems to have had the least intention himself of sailing Indian waters, returned to St. Helena, arriving on August 17.

His mood was relaxed. Whereas, at La Praya, Johnstone had declined all invitations to the round of dinners and dances arranged at that time, now, at St. Helena, he arranged a dinner and ball aboard the *Romney* and amused himself with a Miss Greerstreet and, later, a Mrs. Dunstan.[61] He gives the impression of one who, his main task done, may concentrate on enjoyment. He gave some attention to the slightly frivolous task of deploying ships to pick up prizes and none to the strategically urgent job of reinforcing the British squadron in India, which had to cope with Suffren. He ordered Captain Grant of the *Hannibal,* which he found waiting at St. Helena, to cruise off the Cape for fourteen days before proceeding to India. As he could legally claim one-eighth of any prize money realized from her captures, Johnstone must have been pleased with the *Hannibal's* good fortune; for on October 26 Grant took a large Mauritius-bound merchantman, the *Sévère,* and a French frigate, the *Neckar* of 28 guns, which struck without a fight and which the British government bought for £12,000.[62] He also found the *Jupiter* and the *Mercury* at St. Helena and sent them to look for prizes off Rio de Janeiro.[63] They were to go by way of the island of Trinidada, where Johnstone intended to establish a British colony which he must have hoped would make passable compensation for his failure to conquer Capetown.

Trinidada was in the South Atlantic about 800 miles east of Rio de Janeiro and was uninhabited. It is only 1 mile wide and 2½ miles long and resembles a mirror image of a diminutive Cyprus. Situated on the sea routes both to India and Cape Horn it could supply ships with water and an anchorage. As founding father of the settlement Johnstone chose Philippe d'Auvergne who, well supplied with livestock, plants, seeds, stores, and cannon, got ashore on October 5, 1781, with twenty-seven of his own men and twenty-four captured Frenchmen. Most unfortunately for them their vessel, the *Rattlesnake,* was almost immediately destroyed in a storm,[64] with the result that d'Auvergne and his companions were in effect marooned on a desert island where, only very occasionally, could a ship be counted on to stop. Johnstone himself visited Trinidada for eleven days in November, having sent back from St. Helena the remains of his command with their prizes. He caught up with this convoy but, on January 17, parted company with it in order to chase a prize of a different shape. On January 21 he landed in Lisbon and ten days later was married there.[65]

So ended the tale of Johnstone's expedition in the classic manner. The hero sallied forth, defeated the enemy, conquered land, and returned to claim the hand of a young and beautiful bride. The summary conceals the flaw in his every achievement. Johnstone's heroism had been tempered with caution and indecision; his enemy had lost tactically but won strategically; and the land Johnstone took was unwanted and handkerchief-sized. Is it any wonder that his bride, Charlotte, young and beautiful as she was, should turn out to be a termagant?

8. Final Appointments

Like 1778, the year 1782 was crucial for Johnstone. For his career the chief event in it was the fall of the North ministry—which meant the end of indulgence for the commodore. As the American war wound down, his naval career was bound to finish anyhow. The struggle at sea ended with a final flash of true glory when Rodney, with great skill and some of his customary luck, destroyed French naval power in the West Indies at the battle of the Saints, eclipsing anything that might have remained of Johnstone's reputation as "the hero of the day."

Even if his ventures in international negotiation had been successful, as a defector to North he would not have been chosen for similar work by North's successors, Rockingham and Shelburne. A prospect of a consular appointment from William Pitt the Younger was never fulfilled, and so Johnstone's diplomatic career, such as it was, also came to an end.

There remained possibilities for him, in Parliament and at East India House, whenever his health permitted, for he was an increasingly sick man during the last five years of his life. Domestic life, too, occupied him more than formerly, partly because illness kept him at home, partly because he had married in 1782.

Not that the first fifty-two years of his life had been monastic. He was "naturally of an amorous complexion," wrote the author of the biographical sketch in *Town and Country Magazine,* and in his early life he had "a variety of amours, and some connexions of a more permanent nature."[1] Without mentioning her name, Hickey threw light on one of Johnstone's mistresses, "a very respectable, accomplished and worthy woman whom he had debauched when quite a child, who had borne him two sons, and conducted herself in the most irreproachable manner." It was common knowledge, he said, that Johnstone had repeatedly promised her marriage even as late as the eve of his voyage to the Cape.[2] Their boys were probably John and George, Johnstone's favorite son, who seem to have been brought up together in France before entering the navy and the East India Company respectively.[3] George went on to prosper as assistant to the resident at Lucknow. In his will Johnstone made provision for three more illegitimate children. James Primrose entered the East India Company in 1790. Sophia inherited the fortune of the childless George and married the duke of Cannizaro. Alexander wed a Miss d'Aguilar and lived to see their son a colonel of the Grenadier Guards.[4]

It is idle to speculate on Johnstone's reasons for marrying Charlotte Dee, daughter of the British vice-consul at Lisbon, at the tailend of his life. It was not for money. The Dees had none, if the indigent condition of his wife's sister, Leonora Dee, is any guide.[5] Charlotte was variously described as "handsome" and "dashing" and was young, although not enough plausibly to be Johnstone's granddaughter, as Hickey claimed, since she was over twenty. Nevertheless his marriage to her must have been arranged when he was in Lisbon in 1780; it was not, therefore, a flash-in-the-pan infatuation. Possibly he married to have a son born in wedlock. If so, he obtained his wish, for a boy, John Lowther Johnstone, was born in 1783. In other respects he was unlucky, for he had married a tartar. The ubiquitous Hickey attended the wedding reception at the house of the British envoy to Lisbon, Sir Robert Walpole. Anxious to return to England, Johnstone told Sir William Burnaby, as soon as the wedding feast was over, to prepare his frigate to sail at first light on the following morning. The bride overheard the order and told Burnaby that he need not hurry. She was not ready to leave Lisbon. Johnstone became angry and a public argument ensued:

"We must, my dear Mrs. Johnstone, embark tonight and sail at daybreak tomorrow."

"My dear Mr. Johnstone, I beg leave to assure you that I will neither embark tonight nor sail at daybreak, or at any other time tomorrow."

"By God, madam, but you must and shall! His Majesty's ship must not be detained at the caprice of any woman!"

"By God, sir, I cannot and, what's more, I will not stir from Lisbon until it is my will and pleasure so to do."

The sequel, according to Hickey, was that the couple did not leave Lisbon for over three weeks, and that Johnstone endured misery for the rest of his life.[6]

Augmenting his misery was disappointment over prize money and prolonged suits against him brought by Captain Evelyn Sutton.

Two of the laden Dutch prizes from Saldanha Bay, the *Honkoop* and the *Dankbaarheyt,* had foundered before reaching England. The latter, richest of all the five captures made in the bay, had lost her masts in a storm when within sight of the Channel, and the prize master, Lieutenant Reid of the *Romney,* had abandoned her after the pumps clogged and she began to fill with water. It must have occurred to Johnstone that if he had stayed with his convoy, instead of digressing to Lisbon, he might have found means of getting her to Plymouth.[7] More serious still was the claim of the army officers accompanying the Cape expedition to a share of the prize money from the Dutch East Indiamen. At the time Captain Pasley had gloated that "no soldier was landed till two o'clock, two full hours after the affair was settled, by which they are deprived of all shadow of hope: the sole, and only Right to the Prizes remains to the Navy alone."[8]

In 1786, the lords of the council, on an appeal from the Court of Admiralty, ruled otherwise. The peculiar circumstances of the capture, particularly the presence of the soldiers, meant that the Dutch East Indiamen did not come under the terms of the Prize Act. They qualified as booty and as such went to the crown. The captors would have to rely on the royal bounty for any compensation which they might eventually obtain.[9]

Another who felt cheated of prize money was Captain Sutton of the *Isis,* first because he was unjustly, or so he thought, relieved of his command by Johnstone; second because he was accused on false charges; and third because, so long was his court-martial delayed, he was neither able to clear his name nor to participate in opportunities for prize money.

The commodore seems to have acted with both malice and that wavering consistency which unfortunately marked his actions on the Cape expedition. Sailing back to La Praya after breaking off action with Suffren, Johnstone had spoken civilly to Sutton through his speaking trumpet, so much so that the whole crew of *Isis* were gratified, at last, at having pleased the commodore. On the following day, moreover, before relieving Sutton of his command, Johnstone showed him favor by offering to let him sail back to England with dispatches. It was Sutton, resentful of a reference by Johnstone to his "extraordinary conduct," who pushed the commodore from conciliation into enmity by insistence on a court-martial.[10] By the time Johnstone wrote his official report of the battle at La Praya, no trace was left of tenderness for Sutton, whom he made sole scapegoat for the delay in pursuing Suffren. Captain Alms of the *Monmouth* was perhaps more blameworthy; unlike the *Isis,* his ship was almost undamaged, yet he had trailed almost as badly. Probably Johnstone was aware that Sutton, who had recently survived a court-martial, had no reputation at the Admiralty: "I have no predilection for Captain Sutton," Sandwich had written, "and think nothing but excessive partiality among his judges could have saved him from being broke, instead of being reprimanded, for not fighting the Dutch Man of War."[11]

Once branded, Sutton enjoyed no concessions. He asked to be court-martialed at La Praya. Johnstone refused: the expedition must not be delayed. He asked to be tried in Saldanha Bay. Johnstone again refused: an enemy port was no place for a court-martial. Finally the commodore offered him a trial at St. Helena, knowing full well that Sutton preferred to stay on the *Isis,* his own ship, which was under orders for India. Once arrived there, Sutton applied for a court-martial to Commodore Hughes, who commanded the British naval forces in Indian waters. Hughes had to refuse, either because he did not know precisely what charges Johnstone had preferred or because the alleged offenses had occurred beyond the geographical area of his jurisdiction. Sutton was therefore sent back to England.[12] It was not until December 1783 that he obtained, on a charge of "delaying and discouraging the public service," the court-martial and acquittal which he had sought for over two years. The decisive evidence, possibly, was given toward the end of the eleven-day session, when the boatswain of the *Isis* testified to the severe damage wrought by French cannon on the masts and rigging of his ship.[13]

Sutton was quite unprepared to let the matter rest there. He alleged that Johnstone had sought from personal malice to ruin his reputation and deprive him of some £20,000 in prize money: he initiated a civil suit against his former commander, which came before Mr. Baron Skynner at the Guildhall, London, on Saturday, June 19, 1784. Sutton's counsel, a Mr. Lee, demanded £30,000 as damages. Johnstone's defense was managed by the attorney general, Richard Pepper Arden, who argued that the case essentially concerned naval discipline and that if Sutton were allowed what he sought, the government would never be able to persuade any senior officer to go on dangerous expeditions. The only proper place for Sutton to have sought satisfaction was his own court-martial, which, he stated in reply to one of the plaintiff's allegations, could not have been conducted at sea, since it would have delayed the expedition to the Cape. The flimsiness of Arden's arguments should have made the trial even shorter than it was. The court first convened at nine o'clock on Saturday morning. The jury returned its verdict at eight o'clock on Sunday morning, after conferring for an hour. It vindicated Sutton and awarded him £5,000 damages.

Johnstone wanted a retrial, and the attorney general applied to the barons of the Exchequer to show cause why the verdict against Johnstone should not be set aside. The barons met on June 30, 1784, to consider the case. Lord Chief Baron Skynner declared that the legal question truly at issue had been ignored when Johnstone was tried. The point was not whether Sutton had actually been guilty of disobedience: rather it was whether his conduct had been such as to justify Johnstone in presuming criminal disobedience of orders. With the concurrence of his colleagues, Barons Eyre, Beaumont, Hotham, and Perryn, he said that the verdict ought to be set aside, "for there was no proof of malice, but clear proof of a probable cause." A new trial was therefore ordered, which took place in the Guildhall on December 11. Although it lasted only three hours there were a great many witnesses, the most influential of whom was an Admiral Edwards. When asked by Johnstone's counsel if he knew of any officer refusing to obey his superior's signal, the admiral replied that he did. He himself had once been ordered to engage the enemy after his ship was disabled and had thought it imprudent to risk the possible loss of the whole fleet by joining battle in a ship that was not fit. He added that such a decision was not contrary to duty; junior officers were not in all cases without discretionary power. The jury evidently agreed, because again it found for Sutton, this time awarding him £6,000 damages.[14]

Johnstone would still not admit defeat. In 1785 he lodged a writ of error with the lord chancellor, who sought the opinion of the two chief justices, Lords Mansfield and Loughborough. The noble judges, as Johnstone might happily have termed them, reversed the earlier decision on two grounds. The first was that Johnstone had been sufficiently punished by the damage done to his reputation in preferring unjust charges against Sutton. Second, to confirm the verdict of the jury courts would cause every man acquitted by a court-martial to bring a civil suit against his accuser.[15] Some argued that legal niceties had nothing to do with the decision. It was simply a case of Scotsmen sticking together.[16] On the eve of Johnstone's death Sutton took his case to Britain's final court of appeal, the House of Lords. There the reversal of judgment decreed by Mansfield and Loughborough was upheld by thirty-four to twenty-one, Lord Howe, of all people, supporting Johnstone with the argument that to do otherwise would be to subvert good order and discipline in the navy.[17]

The vote of the House of Lords was on May 22, 1787. Two days later, Johnstone died.[18] He had won his case but had probably lost a good deal of his fortune in fighting it, for the estate he left was meager.

Litigation, however, had not occupied all his time after his return from voyaging in 1782. Initially he had worked hard to interest the administration in the formal annexation of Trinidada. With an enthusiasm reminiscent of the ardor with which he once wrote of Florida, he seemed genuinely to believe that Trinidada could become "an invaluable Jewell in His Majesty's Crown," and interested himself in the settlement in the type of minute detail which he reserved for subjects which captured his fancy. He personally planned a garden there and ordered the importation of "Sheep, Goats, Cocks, Hens, Ducks, Turkeys . . . Guinea Fowls . . . a Jack and two she asses." A Lieutenant Hamilton was to make drawings of the island, which Johnstone said were intended for "a particular person." He evidently thought that royal eyes would see the sketches.

Shelburne, at the time secretary of state for home and colonial affairs, was immersed in peace negotiations. Johnstone importuned him at least twice and Hillsborough at least once in an attempt to get one of them to do something about the island. At last, in April 1782, prompted by the consequences of inaction for the marooned d'Auvergne, Shelburne interviewed Pasley, who had twice been to the island, and in May agreed to set up an ad hoc committee whose composition was suggested by Johnstone. The members were Vice-Admiral Campbell, Commodore Elliott, and from the East India Company, Sir Henry Fletcher, Richard Hall, James Moffat, John Smith, and William Dalrymple. They heard testimony from Johnstone and Pasley at East India House on May 28.[19] Their decision was that, such was the evidence before them, they could make no decision to annex Trinidada. In consequence the Union Jack would be lowered at Fort Johnstone and the island evacuated.

The fact that Trinidada was Portuguese would not have hindered its acquisition had the administration really wanted it. The Portuguese had claimed but not occupied the island. Portugal was in any event a minor power whose rights could be infringed with impunity. Portuguese neutrality had not prevented Boscawen from entering Lagos Bay in 1759 nor Suffren Praya Bay in 1781. The Rockingham administration did not annex

Trinidada because 1782 was the wrong time for claiming a new colony even if, as was untrue in this case, it could do so with impeccable legality and even if the founder had been, unlike Johnstone, untainted by close association with the discredited North.

One must suspect that Johnstone had lost interest in Trinidada before the outcome. When writing to Philip Stephens, the secretary to the Admiralty, about his attendance on the Trinidada committee he suggested that Lieutenant Hamilton should be present, because he *opposed* acquisition of the island; he hoped, too, that the discussion would be over by two o'clock so that he could attend the House of Commons at three, probably to vote in favor of his absent friend Rodney.[20]

There is no doubt that Johnstone enjoyed his parliamentary activities, particularly because he was once more in Opposition, for which his temperament suited him, and at this time in his career he spoke often. In the parliamentary session of 1782/3 only four members, Burke, Fox, North, and Pitt, made more speeches. But frequent oratory did Johnstone's career little good. Politically he was in decline. His former colleagues Fox, Burke, Richmond, and Barré all attained office while he remained in the wilderness. As a "man of business," others of superior caliber—Robinson, Jenkinson, Dundas—all eclipsed him. It was not his age which made him a spent force. He was still in his early fifties, although declining health did not help. Neither was it his apostasy to North; few of his political contemporaries had not turned their coats at some time. Two factors, above all, damaged him. One was his acceptance of naval commands which had taken him far from the center of political activity. The other was his lack of anything to say.

His strength in debates of the past came from positions on America and India which evoked considerable support. Now his unabated refusal to consider complete independence for America, even as Shelburne's peace treaty was discussed, sounded forlorn.[21] America was a dying issue. India certainly was not, but Johnstone's undiminished conservatism on India was as dated and unrealistic as his views on America. Every major political group had its own reform plan for Indian affairs; increased governmental control of the East India Company was implicit in them all. Johnstone would still find support for his prolonged refusal to admit further governmental interference in the company's affairs in its Court of Proprietors, but none that mattered in Parliament.

Many of Johnstone's speeches in the later phase of his career were less concerned with issues than with personalities. Sometimes, as in the case of Rodney, he praised, but more often he attacked. He was not normally waspish, although, as when he opined that the people of America should erect a statue to Fox, he could sting. Burke found an apter mataphor for him. "The hon[orable] gentleman," he said "could give broadside for broadside: and he knew how to open his lower deckers as well as any man in that House." Johnstone used his broadside, in this case in answer to a pistol ball, in a debate concerned with raising the allowance of Fox's patron, the Prince of Wales. Fox had laughed at what Johnstone had intended to be a serious opinion on the need for economy. At once Johnstone digressed. According to Cobbett he said that he knew full well that every sum, of whatever magnitude appeared as a mite in the eye of the Right Honorable Secretary Fox, who set all human ideas at defiance, both in the modes of dissipating and maintaining his private expense; and now he had adopted this last desperate mode of supplying the means of his extravagance i.e., Fox stood to gain financially from an increase in the prince's allowance.[22] If laughter rather than challenges or appeasing offers of employment now greeted his speeches, Johnstone was clearly no longer the force he had been, however violent his language. He was "unacquainted with party," he boasted in December 1782, but during the following year he must have decided that to gain political weight he would have to strike up an acquaintance with party after all. By December 1783, although he was still calling himself "an independent man," he was in fact supporting the party of young William Pitt, whom he praised for his integrity and public character and whose measures, surely at some cost even to his flexible conscience, he supported.

Johnstone, for example, had never shown much enthusiasm for constitutional innovation except with regard to America. He had denounced Burke's scheme for economical reform because "it took from the crown the power absolutely necessary to carry on government."[23] Yet he voted for Pitt's abortive plan for parliamentary reform. To support Pitt's India bill, as he also did, must have strained his principles even more for, as ever, he had been busy at East India House organizing opposition to attempts to extend governmental control over the company.

North's Regulating Act of 1773 and his moderate Charter Act of 1781 had not solved the problems of the British in India. Under the governor generalship of Warren Hastings, it is true, threats to the British presence from the Mahrattas and the French had been beaten back. The price had been high. The finances of the East India Company were once again in disarray, the council in Bengal was divided, while Hastings had used his power, on occasion, like a tyrant.

On the fall of North in March 1782, action to reform Indian affairs was inescapable. A select committee to investigate the Indian situation had been chosen by the Commons as early as February 1781. It was dominated by opponents of North, and its reports and the oratory of its leading member, Edmund Burke, ensured that abuses in India would arouse humanitarian public opinion. In May the House appointed a secret committee, ultimately with the same object as the select committee, but with a much more constructive approach. The administrative expertise and knowledge of Indian affairs among its members was impressive; they included John Robinson, Charles Jenkinson, and Henry Dundas.[24] Both committees began life with rather narrow aims which each managed to extend to general considerations of Indian problems and their solution.

No sooner had the North government fallen and Rockingham acceded to power than Dundas introduced a resolution for the recall of Warren Hastings which passed the House of Commons but was of no effect because a majority of the East India Court of Proprietors defied this attempt to encroach on company concerns. It was the opening shot of a battle in which Johnstone, as a leading supporter of Hastings, would be in the van. The death of Rockingham only four months after taking office and his replacement as first lord of the treasury by Shelburne in July 1782 did little to change the situation. Although formerly Shelburne had backed Hastings, he reluctantly agreed to attempt his recall for the political reason that he wanted to retain the support of Henry Dundas. Again the Court of Proprietors, with Johnstone in the lead, defied the government demand.[25] It was on this occasion that Johnstone successfully besought Lord North, now in the Opposition but who had been hoping to stay on the sidelines in this controversy, to "interfere in the ballot," that is to get Robinson to muster all Northites to vote according to instructions, in the interest of Hastings.[26]

Shelburne got nowhere in attempts at Indian reform before his resignation in February 1783. The accession to power of the Fox-North coalition in April posed much more of a threat to the independence of the company, because it was known that Fox and his friend Burke would attempt a thoroughgoing reform in contrast to the more moderate ones favored by most political leaders. A preliminary step might well be, it was thought, an attempt at the imminent company elections to oust opponents in the existing directorate. To thwart this possibility Johnstone resorted to a typically crude expedient. He headed a deputation which sought to hold Lord North to a verbal promise which he had once made to use the Robinson machine for the reelection of Sulivan, now once more an ally of Johnstone, to the directorate. The delegates found North chatting in his anteroom with Fox, Burke, and Portland. Hustling North into his bedroom, they extracted a written pledge of support for Sulivan and fellow directors of what was now called the "Old Interest" at East India House. As a result, and no doubt to the chagrin of North's coalition partners, the election was a triumph for the "Old Interest."[27]

Fox's India bill, which gestated during the summer of 1783, contained the most sweeping provisions of any of the eighteenth-century reform plans for the company. Its most notorious feature was the government's intention to appropriate the entire patronage of the company by making appointments the responsibility of a proposed commission of seven. The commissioners' names were specified in the India bill. Four were partisans of Fox and three of North. Critics accused Fox of trying to perpetuate the power of the coalition of which he was a member by enormously increasing the number of jobs at its disposal. Violating the charter and traditional privileges of an ancient company, as the bill certainly threatened to do, had sinister implications, it was also charged, for every chartered body in the country.

The lamb is not usually asked if it wants to be shorn, and the ministry did not consult the East India Company about the India bill. Fox successfully kept its provisions secret throughout the summer, and rumors of their nature abounded by the fall. Nevertheless the company did not fully learn how drastic were the intentions of Fox until Parliament assembled. That minister made Indian reform the first business of the session, and exactly one week after the members formally met on November 11, the India bill was introduced, even before all M.P.s were up from the country. As simultaneously the bill was making easy headway through the Commons and East India stockholders first grasped the likely fate of their company, vigorous and angry retaliation began to take shape in Leadenhall Street. The Foxite chairman of the directors, Sir Henry Fletcher, was forced to resign, while a General Court on November 21 established a committee of nine proprietors to defend company interests. Johnstone was chosen to be its chairman.[28]

The selection of the governor was appropriate because of his invariable and ferocious hostility to encroachments on the company's privileges. But, preparing as he then was for Sutton's court-martial, he could not be as active in the affairs of the committee as another member, Richard Atkinson, a prime "man of business" who had made a fortune supplying rum to the British army during the American war.

The committee prepared a case against Fox's India bill for presentation in the House of Lords and organized petitions against it from corporate bodies throughout Britain. Of more consequence for the future, however, was its liaison with Opposition politicians, including Charles Jenkinson and John Robinson, both defectors from North in favor of the rising political star, William Pitt, who was woefully short of supporters but who enjoyed one priceless asset which North had lost and Fox had never possessed, the goodwill of the king. Henry Dundas was another company ally in Pitt's entourage, a strange one, both in that he opposed Warren Hastings, a company favorite, and because he had used his experience on the secret committee of the House of Commons to shape a bill for the reform of the East India Company. Stalwart company conservatives like Johnstone were placed in a dilemma. To work with the Pittites would pave the way for an act which would curtail company rights. To refuse to work with them would perhaps ensure passage of Fox's bill, which had a similar purpose. What Pitt and his agents, all excellent "men of business" achieved was to persuade the committee of nine that their advent to power would result in a reform which would affect company privileges less than Fox's measure. Johnstone may have felt uncomfortable about having to make a choice but, having made it, was wholehearted in sticking to it. It is no accident that at this time the governor began to compliment Pitt in his speeches in the Commons while lambasting Fox's bill, which would, he declaimed, "destroy the British Constitution."[29]

One of the arguments used by Fox to justify the extremity of his bill was that the East India Company was on the edge of bankruptcy. The directors believed, on the contrary, that return to normal peacetime operations, accompanied by payment of certain government debts and curtailment of tea smuggling, would reveal that the company finances were perfectly healthy.[30] In the meantime there was no denying that John Company was financially embarrassed.

Traditionally, the vast expanses of time and distance characteristic of its trade had forced the company into heavy reliance on credit. To pay for administrative expenses and the purchase of goods for eventual sale in England and elsewhere, local funds in India were customarily obtained in exchange for bills drawn on the company in London. In time of peace the proceeds of sales of East Indian merchandise in England enabled the bills to be met when presented. But the years prior to 1783 had been a time of war. Extraordinary expenditure had been necessary to cope with the French, Hyder Ali, and the Mahrattas, while the trade which would help meet its expenses had been interrupted and diminished by the hostilities. The demands of unpaid bill-holders strengthened Fox's allegations of virtual bankruptcy, and Pitt was as concerned as the company to allay their complaints.

He wrote to Johnstone on November 25 suggesting that the financial credibility of the company would be enhanced if a meeting of its creditors could be organized at which they would declare themselves prepared to wait for payment. In his reply Johnstone pointed out the weaknesses in Pitt's scheme, which could easily backfire. The opposite of the intended purpose would be achieved if a number of bill-holders combined to refuse to give any such declaration. Second, the suggested meeting would be of dubious legality without the assent of the lords of the treasury—which would certainly be withheld while the Fox-North coalition retained power. Johnstone observed that most of the money involved had been furnished by company servants who had benefited from the traditional system and who would probably be content, in exchange for their bills, to receive bonds bearing 5 percent interest.[31]

Such expedients took time, and Fox attempted to move with such speed as to deny his opponents time. The second reading of his India bill passed the Commons on November 27 and the final reading on December 9; on the same day it had its first reading in the Lords. The Upper House was now the only place where Fox's bill could be stopped, for George III would not have been ready blatantly to flout the constitution by refusing his signature to a bill that had received the approval of both the Commons and the Lords.

He was prepared to flout it covertly. The famous action whereby the king let the peers know that he would consider any of them who voted for the India bill his enemy killed not only the legislation but also the Fox-North ministry. George III would not have done it had he not been told by Pitt that he was ready to form a government, an assurance that he might not have received were Pitt not convinced that he had company backing for an India bill of his own. It was probably not a pure coincidence that a member of the company's committee of nine, Atkinson, met secretly with Pitt, Dundas, and Robinson on the eve of Fox's defeat in the Lords.[32]

The services of Atkinson and Johnstone had been appreciated. John Robinson wanted to perpetuate the alliance between the "Old Interest" in the company and Pitt's government and used his talents to gull Laurence Sulivan who, at seventy, was still a force in Leadenhall Street, into helping him. With his aid, at an extraordinary election on January 14, 1784, resulting from the resignations of Fletcher and another Foxite, both of the most cooperative members of the committee of nine, Richard Atkinson and George Johnstone, became directors of the East India Company.[33]

The governor seems to have anticipated the result. An aunt had evidently become concerned that he had not summoned her husband (probably General James Murray) to London to cast his vote in the secret ballot for the new directors at East India House. On the day before the election Johnstone replied courteously and serenely that he hoped he had a stronger sense of duty to an aged uncle than to drag him sixty miles in dead of winter on such an errand.[34]

His confidence that he would be elected did not rest on the voting power of the once famous Johnstone group, for it was much diminished. His brother John was, by 1784, only a minor stockholder, while George himself owned only the bare minimum necessary as a formal qualification for any director, £2,000 worth of stock. Without the combined support of Robinson and Sulivan he could not have been elected, but he knew he had their backing. Undoubtedly part of the understanding implicit in their elevation to the horseshoe table was that the new directors would support an administration plan for Indian reform; which explains why Johnstone voted for Pitt's first India bill. He did so with no great enthusiasm. As he explained to his brother he preferred to regard himself as an enemy of the late administration rather than one of the "friends of the Present ministers."[35] As has been noted, Pitt had foreseen the benefits of consulting the lamb before shearing it and had been wise to conciliate key men in the company before attempting to push through reform legislation not altogether dissimilar from the reforms which his predecessors had failed to make law.[36] As an inveterate, vociferous, and effective opponent of governmental intervention in Indian affairs, Johnstone was, perhaps, the first proprietor that Pitt sought to win over. Johnstone would undoubtedly have spoken in Parliament for Pitt's second, successful, India bill if he had been given the opportunity to do so, but he could not, having been defeated in the general election of March 1784.

He had stood for the Haddington Burghs, the only time in his career when he contested a Scottish constituency, perhaps because he was sentimentally attached to the area; Haddington was near Ballencrieff, Lord Elibank's country estate. Precisely why the Pitt political machine did not nominate him for a safe seat like a crown borough in Cornwall is unknown, although it may be that the state of his health, which was poor at this time, made it uncertain, when electoral strategies were planned, that he would be able to continue a parliamentary career. Whatever his reason for attempting it, Haddington Burghs was a difficult seat to win. His opponent, Francis Charteris, had already represented the constituency for four years, was well entrenched, and thus able to hold it against Johnstone in 1784.

It was in an uncharacteristically languid manner that the governor wrote to his brother William, asking him to present a petition to the Commons contesting the Haddington result. Whatever its outcome, he wrote, he did not expect to be seated, although he was confident that any investigation would cause Charteris to be ousted. His own preference, he alleged, was to get clear of the whole business, provided that he could be compensated for the £287 which the election had cost him, so that the money could be distributed among those who had supported him. He was even prepared to drop the petition if Charteris would agree to pay half of his election expenses, but only if Henry Dundas approved the arrangement and would see to the disbursements among his supporters,[37] a significant reservation indicating that his choice of a "difficult" borough had not resulted from a break with the Pitt political organization.

Further proof is that Pitt contemplated sending Johnstone to Lisbon as the British minister to Portugal in September 1784. He may have favored Johnstone's promotion as a means of translating a turbulent and unpredictable ally far from centers of political action. Pitt's need for Johnstone had been much reduced by his sweeping victory in the general election of March. For his part Johnstone would have welcomed the Portuguese posting for the sake of his health, his pocket, and his wife. But it was not to be. The foreign secretary, the young marquess of Camarthen, objected most strongly to the proposed appointment, whereupon Pitt seems to have abandoned it.[38]

His diplomatic aspirations dashed, Johnstone sought to get back into Parliament by standing for Ilchester in Somerset in February 1785. In this by-election the governor had the backing of a powerful local figure, Samuel Smith, who was related to the Lockyer family, which traditionally controlled the borough. Johnstone had probably made Smith's acquaintance in East India House, where he was a fellow director. The governor believed that he had a genuine majority of thirty in the balloting, but he was thwarted by a "most baneful iniquitous" returning officer who enfranchised a number of voters "unknown to the Antient Constitution of Ilchester," all of whom voted against Johnstone.[39] William Pulteney and Smith helped him present a successful petition against the result, and Johnstone was seated for Ilchester, but not until February 1786. A year later his health compelled him to resign in the conventional way by applying for the Chiltern Hundreds.

Meanwhile he had been active in East India Company affairs in which his career reached its culmination when he was elected to the directorate. By 1784 the position of a director was both powerful and more permanent than it had been in the days of the bouts between Sulivan and Clive. Following North's Regulating Act of 1773, election to the Court of Directors was formally for four years; in practice it usually meant tenure for life. Pitt's India Act, on the other hand, which became law in July 1784, was designed to repair the flaws observed in Fox's India bill, of which the chief criticism had been that company patronage would be indirectly distributed by the government. Pitt therefore had thought it wise to let company appointments remain a directorial responsibility. In one important respect, therefore, Johnstone possessed power which could be compared only with that of a governmental minister. Once in this position for which he had served such a long apprenticeship, however, Johnstone fell out with his colleagues. In a private letter to Henry Dundas at the beginning of 1785, Richard Atkinson gave an acidulous commentary on Johnstone's performance as a director:

> Whether we are still to have every measure blasted by him is not for me to determine. He has already done irreparable damage in the military appointments. . . . unless he can be publicly placed in some situation inconsistent with his continuance in the direction, before the negotiations herein pointed out are set on foot, they cannot in my opinion fail of being abortive.

Initially it had appeared to Atkinson that Johnstone's main fault had been adherence to Sulivan, with whom, after a temporary alliance against the Foxites, the supporters of Pitt had quarreled, denying him the chairmanship of the East India Company which he sought. Subsequently Johnstone broke with him too: "It would be a great point with Sulivan," wrote Atkinson, "to get clear of Johnstone with whom he has no cordiality, and he sees the impossibility of any place at a Board where Johnstone is a member."[40]

Despite Atkinson's comments, there was one disastrous military appointment, at least, which Johnstone avoided. Benedict Arnold, still only forty-three and without an outlet for his considerable military talents, wrote to Johnstone seeking an appointment in the army of the East India Company. By implication he likened his own thoughts on the American Revolution to the director's. When its object had been redress of grievances he had supported it, but when the object of the revolutionaries became separation from Great Britain he had repudiated it. The language of Johnstone's reply was kind. It was hardly possible, he wrote, to regard Arnold's past conduct with a higher degree of admiration than he did. However, although Johnstone was satisfied with the purity of his motives, "the generality do not think so," and while that was the case no power in Britain could suddenly place Arnold in the position he sought. "I can by no means engage to take the lead in proposing it." After this rebuff Arnold seems to have dropped the matter and channeled his ambitions toward commerce.[41]

In his later years Johnstone was increasingly troubled by ill health. In 1778 he complained of giddiness, aggravated by bloodletting and a meager diet. In the following year he referred to recent illness to explain absence from the House of Commons. In 1781 a pattern of affliction and remission was discernible, as the troubles brought on by his hardened throat gland abated on his return from the Cape. He seems to have been suffering again in 1782 but rejected his brother's suggestions of medicine and preferred to trust in exercise and diet. He had a doctor attend him, but only to quiet "Miss" (either his wife or her sister Leonora); sooner than incur family disapproval by refusing medical care he would eat ratsbane.[42]

Johnstone's health began to deteriorate rapidly in 1785, although he persisted in distrusting physic: "The natural elements are best for the natural health, altho the Wheel of Life may require a touch one way & the other now and then." On June 24 he gave poor health as his reason for not calling on Warren Hastings, a visit he would certainly have managed if it had been physically possible. By October he was convinced that death was imminent. From his sickbed he wrote bitterly of Robinson, Sulivan, and above all of Henry Dundas, who was "now Lord Paramount of East India affairs, with a sway more absolute tho less Noble because not avowed, than Ch. Fox on his Triumphal Elephant."[43]

The governor rallied but was still very weak. On medical advice he went to Malvern to take the waters in November. He benefited by a remission of his illness to such an extent that in the following month his brother complained that he was "not very governable, and has over-fatigued himself with exercise beyond his strength. . . . He has been on horseback two days at the top of the highest mountain. . . . He has had no pain till last night but he eats enough to give a man in health a fever."[44]

Although information about his symptoms is fragmentary, Johnstone was possibly suffering from Hodgkin's disease, a progressive enlargement of the lymphatic glands accompanied by anemia, which, even now, is a fatal malady, although the afflicted usually survives for a few years after contracting it and enjoys periodic remissions from its ill effects.[45]

Johnstone did not delude himself with false hopes of recovery. In January 1786 he wrote to John Wilkes asking for repayment of old debts because of the state of his health. Trips to London from Taplow in Buckinghamshire, where he had maintained a cottage since his marriage, were now a great strain. He did not attempt to speak in Parliament—his affliction had affected his ability to articulate words. In August he returned to Malvern. For the winter, in company with his wife and their son, he adjourned to Clifton, near Bristol, attended by several physicians, brooding on the progress of his legal battle with Sutton, and writing codicils to his will. He made provision for all of his children and remembered his old friends John Home, Sir James Lowther, Adam Ferguson, Rodham Home, and John Irving.[46] For his wife he wanted his executors to create a trust fund from the sale of his London property from which she would receive £500 a year. Such an income was not generous for a widow with social pretensions, but the young and handsome Charlotte remarried, again to a naval officer, Charles Edmund Nugent, who ultimately rose to be the senior admiral of the Royal Navy. They had one child, Georgina-Charlotte.[47] Johnstone hoped that there would be enough left over to provide £200 a year for his only legitimate son, John Lowther Johnstone, who, he specified, should remain with his mother until the end of his sixth year, after which he was to be educated in Scotland. Finally, he desired that his body should be buried in his native village in Dumfriesshire, carried there by six paupers, each of whom was to receive a grey suit and two guineas. After his funeral he wanted ten guineas to be spent on drink for the mourners.[48]

Johnstone's last days were spent at the Hot Wells at Bristol, where he died on May 24, 1787.[49]

9. Conclusion

George Johnstone has been described as "an enigmatical character."[1] The purpose of this biographical study has been partly to assess the significance of his splintered career but also in part to decipher the enigma.

Although many questions still remain unanswered, the recurring patterns discernible in his varied activities give the clue to some aspects of his complex personality. They suggest that, although intelligent, he was not so much a cerebral as an emotional being, a man of passions in the Age of Reason. Examples of pride, courage, anger, and affection abound in Johnstone's life, but ambition, developed to the point where it is not too strong to describe it as a passion, was salient: ambition for money, place, and prestige. Horace Walpole epitomized the man when he called Johnstone one who went "upon the highway of fortune."[2]

Considering the strength of his ambition, Johnstone must have been disappointed at his life's achievements. He had been a governor, it is true, but of a lesser colony and had been soon recalled. He had been a commodore in the navy, but not an admiral. In diplomacy success had evaded him. In politics he had served in no administration. In the East India Company he had failed to ward off that governmental intervention against which he had fought for years. Above all he died possessed of only moderate means.

Yet, considering the disadvantages under which he labored, the wonder is not that he achieved so little but that he achieved so much. He came from a good but unimportant family. He had to educate himself; unlike so many of his colleagues, he lacked the political advantages of friendships formed in the halls of Eton, Trinity College, or Leiden. He lacked wealth too, for although he acquired considerable sums from prizes and from his naval and diplomatic appointments, he also lost much through litigation and the confiscation of his land in West Florida and Grenada, while as the father of six children he had many commitments. A frugal life-style was always difficult for Johnstone, since one of his brothers had married the richest heiress in England and another was a nabob. His comparative poverty may have tempted him into decisions which were politically unwise. Had he possessed a private fortune in 1779, for example, he might well have held out for a post in the administration instead of accepting command of the *Romney.* His connections, too, so very important a ladder for any ambitious man in the eighteenth century, were second or third rate when he was young, with the exception of Bute, who was for a very short time the weightiest subject in Britain. In later years, it is true, his circle of influential friends was such that he was safe from the inconveniences which might befall the friendless, and to take a case in point, he was not court-martialed, as he might and perhaps should have been, for failing to attack Suffren. Finally, to conclude this list of hindrances to Johnstone's ambition, there was his nationality. The anti-Semitism of eighteenth-century

England was prejudice against Scots and was often present when not avowed.

It was because Johnstone was fiercely ambitious that he was prepared to put his undoubted courage, proven by his gallant behavior at Port Louis and Saldanha, at the service of others. There seems little doubt that in fighting Germain he risked his life to serve his patron Lowther, although he probably hoped to acquire éclat for himself as well. Other duels or affairs, as with Captain Crookshanks or Lieutenant Governor Browne, he would certainly have regarded as undertaken in defense of his honor, although they more truly bear testimony to the deep-seated anger of which he was capable when thwarted. As Wraxall said, he was "an implacable enemy." When he was an officer of the crown, Johnstone's animosity often expressed itself in dismissals or courts-martial, a pattern evident when he was lieutenant on the *Tryal,* abundantly repeated in Florida, and renewed on the voyage to the Cape. It has been noted how the special anger reserved for former associates persuaded him to urge the extermination of the Creeks in 1766 and a war of desolation against the Americans in 1778. In a system where he might have exercised absolute power he would have been a very dangerous man. Nevertheless, great animosity was only one side of a medal which had great amity on the other.

All the same, the fact that Johnstone enjoyed lifelong personal friendships with certain individuals should not obscure the mercurial nature of his political friendships. Whether in East India House or St. Stephen's chapel, he formed and broke alliances with different groups with great facility and purely for political advantage. This was common practice in the eighteenth century. Where he was slightly, although not excessively, unusual was in the readiness with which he abandoned oft-proclaimed principles for political reasons. In American affairs he moved from support for the Stamp Act through denunciation of all taxation of Americans to advocacy of a war of fire and sword against them; in East Indian affairs from denial of the right of Parliament to pass laws even remotely affecting John Company to support of Pitt's India bill, which set up a board to control it. This fluidity implies that Johnstone was prepared to subordinate his convictions to his ambition or that his convictions changed remarkably as he matured, or most likely, that he had no deep-seated convictions. Whatever he may have said in Opposition, as Walpole phrased it, "he never lost sight of the promised land."[3]

Nevertheless, he could assume an excellent pretense of deeply felt belief. In modern times when adherence or otherwise to the party line is the most significant feature of a parliamentary speech, it is easy to forget how much more important in the eighteenth century than now was oratorical prowess. Johnstone was a synthetic Cicero and was not esteemed for beautifully shaped, intellectually satisfying speeches, but his rhetoric was effective.

Like a cavalry charge or a cannonade, it was less finesse than force that counted. Whether his arguments were sound or false, his own feelings sincere or mock, he undoubtedly had the gift, as Wraxall put it, of "powerfully affecting his hearers."[4] In a later period of more popular politics Johnstone's talent for mob oratory might have made him more formidable than he was in the eighteenth century when his chief audience had to be the House of Commons. It is significant that Johnstone was, on balance, more effective in the Court of Proprietors, where his listeners would be less sophisticated, than he was in Parliament. Yet even there he was respected because, better in attack than defense, he could effectively wound and intimidate. He could always find allies because nobody wanted him as an enemy. Charles Townshend likened him to an ape: "If I'se hold him, he will bite you; if you hold him, he will bite me."[5] It was a parliamentary version of a one-man protection racket. This partially explains why he was eventually and at different times on cordial terms with North and Rockingham, Clive and Sulivan, Richmond and Portland, Fox and Sandwich.

Another factor is that, although at times choleric and vindictive, he could also, as Thomas Pasley wrote, "be mighty civil."[6] His letters to those whose favor he craved were charming if fulsome. The best testimony to his considerable social expertise was the fact that although he broke politically with him, he remained on good personal terms with Sir James Lowther all his life, a feat few men achieved. Wherever he went he attracted adherents and also, unfortunately for him, opponents. His impact was divisive; the result was that he was much more effective in opposition than in power. Nevertheless, Johnstone's ambition drove him to pursue responsibility in his career—or careers—for, although they occasionally impinged on one another, Johnstone had five careers: in the navy, in colonial government, in diplomacy, in Parliament, and in East India House. A final judgment is difficult because, in some cases, his ends were negative, his intention to spoil.

His most positive achievements, though far short of his hopes, were as governor of West Florida. Despite incredibly poor relations with the soldiers in his province, he negotiated ably with the Indians, kept order among a lawless pioneer population, established the forms of civil government, and laid the basis for an expanding economy. It was with some justice that he was called Governor Johnstone for the rest of his life.

His naval career fell into two parts, the first positive, the second, in the end, negative. In the earlier phase he rose from midshipman to captain and showed courage, initiative, and competence to manage a sloop in time of war as well as an ability successfully to operate the patronage system to his own benefit in spite of a tendency to insubordination. It was on the basis of this generally creditable but by no means extraordinary performance that he embarked on the second phase of his naval career during the American war. Among the Channel Islands and off the coast of Portugal in command of a small squadron with limited aims he again served with credit, losing no ships of his own but capturing several of the enemy's, safely escorting valuable convoys through dangerous waters, and all the while supplying the Admiralty with good intelligence. Critics of his final naval appointment have usually ignored this earlier period as a commodore in which Johnstone did his duty efficiently. It was when he was entrusted with the larger responsibility of capturing the Cape of Good Hope that he revealed inadequacy as a naval leader. He lacked the ability to unify a large command; it was symbolic that he preferred to fly his commodore's pendant from a mere 50-gun ship, rather than a ship of the line. Disheartened by division among his subordinates, he passed up a chance to destroy the enemy and showed the pettiness of his strategic vision by treating too lightly the French threat to his fleet and to the Cape of Good Hope. The results were not disastrous. It is true that the Cape (which never had been British) did not become so for another fourteen years, but India, for which alone the Cape was important, was not lost. Although the pundits sneered, as far as his sailors and the British public were concerned, Johnstone more than made up for his failure to take the Cape by his skillfully managed coup in Saldanha Bay.

Accidents of time and place are very important in the careers of men who live by war. How high would Napoleon have risen if he had been born in 1739 instead of 1769? It was Johnstone's fate to possess many of the talents necessary for success as a naval officer but, at several critical times in his life, to have no opportunity to use them. His brave behavior at Port Louis might have been the prelude to an early command had it not occurred at the tail end of the War of the Austrian Succession. Another war was all but played out when he finally obtained his post captaincy in 1762. During the following decade and a half Johnstone was probably at the height of his powers, but could not employ them in pursuit of his chosen profession. By the time that he entered the navy again, he was not old but was already in the grip of a fatal disease. The errors of judgment to which it made him prone probably contributed to his fumbling the best opportunity of his naval career, when he encountered Suffren in 1781.

In Parliament he was conservative on East Indian questions although, until 1778, among the avant-garde on American problems in that he supported colonists' rights. He was certainly influential, not simply because of his rhetorical skill but also because he was well informed, particularly on India—but how influential is impossible to measure. He was one of the most formidable Opposition politicians in the 1770s, of sufficient weight for North to buy him off. His imperial theories were practical rather than theoretical and had some merit; they were not necessarily vitiated by the conversion of their author into a hawk of the crudest kind after 1778, although his volte-face certainly did little to hasten their acceptance, and must disqualify him from the title conferred on him recently as one of the "transatlantic heroes of the Revolution."[7]

His first diplomatic venture, in that same year, 1778, was a fiasco. He misjudged American opinion, and his unorthodox diplomatic approaches failed as dismally as the conventional ones of his colleagues Carlisle and Eden. His shady overtures were not merely rejected but publicized. For the history of the world Johnstone's diplomatic gaucherie and the Carlisle commission as a whole had no significance. They never had the slightest chance of success. For Johnstone's personal career his experiences on the peace commission were highly significant in that they helped to propel him from the Opposition into North's camp. If his dabbling in Portugal was not merely a cover for intelligence work, it was certainly not a serious diplomatic venture and was of small importance.

His later parliamentary career was much concerned with India. He lacked the political weight which he had enjoyed in the 1770s but no doubt had an effect both in Parliament and in the East India Company's General Court of Proprietors in slowing down attempts by the government to reform the company. In many ways, particularly if Johnstone's main importance is seen as a "spoiler," his career in the East India Company, in which he was active from 1763 until 1786, is the main success of his many-faceted life. He helped scotch the company's attempt to punish his brother for exploiting Indians. He assisted in the destruction of Clive's prestige. For his contribution in helping to thwart the most radical of the various India bills, he was rewarded with a company directorship for the last three years of his life.

One final aspect of George Johnstone deserves mention in this assessment. It is his conviction that he was fundamentally honest.

> I always distinguish [he wrote toward the end of his life] the Crimes of the heart from those of the Passions, forgiving to the last, but desiring a total seperation of all intercourse with the other Class of Mortals or as the Scotch call them children of the Devil.[8]

Johnstone would probably have admitted that he was sometimes led astray by passions, but being a self-righteous type of man, would not have ranked himself with the devil's children. No commentator should be as quick as Johnstone probably was to dismiss lightly the effect of his own errant passions. At times they carried him to deeds of daring. At others, during his governorship and the American war, they might, if unchecked, have caused Johnstone to be remembered for massacres rather than duels. His career demonstrated how the eighteenth-century system, connection-ridden racket that it was, enabled a man to rise to heights where he had no business to be. It showed, too, that there was in the system, biased against extremity as it also was, the means to prevent such a man from staying too high too long, or from doing irreparable damage.

Notes

Preface

[1]*Dictionary of National Biography,* 4th ed. (cited hereafter as *DNB*), s.v. Johnstone, George.

[2]Lord Loughborough to John Robinson, September 8, 1780, Marquess of Abergavenny, *Abergavenny MSS,* p. 36 (cited hereafter as *Abergavenny MSS*).

[3]Dunbar Rowland, *Mississippi Provincial Archives, 1763–1766: English Dominion,* (cited hereafter as *MPAED*).

[4]Johnstone to Pulteney, n.d., Pulteney Papers, no. 467, Huntington Library, San Marino, Calif.

Chapter 1

[1]John Burke, *History of the Commoners of Great Britain and Ireland,* 2:302, and James Ralfe, *The Naval Biography of Great Britain,* 1:364.

[2]Sir James Johnstone to Professor Charles Mackie, October 18, November 23, 1742, Laing MSS, La. II 91, Edinburgh University Library, Edinburgh.

[3]William Cobbett, *The Parliamentary History of England from the Norman Conquest in 1066 to the Year 1803,* 20:343.

[4]Adm. 107/4, Public Record Office, London. It was common, if illegal, for boys to have their names entered on ships' books without actually serving (see J. C. Beaglehole, *The Life of Captain James Cook,* p. 141) and it is possible that Johnstone "earned time" for a year in this way. All Admiralty documents are from the Public Record Office, London (abbreviated hereafter to P.R.O.), unless otherwise stated.

[5]George Murray (1706–85) entered the Royal Navy in 1721, was promoted to captain in 1740, and sailed with Anson but returned with the *Pearl* after reaching Cape Horn (Lord Anson, *Lord Anson's Voyage Round the World 1740–1744,* pp. 52, 92). Murray became a rear admiral in 1756, and on his brother's death in 1778, he became the sixth Lord Elibank.

[6]*Town and Country Magazine* 13 (Oct. 1781):513. The biographical sketch of Johnstone in the notorious "Tête à Tête" series in *Town and Country Magazine* is the only one apparently attempted in the eighteenth century. It is not as valuable as it might have been, since its aim was purely laudatory. Its probable author was Charles Caraccioli, an enemy of Clive who would have been uncritical of Johnstone because he, too, opposed Clive. Horace Bleakley, "'Tête à Tête' Portraits in 'The Town and Country Magazine,'" pp. 241-2.

[7]Ralfe, *Naval Biography,* 1:364.

[8]*DNB,* s.v. Johnstone, George.

[9]Adm/L/C 39, National Maritime Museum, Greenwich.

[10]*London Gazette,* May 3, 1748.

[11]Johnstone to a "lady of rank," November 14, 1751, Laing MSS, La. II. 73/64.

[12]The author of the sketch of Johnstone in *Town and Country Magazine* 13 (Oct. 1781):513–6 suggested that this course in self-education took place in 1762. More plausibly it began much earlier; Johnstone had more leisure after 1749 than in the period preceding his governorship of West Florida.

[13]Johnstone to William Johnstone Pulteney, Feb. 18, 1761, Pulteney Papers, no. 453.

[14]James Boswell, *Boswell for the Defence, 1769–1774*, p. 89.

[15]John Ramsay, *Scotland and Scotsmen in the Eighteenth Century, 1:318*–20.

[16]Johnstone to an unnamed lady, n.d., Laing MSS, La. II. 73. The lady referred to as Miss Pratville may be a Miss Pratveal who married Sir Charles Asgill, a future lord mayor of London, in 1755. See *Gentleman's Magazine* 25 (Dec. 1755):571.

[17]*Town and Country Magazine* 13 (Oct. 1781):514.

[18]Cf. Peregrine Pickle, who amused himself "with little intrigues, which, in the opinion of a man of pleasure, do not affect his fidelity to the acknowledged sovereign of his soul," Tobias Smollett, *Peregrine Pickle,* p. 166.

[19]A document of November 10, 1753, whereby one Ann Ferguson conferred a power of attorney on Johnstone; Laing MSS, La. II. 73.

[20]Adm/L/B 89, National Maritime Museum, and Adm. 1/511.

[21]Adm. 1/5296, pt. 1.

[22]Adm. 12/22.

[23]Arthur Forrest to John Cleveland, June 18, 1758. Original Letters Collected by William Upcott of the London Institution, "Naval Characters," vol. 2, 1718–1756, National Maritime Museum, Greenwich, England (cited hereafter as Upcott Collection). I am very grateful to Dr. Robert R. Rea of Auburn University for detailed notes relating to Johnstone from this little-known manuscript collection.

[24]Robert Beatson, *Naval and Military Memoirs of Great Britain from 1729 to 1783*, 2:42–47.

[25]Forrest to Cleveland, June 18, 1758, Upcott Collection.

[26]Johnstone to Forrest, June 12, 1758, ibid.

[27]Cleveland to Forrest, August 28, 1758, ibid.

[28]Forrest to Cleveland, June 18, 1758, ibid.

[29]Sir Gilbert Elliott to James Johnstone, November 23, 1759, Laing MSS, La. II. 73/72.

[30]Adm/L/T 217, National Maritime Museum.

[31]Fragmentary court-martial articles in rough draft in Johnstone's hand for the trial of Cookson, as well as the letter from James Douglas to Johnstone of January 6, 1759, which refers to press reports of the forthcoming trial, may be found in Laing MSS, La. II. 73. The court-martial proceedings against the purser are in Adm. 1/5298.

[32]Lady Johnstone to Johnstone, January 1, 1759, Laing MSS, La. II. 73/71.

[33]David Hume to Lord Elibank, April 2, 1759, in E. C. Mossner, "New Hume Letters to Lord Elibank, 1748–1776," p. 449.

[34]Guildford to Johnstone, September 3, 1759, MS 1:580, no. 391, f. 104, National Library of Scotland, Edinburgh.

[35]Elliot to James Johnstone, November 23, 1759, Laing MSS, La. II. 73/72. Sir Gilbert Elliot (1722–77) was a lawyer, statesman, philosopher, and poet. He became M.P. for Selkirkshire in 1753, a member of the Admiralty board in 1756 and of the treasury board in 1761. In 1762 he

became treasurer of the chamber and served as treasurer of the navy from 1770 until his death. In 1762 he helped to found the Poker Club, to which at least three of Johnstone's relatives belonged.

[36]Johnstone to Cleveland, March 19, 1760, Adm. 1/1985.

[37]Johnstone to Pulteney, October 1, 2, 30, 1759, Pulteney Papers, nos. 461, 450, 451.

[38]Ralfe, *Naval Biography,* 1:364.

[39]Johnstone to Admiralty, March 19, March 26, May 25, and June 22, 1760, Adm. 1/1985. See also, for the *Hornet*'s log, Adm. 51/458, pt. 5.

[40]Johnstone to Admiralty, October 6, 1760, Adm. 1/1985.

[41]I am grateful to Dr. Robert R. Rea of Auburn University for notes on the log of the *Hornet* (Adm. 51/458, pt. 5) as well as on the court-martial proceedings, which may be found in Adm. 1/5299, pt. 4.

[42]Johnstone to Admiralty, January 8, 1761, Adm. 1/1985. A snow was a small briglike sailing vessel with supplementary trysail mast.

[43]A brigantine was a two-masted vessel with squaresailed foremast and fore-and-aft mainmast.

[44]Johnstone to William Johnstone Pulteney, Lisbon, February 18, 1761, Pulteney Papers, no. 453.

[45]William C. Atkinson, *A History of Spain and Portugal,* pp. *230, 243–7.*

[46]Ibid., pp. 231–2.

[47]Joseph Baretti, *A Journey from London to Genoa through England, Portugal, Spain, and France,* pp. 128, 187-92.

[48]Johnstone to Pulteney, February 18, 1761, Pulteney Papers, no. 453.

[49]In his attempt to make a classical allusion, Johnstone appears to have made a slip. In imperial Rome the gates of the temple of Janus on the Janiculum were kept open in time of war and closed in time of peace.

[50]Johnstone to Pulteney, Dover, October 2, 1759; Lisbon, February 18, 1761, August 9, 1761, Pulteney Papers, nos. 450, 453, 454.

[51]This discussion of post captaincy is based on Michael Lewis, *A Social History of the Navy, 1793–1815,* pp. 186–9, 318.

[52]Johnstone to Admiralty, January 29 and November 7, 1761, Adm. 1/1985.

[53]Ralfe, *Naval Biography,* 1:365.

[54]Johnstone to Pulteney, August 9, 1761, Pulteney Papers, no. 454.

[55]Rodney to Mickle, May 16, 1788, in Catherine L. Johnstone, *Supplement to History of the Johnstones,* p. 49.

[56]C. R. Boxer, *The Portuguese Seaborne Empire, 1415–1825,* p. 167. Statistics may be found in H. E. S. Fisher, "Anglo-Portuguese Trade 1700–50," p. 221.

[57]Johnstone to Admiralty, May 19, 1762, Adm. 1/1985.

[58]Adm. 51/458, pt. 5.

[59]Johnstone to Admiralty, August 23 and October 8, 1762, Adm. 1/1985. Although not referred to as a relative, this James Johnstone was probably George's nephew, who was subsequently provost marshal in West Florida (*MPAED*, 1:300), and whom Johnstone remembered in his will, Prob. 11/1154, P.R.O., London. Johnstone's relationship to Crawford remains obscure, although a connection undoubtedly existed, and Johnstone helped the boy progress in the navy: see Henry Crawford to Johnstone, February 6, 1763, and Gilbert Elliot to Johnstone, July 21, 1763, in Laing MSS, La. II. 73/87.

[60]Johnstone to Admiralty, November 8 and December 7, 1762, Adm. 1/1985.

[61]Ralfe, *Naval Biography*, 1:365.

[62]The feigned letter from the Pretender was written for the *North Briton* of February 19, 1763, and is reproduced in its entirety in *Scots Magazine* 25 (Feb. 1763):69–72. John Ramsay implied (*Scotland and Scotsmen*, 1:322) that there would have been remonstrances against his appointment by peers even without the Wilkes article.

[63]Mossner, "New Hume Letters," pp. 435–6.

[64]Alexander Carlyle, *Autobiography of Alexander Carlyle*, p. 409.

[65]Henry Mackenzie, *An Account of the Life and Writings of John Home, Esq.*, pp. 32–51.

[66]James Boswell, *Boswell in Search of a Wife, 1766–1769*, p. 286.

[67]James Boswell, *Boswell's London Journal, 1762–1763*, pp. 123, 125, 237, 244.

[68]Carlyle, *Autobiography*, p. 409.

[69]Prob. 11/1154. There is no evidence to support Sir Julian Corbett's claim that Johnstone received his governorship for warning Rodney of Spanish entry into the Seven Years War. Sir Julian Corbett, *England in the Seven Years War*, 2:235.

[70]Johnstone to Bute, June 16, 1763, Charles Jenkinson, *Jenkinson Papers, 1760–1766*, p. 157.

[71]Egremont to the lords of trade, July 14, 1763, C.O. 5/65, f. 205, P.R.O., London.

[72]Home to Bute, August 27, 1763, and Elibank to Bute, October 22, 1763, letters 160 and 192 in Bute Correspondence, Glamorgan Central Library, Cardiff, Wales.

[73]Wilkes to Earl Temple, October 18, 1763, in George Grenville, *The Grenville Papers*, 2:137. See also *Gentleman's Magazine* 33 (Oct. 1763):516; *An Appeal to the Public in Behalf of George Johnstone, Esq., Governor of West Florida; Monthly Review* 29 (Nov. 1763):391–2; *London Magazine* 33 (Oct. 1763):560; and (for the barber variant) *Scots Magazine* 25 (Nov. 1763):626. I am indebted to Dr. Robert R. Rea of Auburn University for some of these references.

[74]*Town and Country Magazine* 13 (Oct. 1781):513.

[75]Johnstone was delighted to accept when Wilkes invited him to dinner on January 11, 1776, and in 1786, when Johnstone knew that he was dying, he wrote to Wilkes in cordial terms asking for the repayment of loans apparently made repeatedly over a long period. Add. MSS, 30872, f. 1, and 30873, f. 4, British Museum (British Library), London.

[76]Both may be found in the Miscellaneous MSS Collection, Library of Congress, Washington, D.C., but are also reproduced in James A. Padgett, "Commission, Orders, and Instructions to George Johnstone, British Governor of West Florida, 1763–1767," pp. 1021–68.

[77]*Town and Country Magazine* 13 (Oct. 1781):513.

[78]For this information and similar facts concerning sales and purchases of East India stock by Johnstone and his circle cited elsewhere in this work I am indebted to Mr. Ian Baxter of the India Office Library and Records, London, who kindly made many transcriptions from the ledgers of the East India Company.

[79]Walpole to Sir Horace Mann, October 29, 1767, Horace Walpole, *Correspondence of Horace Walpole,* 12:560.

[80]James M. Holzman, *The Nabobs in England,* p. 148; Catherine L. Johnstone, *History of the Johnstones, 1191–1909,* p. 182; *Scots Magazine* 35 (Mar. 1773):165.

[81]Johnstone, *History of the Johnstones,* p. 179.

[82]Holzman, *Nabobs in England,* pp. 10, 148; S. C. Hill, *Bengal in 1756–7,* 1:70 and 3:75.

[83]This description of the situation and its effects is based on Keith Feiling, *Warren Hastings,* pp. 10–53.

[84]Holzman, *Nabobs in England,* p. 10.

[85]William Bolts was a Dutch adventurer. Between the time that he entered the service of the East India Company in 1760, and the year 1766, when Bolts decided that it would be more profitable to trade as a merchant outside the company's jurisdiction, he accumulated £90,000. Feiling, *Warren Hastings,* p. 45, and Abdul Majed Khan, *The Transition in Bengal, 1756–1775,* p. 140. For a comprehensive study of Bolts's activities, see N. L. Hallward, *William Bolts.*

[86]Sir Lewis B. Namier and John Brooke, *The House of Commons, 1754–1790,* 2:687. Hallward, *William Bolts,* pp. 5–8, and John Malcolm, *The Life of Robert, Lord Clive,* 2:341.

[87]Lawrence H. Gipson, *The British Empire before the American Revolution,* 9:303–7.

[88]Johnstone to William Johnstone Pulteney, February 2, [1764], Pulteney Papers, no. 468.

[89]*Pennsylvania Gazette,* April 19, 1764.

[90]Alexander Johnstone to [?], February 11, 1764, MS 1:1006, f. 11, National Library of Scotland.

[91]C. H. Philips, *The East India Company, 1784–1834,* p. 3.

[92]General Court minutes for March 12 and May 2, 1764, B/256, ff. 301, 317, India Office Library and Records, London.

[93]*London Magazine* 31 (Mar. 1764):159.

[94]George Johnstone and Lord Elibank, the nuclear members of the Johnstone group, first bought stock in 1763; they were joined by William Johnstone Pulteney in February 1764, Baxter Transcripts, India Office Library and Records, London.

[95]European MSS, G37, boxes 32, 37, India Office Library and Records, London.

[96]*London Magazine* 31 (Mar. 1764):215–6.

[97]Lucy Sutherland, *The East India Company in Eighteenth-Century Politics,* pp. 117–31; General Court minutes for May 2 and 18, 1764, B/256, ff. 317, 332.

[98]Charles Caraccioli, *The Life of Robert, Lord Clive,* 2:182–3; *Scots Magazine* 26 (June 1764):344.

Chapter 2

[1]Gipson, *British Empire,* 9:222, 230, 231.

[2]For a summary of ministerial postwar policy changes, particularly with respect to the trans-Appalachian region, in which West Florida was situated, see Vincent T. Harlow, *The Founding of the Second British Empire, 1763–1793,* 1:162–98.

[3]Cecil Johnson, *British West Florida, 1763–1783,* p. 12.

[4]"Thoughts Concerning Florida," n.d., P.R.O. 30/47/14/3, ff. 88–9, P.R.O., London. See also my "George Johnstone and the 'Thoughts Concerning Florida'—A Case of Lobbying?" pp. 164–76.

[5]Cobbett, *Parl. Hist.,* 23:473.

[6]Johnstone to Halifax, June 11, 1765, *MPAED,* 1:256–7.

[7]Johnstone to Egremont, July 20, 21, 1763, P.R.O. 30/47/14/3, ff. 84, 86.

[8]Johnstone to Pownall, July 27, 1763, C.O. 05/574, ff. 1–4.

[9]Padgett, "Commission," pp. 1034–5.

[10]Johnstone to Pownall, January 29, 1764, C.O. 5/574, f. 7.

[11]*Journal of the Commissioners for Trade and Plantations from January 1764 to December 1767,* pp. 7, 12, 60–1.

[12]Johnstone to Tayler, July 31, 1766, Mississippi Provincial Archives, English Dominion, 2:538, Jackson, Mississippi.

[13]C.O. 5/574, f. 83; Hoggan to Johnstone, January 18, 1760, Laing MSS, La. II. 73/77.

[14]Clinton N. Howard, *The British Development of West Florida, 1763–1767,* pp. 63, 76, 80–1.

[15]Florida Land Register, 1764–1768, C.O. 5/601, p. 222; James Dallas to Johnstone, January 6, 1776, Laing MSS, La. II. 73/123.

[16]Johnstone to Pownall, September 3, 1764, C.O. 5/574, f. 99.

[17]Johnstone to Halifax, August 4, 1764, *MPAED,* 1:152.

[18]Johnstone to Pownall, September 3, 1764, C.O. 5/574, f. 100. The priority he gave to conciliating the Indians was reasonable, in that West Florida would be a miserable province if Indian friendship and land could not be won. As Willsom Forbes put it: "We are informed there is a Governor appointed, but . . . untill the Country is greatly improved, I know nothing he has to Govern," Forbes to [secretary of state?], Pensacola, January 29, 1765, C.O 5/582, f. 190.

[19]Johnstone to Pownall, September 3, October 31, 1764, C.O. 5/574, ff. 100, 120.

[20]Johnstone to Balfour, March 25, 1763, Laing MSS, La. II. 73/86. "Buckara" or "buckra" was a Creole word for white man.

[21]Johnstone to Pownall, September 25, October 31, 1764, C.O. 5/574, ff. 104, 107, 117.

[22]Prévost to secretary at war, September 7, 1763, Forbes, "Report on Pensacola," January 30, 1764, and Farmar to secretary at war, March 2, 1764, *MPAED,* 1:136-7, 112-4, 115.

[23]Newton D. Mereness, ed., *Travels in the American Colonies,* pp. 381–7.

[24]*Scots Magazine* 27 (January 1765):51–2.

[25]The position of naval officer seems to have been always combined with that of register in West Florida.

[26]Johnstone to Halifax, September 14, 1765, *MPAED,* 1:289.

[27]Padgett, p. 1029.

[28]In the letter quoted here (Johnstone to Halifax, September 14, 1765, *MPAED,* 1:289), the relation to whom he refers was probably his nephew James, who subsequently acted as provost marshal. Despite the ambiguous wording, Johnstone's secretary, Primrose Thomson, was not a relative of the governor but a lifelong friend and godfather to his natural son John (Thomson to Johnstone, March 16, 1777, Laing MSS, La. II. 73/135.

[29]Conway to Johnstone, March 13, 1766, *MPAED,* 1:297.

[30]For example, Farmar was annoyed that when the French commandant handed over his forts, cannon had not been left there. Farmar to the secretary of war, January 24, 1764, *MPAED,* 1:10.

[31]For a good summary of this period see Clinton N. Howard, "The Interval of Military Government in West Florida, 1763–4," pp. 18–23.

[32]James Adair, *History of the American Indians,* p. 309.

[33]The role of Farmar rather than of the Pensacola commandants has been emphasized here because, during the period of military government, inhabited Mobile rather than deserted Pensacola was the *de facto* capital of the province.

[34]Neyon de Villiers to d'Abbadie, April 20, 1764, Clarence W. Alvord and Clarence E. Carter, eds., *Illinois Historical Collections,* 10:242. See also Farmar to Wellbore Ellis, January 24, 1764, *MPAED,* 1:17.

[35]Johnstone to the Board of Trade, May 30, 1764, *MPAED,* 1:150.

[36]Johnstone to Pownall, April 1, 1766, *MPAED,* 1:465.

[37]For details of the extent to which disease ravaged army units in West Florida see Robert R. Rea, "Graveyard for Britons."

[38]Halifax to Johnstone, September 8, 1764, *MPAED,* 1:151.

[39]Johnstone claimed that half of the population of Spanish Louisiana would come to settle in West Florida if military protection could be assured them. Johnstone to Halifax, Feb. 19, 1765, *MPAED,* 1:255.

[40]His testiness was evidenced by altercations with John Stuart, whom Farmar called "cavalier" and whose hand he refused to shake (John R. Alden, *John Stuart and the Southern Colonial Frontier,* pp. 196, 199); Stuart had wit and skill enough not to let the enmity harden.

[41]Smollett, *Peregrine Pickle,* p. 162.

[42]Padgett, "Commission," pp. 1026, 1030, 1032.

[43]Captain Robert Mackinnen to Johnstone, November 6, 1764, *MPAED,* 1:163.

[44]Halifax to Johnstone, February 9, 1765, *MPAED,* 1:173.

[45]Gage to David Wedderburn, and Gage to David Simpson, July 31, 1765, *MPAED,* 1:389, 392.

[46]In contrast to Johnstone, John Stuart, the Indian superintendent for the South, whose position with respect to Gage was more awkward, legally, even than the governor's, obtained friendly cooperation from the commander-in-chief. See Alden, *John Stuart*, p. 149, and Howard, *British Development*, p. 23, for a description of how Johnstone used every possible legal pretext to delay Farmar's expedition up the Mississippi for the important task of reassuming control of the Illinois country in the wake of Pontiac's rebellion.

[47]Robert R. Rea, "Outpost of Empire," p. 222, and Gage to Wedderburn, January 27, 1766, *MPAED,* 1:392–395.

[48]For a fuller account, see Johnson, pp. 49–56, and Clarence E. Carter, "The Beginnings of British West Florida," pp. 330–1.

[49]Montfort Browne to Conway, March 27, 1766, *MPAED,* 1:298.

[50]Johnstone to Mackinnen, November 3 and 7, 1764, *MPAED,* 1:159, 165.

[51]Johnstone to Pownall, February 19, 1765, C.O. 5/574, f. 244, and Farmar to Gage, March 11, 1765, Alvord and Carter, *Illinois Historical Collections,* 10:465.

[52]Johnstone to Conway, October 24, 1765, *MPAED,* 1:293.

[53]Johnstone to Gage, June 20, 1765, *MPAED,* 1:385–6.

[54]Deposition of George Johnstone before Chief Justice Clifton, February 1, 1766, *MPAED,* 1:455.

[55]Johnstone to Pownall, August 7, 1766, *MPAED,* 1:319.

[56]Johnstone to Pownall, April 1, 1766, C.O. 5/574, f. 477.

[57]Johnstone to Conway, October 24, 1765, *MPAED,* 1:293.

[58]Peter Force, ed., *American Archives,* 4th series, 1:54–5.

[59]Memorial from several of the inhabitants of West Florida to John Pownall, April 1766, *MPAED,* 1:305.

[60]Johnstone to Pownall, April 1, 1766, *MPAED,* 1:450.

[61]Johnstone to Halifax, June 11, 1765, *MPAED,* 1:257.

[62]The governor never doubted the legality of the Stamp Act. In February 1766, he derided arguments against it as having no "foundation either in experience or common sense." In April when he confessed to misgivings about enforcing it, it was merely because all formalities were incomplete. He would have preferred the stamp money to have been spent in the province where it was collected. Years later when, in 1774, he denigrated the Stamp Act as "unnecessary and dangerous," he did not deny its legality. Johnstone to Board of Trade, Feb. 26, 1766, *MPAED,* 1:417; Johnstone to Pownall, April 1, 1766, in Howard, *British Development,* p. 124; and Force, *American Archives,* 4th series, 1:56.

[63]Johnstone to the secretary of the Board of Trade, April 1, 1766, *MPAED,* 1:462; Caminade to Halifax, February 18 and June 15, 1765, *MPAED,* 1:179, 285; Adair, *History,* pp. 311, 324.

[64]For example, Johnstone to Conway, October 24, 1765, and Johnstone to the secretary of the Board of Trade, January 28, 1766, *MPAED,* 1:293, 345; Johnstone to Boddington, July 19, 1766, Mississippi Provincial Archives, English Dominion, Vol. 2.

[65]Baron de Montesquieu, *The Spirit of Laws,* p. 194.

⁶⁶Johnstone to the secretary of the Board of Trade, January 28, 1766, and Johnstone to Pownall, April 1, 1766, *MPAED,* 1:346, 444.

⁶⁷Johnstone to the secretary of the Board of Trade, January 28, 1766, *MPAED,* 1:346.

⁶⁸Johnstone to Pownall, April 4, 1766, in Howard, *British Development,* p. 126.

⁶⁹A score of malcontents complained of Johnstone to John Pownall in April 1766; one charge was that while other colonists had foreign cargoes seized, the governor allowed the favored Wedderburn to import French wine and brandy with impunity. *MPAED,* 1:304.

⁷⁰Many crimes were committed in West Florida, but many criminals were imprisoned; in January 1766 at least a dozen were in the Pensacola jail for capital offenses. Johnstone to Conway, January 28, 1766; *MPAED,* 1:295.

⁷¹Johnstone to Halifax, June 11, 1765, *MPAED,* 1:256–7.

⁷²A list of these papers may be found in *MPAED,* 1:6–7.

⁷³For a consideration of the trend in the period 1763–75, see Jack Sosin, *The Revolutionary Frontier, 1763–1783,* pp. 20–38.

⁷⁴Apart from Harlow, noted elsewhere, see Clarence W. Alvord, *The Mississippi Valley in British Politics, 1:157*–210.

⁷⁵Farmar's correspondence and papers relating to Indians during the interval of military government may be found in *MPAED,* 1:80–97.

⁷⁶Chevalier Montault de Montbéraut, *Mémoire justificatif,* p.11.

⁷⁷Memorial of George Johnstone to the Board of Trade, May 30, 1764, *MPAED,* 1:150.

⁷⁸The fullest biographical treatment available is in Alden, *John Stuart,* pp. 156–71.

⁷⁹The best summary of the chevalier's life may be found in his *Mémoire,* pp. 15–58.

⁸⁰Ibid., pp. 19, 20, 22, 50.

⁸¹Adair, *History,* p. 306.

⁸²A high moral tone pervades the arguments of Helen L. Shaw in *British Administration of the Southern Indians, 1756–1783,* pp. 25–6) against present giving. In fact, apart from being in the European diplomatic tradition, it was probably an essential lubricant, given Johnstone's weak position, if the machinery of Anglo-Indian relations were to function at all.

⁸³Speeches and documents relating to the Congress are in *MPAED,* 1:184.

⁸⁴*MPAED,* 1:220, 248.

⁸⁵Montbéraut, *Mémoire,* pp. 33-4.

⁸⁶Johnstone and Stuart to Halifax, June 12, 1765, *MPAED,* 1:184.

⁸⁷For proceedings of the congress and text of the resultant treaty, see *MPAED,* 1:188–215.

⁸⁸Johnstone to Conway, June 23, 1766, *MPAED,* 1:513.

⁸⁹Campbell to Lord Adam Gordon, June 14, 1767, Atholl MSS 49 (6):99, Blair Castle, Perthshire. For a discussion of Campbell and Hannay's sojourn among the Creeks see Robin F. A. Fabel and Robert R. Rea, "Lieutenant Thomas Campbell's Sojourn among the Creeks," pp. 97–111.

[90]*MPAED,* 1:199, 205.

[91]Alden, *John Stuart,* p. 206.

[92]Johnstone and Stuart to Halifax, June 12, 1765, *MPAED,* 1:184–8.

[93]Gipson, *British Empire,* 9:222.

[94]Johnstone to Bute, June 12, 1765, letter 143, Bute Correspondence.

[95]Johnstone to Halifax, June 11, 1765, *MPAED,* 1:257.

[96]Sir Jeffrey Amherst's "Distribution of Troops, 1763" and Johnstone to Pownall, February 19, 1765, Alvord and Carter, *Illinois Historical Collections,* 10:9, 438.

[97]D'Abbadie's journal for August, 1764, ibid., 10:195–6; Farmar to Wellbore Ellis, January 24, and April 7, 1764, and Campbell to Johnstone, December 12, 1764, *MPAED,* 1:13, 117, 265–6.

[98]Estimate of the cost of Fort Bute, n.d., C.O. 5/582, f. 489.

[99]Minutes of the meeting and Lindsay's letter to Johnstone of January 2, 1765, may be found in *MPAED,* 1:13, 117, 266–7.

[100]Pownall to Johnstone, October 3, 1765, *MPAED,* 1:270.

[101]Archibald Robertson, *Archibald Robertson,* pp. 12–15.

[102]Johnstone to Robertson, October 1, 1765, and Johnstone to the commander of Fort Bute, October 2, 1765, C.O. 5/574, ff. 917, 909–11.

[103]Johnstone to Lindsay, December 10, 1764 C.O. 5/582, f. 499. The governor overestimated the period each year when the Iberville would be navigable. A contemporary who actually went there observed that the Mississippi did not even begin to rise until the end of April and that as early as July 22, 1766, the Iberville was almost dry (from an anonymous manuscript reproduced in Isabel M. Calder, ed., *Colonial Captivities, Marches, and Journeys,* pp. 232–3). Johnstone was probably misled by the river's remaining unusually high in 1764. It did not begin to recede until August 20. See D'Abbadie's journal, August 1764, Alvord and Carter, *Illinois Historical Collections,* 10:196.

[104]Gage to Shelburne, December 23, 1766, Alvord and Carter, *Illinois Historical Collections,* 11:462.

[105]D'Abbadie to the minister, January 29, 1765, and Gordon's journal entry for October 14, 1766, ibid., 10:425 and 11:303.

[106]Howard, *British Development,* p. 116.

[107]Gipson, *British Empire,* 9:217; Peter J. Hamilton, *Colonial Mobile,* p. 226.

[108]Thomas Hutchins, *An Historical Narrative and Topographical Description of Louisiana and West Florida,* p. xxiv.

[109]Entry in Gordon's journal for August 5, 1763, in Mereness, *Travels,* p. 382.

[110]Johnstone to Pownall, February 19, 1765, T.I. 437, P.R.O., London.

[111]Cecil Johnson, "Pensacola in the British Period," p. 271.

[112]Johnstone to Pownall, Kingston, September 25, and Pensacola, October 31, 1764, *MPAED,* 1:167–71.

113The text of this act of 1763 may be found in C.O. 5/65, f. 185.

114Figures from Howard, *British Development,* p. 43; minutes of the council and of the only assembly of Johnstone's governorship are published in *Louisiana Historical Quarterly* 22 (1939):311–84.

115Howard, *British Development,* pp. 34, 38, 50–101.

116Charles A. Gauld, "A Scottish View of West Florida in 1769," pp. 63, 66.

117Howard, *British Development,* pp. 32–4. Johnstone to Pownall, February 19, 1765, C.O. 5/574, f. 243.

118Johnstone to Pownall, April 2, 1766, C.O. 5/574, f. 960.

119*Scots Magazine* 27 (July 1765):385.

120Ibid. (Feb. 1765):105–106, and 28 (June 1766):323.

121*Scots Magazine* 28 (Jan. 1766):66.

122Ibid. (Feb. 1766):163.

123Ibid. (May 1766):271–2.

124Ibid. (Jan. 1766):50.

125John D. Born, Jr., "Charles Strachan in Mobile," p. 32.

126Johnstone to Board of Trade (?), December 29, 1765, C.O. 5/574, ff. 951–4.

127*Scots Magazine* 28 (Feb. 1766):105.

128Ibid. (June 1766):382.

129Ibid. (Dec. 1766):663.

130Gipson, *British Empire,* 9:249.

131Johnstone to Pownall, February 19, 1765, C.O. 5/574, f. 249.

132Minutes of West Florida council meeting December 13, 1765, C.O. 5/574, f. 947.

133Robert E. Gray, "Elias Durnford, 1739–1794," pp. 21–3.

134Johnstone to Pownall, April 2, 1766, C.O. 5/574, f. 969.

135*Scots Magazine* 29 (Jan. 1767):51.

136Ibid. (Feb. 1767):162.

137*Scots Magazine* 28 (May 1766):272. For the rise and fall of Campbell Town, see J. Barton Starr, "Campbell Town."

138Johnstone to Pownall, April 2, 1766, C.O. 5/574, f. 968.

139Johnstone to Pownall, February 19, 1765, and April 1, 1766, C.O. 5/574, f. 233, and C.O. 5/583, f. 433.

140*Scots Magazine* 28 (Sept. 1766):495; Johnstone to Pownall, February 19, 1765, and April 2, 1766, C.O. 5/574, ff. 233, 960–6.

141*Scots Magazine* 28 (June 1766):381–2.

[142]Calder, ed., *Colonial Captivities,* pp. 228-30.

[143]Gauld, "Scottish View," p. 64.

[144]Gipson, *British Empire,* 9:197.

[145]Aubry to the minister, February 12, 1765, Alvord and Carter, *Illinois Historical Collections,* 10:435.

[146]Namier and Brooke, *House of Commons,* 2:684.

[147]Shaw, *British Administration,* p. 41; Johnson, *British West Florida,* p. 60; Howard, *British Development,* p. 22. Gipson quoted more of the relevant factors (Gipson, *British Empire,* 10:229-30), but even he made too much of Indian relations and omitted other important considerations.

[148]Sutherland, *East India Company,* pp. 120–1.

[149]John Norris, *Shelburne and Reform,* pp. 26, 36, 38.

[150]Dennys De Berdt to Thomas Cushing, September 19, 1766, *Letters of Dennys De Berdt, 1757–1770,* p. 324.

[151]*Journal of the Commissioners for Trade, 1764 to 1767,* pp. 328, 343; Gipson, *British Empire,* 9:228.

[152]Mississippi Provincial Archives, English Dominion, 10:665.

[153]The letter was never actually sent because Chatham, Shelburne's superior, changed his policy.

[154]William Tayler to John Stuart, June 24, 1766, John Stuart to the Board of Trade, July 10, 1766, and Gage to [?], August 30, 1766, in C.O. 5/67, ff. 41, 102, 231.

[155]Johnstone to Stuart [?], May 19, 1766, C.O. 5/67, f. 45.

[156]Johnstone to Conway, June 23, 1766, *MPAED,* 1:511-2.

[157]Johnstone to Stuart, September 30, 1766, C.O. 5/67, f. 423.

[158]Minutes of the Committee of the Council, October 30, 1766, C.O. 5/584, f. 242.

[159]Johnstone to Stuart, September 30, 1766, C.O. 5/67, f. 423.

[160]Barrington's Plan for the West, May 10, 1766, Alvord and Carter, *Illinois Historical Collections,* 11:241.

[161]Shelburne to Chatham, February 17, 1767, P.R.O. 30/8/3, f. 189.

[162]*Pennsylvania Gazette,* March 5, 1767.

[163]Shelburne to Johnstone and Shelburne to Browne, February 19, 1767, Mississippi Provincial Archives, English Dominion, 10:665, 668.

[164]Johnstone to Bute, July 25, 1765, letter 144, Bute Correspondence.

[165]Montfort Browne to Conway, March 27, 1766, *MPAED,* 1:302. Despite the principle hinted at in his letter, Browne, after succeeding to the governorship, lost his post and was shipped back to England for challenging and all but killing a political opponent; see Robert R. Rea, "Pensacola under the British (1763–1781)," p. 66.

[166]Johnstone to Conway, June 23, 1766, *MPAED,* 1:511.

Chapter 3

[1]Sutherland, *East India Company,* pp. 110–1.

[2]Campbell to Johnstone, 1767[?], Laing MSS, 2:509. References to Campbell's friendship with Johnstone in Florida and details of his literary career may be found in Robert R. Rea, "Belles Lettres in British West Florida," pp. 145–9.

[3]*Diwani* was the right of receiving as *diwan,* or finance minister, the revenue of Bengal, Behar, and Orissa.

[4]Sutherland, *East India Company,* pp. 145–6.

[5]Shelburne to Johnstone, September 22, 1766, Mississippi Provincial Archives, English Dominion, 10:665. Evidence is lacking to determine with precision what Johnstone did after his return to England on March 18, 1767 (*Scots Magazine* 29 [Mar. 1767]:162.) It may be presumed that he collaborated with other Johnstones in their destructive tactics in East India House. It would be especially piquant to know exactly how he greeted Shelburne when they met (if they indeed did) and to know how he was persuaded to work in the same cause with him in East Indian affairs.

[6]Sutherland, *East India Company,* pp. 153–73.

[7]General Court minutes for May 6, 1767, B/256–9.

[8]Duke of Grafton, *Autobiography and Political Correspondence of Augustus Henry, Third Duke of Grafton,* pp. 125–6.

[9]*Town and Country Magazine* 13 (Oct. 1781):513–4.

[10]J. S. Watson, ed., *Cicero's Oratory and Orators,* p. 254.

[11]A reference, presumably, to the victories of Major Thomas Adams at Sooty and Oondwa Nullah in 1763, of Major Hector Munro at Buxar in 1764, and to Sir Richard Fletcher's conquest of Oudh in 1765.

[12]George Johnstone, *Speech of Mr. George Johnstone in the General Court of Proprietors of East India Stock upon the Subject of Restitution for Private Losses in the War against Cossim Ali Cawm.*

[13]*Critical Review* 26 (Aug. 1768):147.

[14]John Home to James Oswald, [1767], James Oswald, *Memorials of the Right Hon. James Oswald,* p. 115.

[15]Horace Walpole to Horace Mann, 1761, Earl of Bute, *A Prime Minister and His Son,* p. 29; Alexander Carlyle, *Autobiography,* p. 418; Brian Bonsall, *Sir James Lowther and Cumberland and Westmorland Elections, 1754–1775,* p. v.

[16]Sir Nathaniel W. Wraxall, *Memoirs,* 2:80.

[17]A detailed account of the legal struggle between Lowther and Portland, biased in the duke's favor, may be found in A. S. Turberville, *A History of Welbeck Abbey and Its Owners,* 2:101–35. See also Portland to Dunning, August 6, 1776, Fitzwilliam MSS, Wentworth Woodhouse Muniments, Sheffield City Libraries, Sheffield.

[18]Details of Elliot's career may be found in Namier and Brooke, *House of Commons,* 2:397, and in *DNB,* s.v. Elliot, John. He is not to be confused with the John Elliot who succeeded Johnstone as governor of West Florida.

[19]Richard S. Ferguson, *Cumberland and Westmorland M.P.'s,* pp. 155–7, 423.

[20]Carlyle, *Autobiography,* p. 483.

[21]Ferguson, *Cumberland,* p. 157.

[22]Ibid. pp. 150–1.

[23]Bonsall, *Sir James Lowther,* pp. 99, 105, 107. As a result of Fletcher's petition, Lowther was unseated in December 1768.

[24]Carlyle, *Autobiography,* p. 419.

[25]Sutherland, *East India Company,* pp. 188–90. Dame Lucy Sutherland has stated that George Johnstone stood for election to the Court of Directors in April 1769. His brother John apparently did, but I have not been able to confirm that the governor did so.

[26]Johnstone to William Johnstone Pulteney, January 27, [1768?], Pulteney Papers, no. 457.

[27]Baxter Transcripts.

[28]*Gentleman's Magazine* 39 (Apr. 1769):211.

[29]Sutherland, *East India Company,* p. 189.

[30]For details of the celebrated Douglas case, see James N. M. Maclean, *Reward Is Secondary,* pp. 95–6, 226–7, 377–9. A Johnstone, probably William, had already in 1763 written a pamphlet on the Douglas case in the interest of the Hamilton claimant. See David Hume to Adam Smith, July 27, 1763, in David Hume, *The Letters of David Hume,* 1:40.

[31]*A Letter to the Proprietors of East India Stock* and *Thoughts on Our Acquisitions in the East Indies.* Internal evidence shows that the author of the latter was Johnstone, although it was published anonymously, and that it was written two years before it was published.

[32]*Gentleman's Magazine* 39 (supplement for 1769):634; Namier and Brooke, *House of Commons,* 2:684; Sir John Fortescue, ed., *Correspondence of King George the Third,* 3:128.

[33]J. Steven Watson, *The Reign of George III, 1760–1815,* p. 142.

[34]Cobbett. *Parl. Hist.,* 16:995–7.

[35]Ibid., 16:1328.

[36]Burke to Rockingham, December 18, 1770, Edmund Burke, *The Correspondence of Edmund Burke,* 2:172.

[37]Bonsall, *Sir James Lowther,* pp. 122–32.

[38]The account of the duel is from *Scots Magazine* 32 (Dec. 1770):724–5.

[39]North to the king, December 17, 1770, Fortescue, *George III,* 2:187; Horace Walpole, *Memoirs of the Reign of George III,* 4:229; Burke to Rockingham, December 18, 1770, Burke, *Correspondence,* 2:172.

[40]Loren Reid classed Johnstone with Fox, Burke, Townshend, and Barré as the most significant Opposition speakers in the parliamentary session of 1777–8. Loren Reid, *Charles James Fox,* p. 84.

[41]Cobbett, *Parl. Hist.,* 16:995-7; Namier and Brooke, *House of Commons,* 2:684.

[42]Elibank to William Young, October 29, November 18, 1771, A. C. Murray, *The Five Sons of "Bare Betty,"* pp. 167–70.

[43]The Johnstone group had fanned public indignation. Two works highly critical of Clive, *A History of Hindustan* and *Considerations on Indian Affairs,* had been published in 1768 and 1770. The authors of each, Alexander Dow and William Bolts, were in the Johnstone orbit. Sutherland, *East India Company,* p. 221.

[44]Dame Lucy Sutherland lays part of the blame for this failure on George Johnstone, who, she claims, would oppose any scheme which might, however remotely, endanger his brother John. Sutherland, *East India Company,* p. 218.

[45]Cobbett, *Parl. Hist.,* 17:366–76.

[46]*Town and Country Magazine* 4 (May 1772):240.

[47]Harlow, *Second British Empire,* 2:50–60.

[48]*London Magazine* 41 (Nov. 1772):529–30.

[49]Burke, *Correspondence,* 2:391.

[50]Richmond to Burke, May 27, 1773, ibid., p. 437.

[51]Rockingham to Burke, January 5, 1773, ibid., p. 401n.

[52]Sutherland, *East India Company,* p. 259.

[53]William Pulteney, *Thoughts on the Present State of Affairs with America and the Means of Conciliation,* Appendix 4, pp. 103, 109.

[54]*New York Gazette,* March 22, July 12, 1773.

[55]Sutherland, *East India Company,* pp. 272–5.

[56]Adair was a lawyer and Wilkesite M.P. who should not be confused with James Adair, the Indian trader. Wier was a dissident director of the East India Company.

[57]Richmond to Adair, December 1, 1773; Alison Olson, *The Radical Duke,* pp. 160–1.

[58]Richmond to Rockingham, April 8, 1774, Johnstone to Rockingham, n.d., Fitzwilliam MSS.

[59]Johnstone to Rockingham, May 16, 1776, Fitzwilliam MSS.

[60]Sutherland, *East India Company,* p. 309.

[61]King to North, November 21, 1776, Fortescue, *George III,* 3:404.

[62]Boswell, *London Journal,* p. 322.

[63]Ringers to Johnstone, April 24, 1775, Pigot to Johnstone, February 5, [1775], Laing MSS, La. II. 73. Johnstone to Rockingham, 23rd of [?], 1775, Fitzwilliam MSS.

[64]Sutherland, *East India Company,* pp. 321, 323.

[65]Portland to Rockingham, August 19, 1776, Fitzwilliam MSS.

[66]Horace Walpole, *The Last Journals of Horace Walpole,* 1:424.

[67]Johnstone to Edmund Burke, May 25, June 4, 1775, Burke Correspondence, Wentworth Woodhouse Muniments, Sheffield City Libraries, Sheffield; Bonsall, *Sir James Lowther,* pp. 141-3.

[68]Duke of Rutland, *Rutland MSS,* p. 134 (cited hereafter as *Rutland MSS*).

[69]Cobbett, *Parl. Hist.*, 17:1188–9, 1281, 1391.

[70]The French did in fact attempt to invade Britain in 1779.

[71]Cobbett, *Parl. Hist.*, 18:60–4.

[72]Rockingham to Johnstone, February 17, March 7, and July 10, 1775. These three letters have survived from what was undoubtedly a more numerous correspondence, Laing MSS, 2:73.

[73]Johnstone to Lowther, June 7, 1775, Earl of Lonsdale, *Lonsdale MSS*, p. 135 (cited hereafter as *Lonsdale MSS*).

[74]Cobbett, *Parl. Hist.*, 18:253–4, 301, 744–7, 817–22.

[75]*The Beauties of the British Senate*, 1:106.

[76]Cobbett, *Parl. Hist.*, 18:1240.

[77]Ibid., 19:156–7.

[78]Ibid., 19:252, 332, 520.

[79]Ibid., 18:817, 819, 822; 19:61, 98.

[80]Peter D. G. Thomas, *The House of Commons in the Eighteenth Century*, p. 149.

Chapter 4

[1]Orders to the earl of Carlisle, Lord Viscount Howe, William Eden, and George Johnstone, April 12, 1778, Benjamin F. Stevens, ed., *Facsimiles of Manuscripts in European Arachives Relating to America, 1773–1783*, no. 440.

[2]Charles R. Ritcheson, *British Politics and the American Revolution*, p. 233.

[3]Cobbett, *Parl. Hist.*, 19:533.

[4]Ibid., pp. 65, 541.

[5]Wentworth was a well-traveled stock-jobber from New Hampshire, who had been a member of the council of, and agent for, that colony until the Revolution, when he entered British service.

[6]Wentworth to Eden, Paris, December 17, 1777, Stevens, *Facsimiles*, no. 231; Ritcheson, *British Politics*, p. 237.

[7]Pulteney to Germain, December 6, 9, 1777, Mrs. Stopford-Sackville, *Stopford-Sackville MSS*, 2:81–3 (cited hereafter as *Stopford-Sackville MSS*). These letters were not prompted entirely by the news of Saratoga. Nine months earlier Pulteney had written to Germain offering to find out from a contact in Paris what terms Franklin would consider for a laying down of arms, Pulteney to Germain, March 5, 1777, ibid., 2:59.

[8]Stevens, *Facsimiles*, no. 1787, dated December 19, 1777. Ritcheson's identification of the anonymous letter writer as Pulteney (Ritcheson, *British Politics*, p. 238) is implausible. The author made no attempt to disguise his calligraphy; indeed he ended his letter by hoping that Bancroft would "excuse the omission of my name; as you will readily know it by the handwriting," which writing bears no resemblance to that of Pulteney, an example of which may be seen in *Facsimiles*, no. 1946.

[9]When Wentworth met Franklin on January 6, 1778, the latter "hinted that his opinion in any question would be that of Congress," Wentworth to Eden, January 7, 1778, Stevens, *Facsimiles,* no. 489.

[10]Johnstone to William Johnstone Pulteney, January 8, [1778], Pulteney Papers, no. 465.

[11]Bathurst offered his resignation but North managed, temporarily, to dissuade him. North to Bathurst, February 19, 1778, Earl of Bathurst, *Bathurst Papers,* p. 17 (cited hereafter as *Bathurst Papers*).

[12]The king to North, February 9, 1778, Fortescue, *George III,* 4:36; North to Dartmouth, February 10, 1778, Stevens, *Facsimiles,* no. 2089; Cobbett, *Parl. Hist.,* 19:718.

[13]Cobbett, *Parl. Hist.,* 19:417. More than a fortnight before this, Edward Bancroft had informed another member of the Opposition that Burgoyne's advance had been halted, and of an engagement [Bennington?] in which 600 of his troops had been compelled to surrender, Bancroft to Thomas Walpole, n.d., received November 3, 1777, Stevens, *Facsimiles,* no. 289.

[14]Morris was "an old acquaintance" of Johnstone, according to his business partner, Thomas Willing, *Willing Letters and Papers,* p. 83. It was his flair with money which would enable the revolutionary cause financially to survive the war with Britain—it did not prevent Morris, however, from ending in a debtor's prison.

[15]Francis Wharton, ed., *The Revolutionary Diplomatic Correspondence of the United States,* 2:487.

[16]Cobbett, *Parl. Hist.,* 19:707.

[17]Samuel F. Bemis, *The Diplomacy of the American Revolution,* p. 61.

[18]David Hunter Miller, *Treaties and Other International Acts of the United States,* 2:3, 35–6.

[19]Cobbett, *Parl. Hist.,* 18:750, 1402.

[20]Marshall Smelser, *The Winning of Independence,* p. 129.

[21]Cobbett, *Parl. Hist.,* 18:626 and 19:65, 237.

[22]Walpole, *Last Journals,* 2:158.

[23]Stevens, *Facsimiles,* no. 67. Subsequently Carlisle became president of the Board of Trade (1779), lord lieutenant of Ireland (1780), lord privy seal (1783) and lord lieutenant of the East Riding of Yorkshire (1799).

[24]Walpole, *Last Journals,* 2:122.

[25]Lafayette to Henry Laurens, June 12, 1778, Marquis de Lafayette, "Letters from the Marquis de Lafayette to the Hon. Henry Laurens, 1777–1780," 9:5.

[26]Ritcheson, *British Politics,* p. 264, and Carl Van Doren in Benjamin Franklin, *Letters and Papers of Benjamin Franklin and Richard Jackson 1753–1785,* p. 27, both suggest that Eden selected Carlisle.

[27]Walpole, *Last Journals, 2:122. Cobbett's Parl. Hist.* omits speeches by Johnstone of any such import.

[28]Earl of Carlisle, *Carlisle MSS,* p. 377 (cited hereafter as *Carlisle MSS*).

[29]Wedderburn to Eden, February 1778, Stevens, *Facsimiles,* no. 356.

[30]Minute by Eden, February 23[?], 1778, Minute by Hatsell, February 23[?], 1778, Memoranda of Dates, February 17 to November 14, 1778, in Eden's writing, Stevens, *Facsimiles,* nos. 374, 375, 372.

[31]Eden was four years older than Carlisle so they would not, probably, have been close friends at school. Nevertheless, the old school tie was much in evidence on the commission. *"Audaces fortuna juvat!* Our old Eton theme was never more applicable than to your present enterprise," wrote Suffolk to Eden on March 1. See Stevens, *Facsimiles,* no. 384.

[32]Carlisle to Ekins, October 1778, *Carlisle MSS,* p. 377.

[33]Jackson had been agent for Connecticut (1760–70), for Pennsylvania (1763–70), and for Massachusetts (1765–70), and had been counsel to the South Sea Company (1764–7).

[34]Jackson to Eden, March 1, 1778, Wedderburn to Eden, March 30, 1778, Stevens, *Facsimiles,* nos. 383, 411.

[35]Carlisle to Ekins, October 1778, *Carlisle MSS,* p. 378.

[36]Eden to North and Eden to Wedderburn, both of March 30, 1778, Stevens,*Facsimiles,* nos. 411, 412.

[37]Contrary to Ritcheson, *British Politics,* p. 266, who says it was Eden who preferred Pulteney.

[38]Wedderburn to Eden, March 30, 1778, Stevens, *Facsimiles,* no. 413.

[39]Eden to Wedderburn, March 31, 1778, ibid., no. 415.

[40]Walpole to William Mason, July 24, 1778, Walpole, *Correspondence,* 28:421.

[41]Wedderburn to Eden, March 31, 1778, Stevens, *Facsimiles,* no. 416.

[42]*Carlisle MSS,* p. 378.

[43]Wedderburn to Eden, April 1778, Stevens, *Facsimiles,* no. 426.

[44]Carlisle to Eden, April 1[?], 1778, William Eden to Morton Eden, April 9, 1778, Stevens, *Facsimiles,* nos. 420, 432.

[45]Eden's "Proposal," April 1778, ibid., no. 421.

[46]The king to North, March 3, April 3, 1778, Fortescue, *George III,* 4:44, 94.

[47]Knox corroborates the king's estimate of Eden's persuasiveness with his own comment on Eden's "most insinuating, gentle manner." *Reports on MSS in Various Collections* 6:266 (cited hereafter as *Various Collections);* the king to North, April 1, 1778, Fortescue, *George III,* 4:93.

[48]The king to North, March 26, 1778, North to the king, April 1, 1778, ibid., 4:80, 91.

[49]Franklin to Pulteney, March 30, 1778, Franklin to Joseph Reed, March 19, 1780. Benjamin Franklin, *The Works of Benjamin Franklin,* 8:253, 443.

[50]Johnstone to Eden, April 5, [1778], Simon Gratz Collection, case 2, box 30/4, Pennsylvania Historical Society, Philadelphia.

[51]Carl Van Doren, *Secret History of the American Revolution,* pp. 79–80, 116.

[52]Temple's engagement, with an explanatory note added by North, both in Eden's hand, April 1778, Stevens, *Facsimiles,* no. 424.

[53]*Scots Magazine* 40 (July 1778):214.

[54]Memorandum by Eden, n.d., Stevens, *Facsimiles,* no. 67.

[55]James Robertson, a veteran of the Seven Years War and the battle of Long Island, was civil governor of New York in 1778.

[56]Joseph Reed, *Remarks on Governor Johnstone's Speech,* pp. 9–12.

[57]Cobbett, *Parl. Hist.,* 19:1085–7.

[58]William Pulteney, *Thoughts on the Present State of Affairs with America and the Means of Conciliation.*

[59]Eden to Wedderburn, April 12, 1778, Eden to Morton Eden, May 4, 1778, Stevens, *Facsimiles,* nos. 441, 446.

[60]*Carlisle MSS,* pp. 322–34.

[61]Harlow, *Second British Empire,* 1:500, 529.

[62]Ritcheson was probably the first historian to praise Johnstone. See Ritcheson, *British Politics,* pp. 225–6, for a tribute to his "creative analysis" of imperial problems.

[63]Johnstone made this speech as early as October 26, 1776, Cobbett, *Parl. Hist.,* 18:749–50.

[64]Jeremy Bentham, *The Works of Jeremy Bentham,* 1:281 k.

[65]Ferguson was professor of moral philosophy at Edinburgh University and a lifelong friend of Johnstone; Lind was a political hack writer employed by Lord Mansfield, who wrote both for and against the American cause. For Lind's attempt to mediate for Bentham see Joseph Reed, *Life and Correspondence of Joseph Reed,* 1:424.

[66]Eden to Morton Eden, May 4, 1778, Stevens, *Facsimiles,* no. 446.

[67]Johnstone to William Johnstone Pulteney, April 21, [1778], Pulteney Papers, no. 455.

[68]The culprit, who had half-severed the mainstay collar and the bowsprit gammon, was never discovered. *Scots Magazine* 40 (July 1778):214.

Chapter 5

[1]Carlisle to Lady Carlisle, June 17, 1778, and Carlisle to Ekins, October 1778, *Carlisle MSS,* pp. 335n, 338, 379.

[2]Stevens, *Facsimiles,* no. 68.

[3]The bishop of Bangor was one of several who thought that it was Eden with whom Johnstone would fall out: "Fitzpatrick lamented . . . that you and Mr. Johnstone did not go on different ships; he apprehended constant quarrels between you." Bangor to Eden, June 3, 1778, ibid., no. 494. Eden to Wedderburn, June 18, 1778, ibid., no. 500.

[4]*Carlisle MSS,* p. 334.

[5]Eden to North, March 30, 1778, Stevens, *Facsimiles,* no. 411.

[6]The president of Congress, Henry Laurens, wrote of Johnstone as "a gentleman who has been deservedly esteemed in America." Laurens to Johnstone, Yorktown, June 14, 1778. *Scots Magazine* 40 (Aug. 1778):431.

[7]Eden's salary memorandum, April 1778, Stevens, *Facsimiles,* no. 421.

[8]Carlisle to Lady Carlisle, June 21, 1778, *Carlisle MSS,* p. 346.

[9]*Scots Magazine* 41 (Aug. 1779): 429.

[10]Johnstone to Carlisle, New York, September 16, 1778, *Carlisle MSS,* p. 366.

[11]Germain to Clinton, March 8, 1778, *Stopford-Sackville MSS,* 2:94–9.

[12]The king to North, March 23, 1778, Fortescue, *George III,* 4:74.

[13]The king to Clinton, March 21, 1778, Stevens, *Facsimiles,* no. 1069.

[14]Germain to Clinton, March 21, 1778, ibid., no. 1068.

[15]*Carlisle MSS,* p. 378.

[16]Carlisle to Eden, March 1778, Add. MSS, 34 415, f. 31, quoted in Alan Valentine, *Lord North,* 1:535. Eden to Wedderburn, April 12, 1778, Stevens, *Facsimiles,* no. 441.

[17]*Carlisle MSS,* p. 379.

[18]Clinton was ordered to replace General Howe as commissioner if Sir William had already sailed for England as he did on May 25, a few days before the arrival of the other commissioners.

[19]*Journals of the Continental Congress,* 4:233, 255.

[20]William B. Willcox, *Portrait of a General,* p. 230.

[21]Carlisle's paper endorsed "Hints of General reasoning from which to form our letter to the Congress," penned on June 1, referred to the French as "a nation . . . notorious for its perfidy and tyranny, who must hate you . . . in whose noxious connection your posterity . . . will imbibe every baleful principle of slavery. . . ." *Carlisle MSS,* p. 340.

[22]Commission to Congress, June 9, 1778, *Annual Register, First Series,* 1758–1862, 21:335–7.

[23]*Journals of Congress, 4:353*–4.

[24]Joseph Galloway (1731–1803) was a wealthy Philadelphia lawyer, Speaker of the Pennsylvania Assembly and a delegate to the First Continental Congress. He served Howe in Philadelphia as superintendent of police and mail. When the city was abandoned, he left for England. Thomas Willing (1731–1821) was a Philadelphia merchant in partnership with Robert Morris. He championed colonists' rights early in the Revolution, was president of the first Provincial Congress of Pennsylvania and a delegate to the Second Continental Congress, but voted against independence and was in Philadelphia during the British occupation, although he rejected the loyalist oath; Ambrose Serle, *The American Journal of Ambrose Serle, 1776–1778,* pp. 307–9; Memorandum of Thomas Willing, November 12, 1777, Thomas Willing Papers, Pennsylvania Historical Society, Philadelphia.

[25]Thomas Johnson (1732–1819) was a member of the Continental Congress known to favor reconciliation with Britain. He was elected governor of Maryland in 1777. William Carmichael (d. 1795) was a Marylander who knew Scotland and England, which he left in 1775. He worked for the Franklin commission in Paris for three years before returning to America in 1778; he became a member of the Continental Congress. The "Maryland gentleman" was possibly Robert Eden, one of whose letters, an introduction of his brother, has survived. Eden to Washington, Piccadilly, April 17, 1778, Jared Sparks, ed., *Correspondence of the American Revolution,* 2:108; *Scots Magazine* 40 (Aug. 1778):430.

[26]Jane Burke to Richard Champion, April 4, 1778, Burke, *Correspondence,* 3:425.

[27]Wraxall, *Memoirs,* 2:68.

[28]*Annual Register,* 22:20.

[29]Johnstone to Laurens, Philadelphia, June 10, 1778, Fitzwilliam MSS, and *Scots Magazine* 40 (Aug. 1778):431.

[30]Laurens to Johnstone, York, June 14, 1778, Edmund C. Burnett, ed., *Letters of the Members of the Continental Congress,* 3:292–3.

[31]In the interests of achieving a reconciliation, Dana had gone to Britain in the fall of 1774 to represent the cause of discontented colonists among their English friends. His brother had married the daughter of Lord Kinnaird, into whose family Johnstone's sister Barbara had also married. It seems likely-that Dana met the governor in 1774 through his sister. He returned to Massachusetts in April 1776.

[32]Johnstone to Dana, Philadelphia, June 10, 1778, *Scots Magazine* 40 (Oct. 1778):530.

[33]Johnstone to Morris, Philadelphia, June 16, 1778, Wharton, *Revolutionary Diplomatic Correspondence,* 2:616.

[34]In September 1778, Wedderburn wrote from England to Eden in America that "Johnstone's letter . . . turned me quite sick. You cannot imagine how much it offends all ranks of People." Stevens, *Facsimiles,* no. 517.

[35]Simon Gratz Collection, case 16, box 14, Pennsylvania Historical Society.

[36]Van Doren, *Secret History,* pp. 41–3.

[37]Ibid., p. 100.

[38]All details of Elizabeth Ferguson's conversations with Johnstone and Reed are from Reed, *Remarks,* and *Scots Magazine* 41 (Dec. 1779):717–8. It should be borne in mind that the marquis of Chastellux, who sympathized with the American cause and knew Reed, believed that he exaggerated the offers made to him. Marquis de Chastellux, *Travels in North America in the Years 1780, 1781, and 1782,* p. 133.

[39]New York Historical Society, *Collections for 1872,* pp. 405–6.

[40]*Journals of Congress,* 4:354.

[41]*Scots Magazine* 40 (July 1778): 366.

[42]Washington to Johnstone, June 12, 1778, George Washington, *The Writings of George Washington, 1745-1799,* 12:52-3. The editor of the collection, John C. Fitzpatrick, believed that the letter of June 18 was a forgery, but does not mention that it appeared in the British press at the time, assigned no motive for forgery, and seemed not to take into account that the British diplomatic position was much worsened by the evacuation of Philadelphia between the twelfth and the eighteenth and that therefore a stronger letter from Washington would have been appropriate in the circumstances.

[43]A clear indication that Washington, by June 18, was aware of the nature of Johnstone's strategy.

[44]*Scots Magazine* 40 (Aug. 1778):430.

[45]Washington to Laurens, Valley Forge, June 18, 1778, Washington, *Writings,* 12:84.

[46]*Journals of Congress,* 4:401.

[47]Ibid., 4:460.

[48]Serle, *Journal,* pp. 309, 329.

[49]Simon Gratz Collection, case 16, box 14, Pennsylvania Historical Society.

[50]John Trumbull, *M'Fingal,* p. 146.

[51]Commissioners to Congress, New York, July 11, 1778, Stevens, *Facsimiles,* no. 1119.

[52]*Scots Magazine* 40 (Oct. 1778): 532.

[53]*Journals of Congress,* 4:416.

[54]*Scots Magazine* 40 (Oct. 1778):533–4.

[55]Stevens, *Facsimiles,* no. 1132. Johnstone had submitted the draft of this declaration to his fellow commissioners for their approval before making it public. See ibid., no. 1131.

[56]*Scots Magazine* 40 (Oct. 1778):604.

[57]Carlisle to Lady Carlisle, New York, July 6, 1778, *Carlisle MSS,* p. 346.

[58]Commissioners to Germain, June 14, 1778, Stevens, *Facsimiles,* no. 1110.

[59]Walpole to William Mason, July 24, 1778, Walpole, *Correspondence,* 28:421.

[60]John Berkenhout was born in Yorkshire in 1730 and served in the Prussian and British armies before acquiring medical qualifications in Edinburgh and Leiden. How his attempt to open up unofficial negotiations with Congress landed him in a Philadelphia jail may be read in his journal in Mereness, *Travels,* pp. 574–82.

[61]Eden to Carlisle, August 20, 1778, *Carlisle MSS,* p. 359.

[62]Draft of a letter from the commission (excluding Johnstone) of September 5, 1778, in Carlisle's hand, and Eden to Wedderburn, September 22, 1778, Stevens, *Facsimiles,* nos. 1146, 526.

[63]Johnstone to Carlisle, New York, September 16, 1778, *Carlisle MSS,* p. 369.

[64]Thomas Jones, *History of New York during the Revolutionary War,* 1:160.

[65]Stuart to Bute, October 17, 1778, Bute, *A Prime Minister and His Son,* p. 137. Major John Bowater to the earl of Denbigh, July 31, 1778, Marion Balderston and David Syrett, eds., *The Lost War,* p. 167.

[66]Beresford was destined to be the most eminent of the trio. After, ironically, capture at Charleston in 1780 and a period as a British prisoner, he became lieutenant governor of South Carolina in 1783 and subsequently a member of Congress.

[67]*Stopford-Sackville MSS,* 2:115.

[68]Laurens to Washington, September 23, 1778, and Laurens to Henry, September 26, 1778, Burnett, *Letters of Members of Congress,* 3:422, 425.

[69]Washington to General Heath, September 27, 1778, Washington, *Writings,* 12:509.

[70]Washington to Major General Sullivan, September 27, 1778, ibid., p. 510.

[71]Washington to Laurens, October 3, 1778, ibid., 13:15–6.

[72]Germain to Clinton, August 5, 1778, *Stopford-Sackville MSS,* 2:15; James Simpson to

Richard Cumberland, September 1, 1778, cited by Piers Mackesy in *The War for America, 1775–1783*, p. 233.

[73]Knowledge of the orders of March 21 was not confined to the officers of highest rank. Colonel Stuart wrote to his father only two or three days before Johnstone was gossiping to Williams that an expedition to the West Indies under Grant with 5,000 men was to sail from New York the following week. Charles Stuart to Bute, Sept. 16, 1778, Bute, *A Prime Minister and His Son*, p. 133.

[74]*Journals of Congress*, 4:555–8.

[75]John Laurens to Henry Laurens, September 29, 1778, *South Carolina Historical and Genealogical Magazine* 6 (July 1905):108.

[76]John R. Alden, *The South in the Revolution, 1763–1789*, p. 240.

[77]Mackesy, *War for America*, p. 221.

[78]He certainly did to Charles Stuart, a comparatively junior officer, who found that the orders countermanding his earlier instructions left Clinton "perplexed beyond words." Stuart to Bute, Sept. 16, 1778, Bute, *A Prime Minister and His Son*, p. 133.

[79]Clinton to Drummond, March 2, 1779, Newcastle MSS, Nottingham University Library, Nottingham.

[80]Johnstone to [?], July 1778, Stevens, *Facsimiles,* no. 1147.

[81]Charles Stuart to Bute, September 16, 1778, Bute, *A Prime Minister and His Son*, p. 132. Carlisle's and Eden's letters in the early stages of the commission suggest that conversion to a war of destruction was a late development. Although Jeremy Bentham mentioned, at third or fourth hand, that during the *Trident*'s voyage Ferguson had urged the commission "to put to death man, woman, and child, as many as they could catch" (Reed, *Life and Correspondence,* 1:424), it should not be taken seriously.

[82]Carlisle to Selwyn, October 23, 1778, George Selwyn, *George Selwyn and His Contemporaries,* 3:339–40 (cited hereafter as *Selwyn*).

[83]*Annual Register,* 21:328–32.

[84]Carlisle to Lafayette, October 11, 1778, Penn MSS, 5:241, Pennsylvania Historical Society, Philadelphia.

[85]Lord Townshend to Edmund Pery, April 3, 1778, *Eighth Report*, pt. 1, sec. 1, p. 196a.

[86]Lord Pembroke to the Reverend W. Coxe, June 6, 1778, Henry Herbert, ed., *Henry, Elizabeth, and George, 1734–80*, p. 120.

[87]Germain to William Knox, July 23, 1778, *Various Collections,* 6:144.

[88]Charles Townshend to Selwyn, November 6, 1778, *Selwyn,* 3:347.

[89]Whitshed Keene to Eden, November 5, 1778, Stevens, *Facsimiles,* no. 541.

Chapter 6

[1]Commissioners to Germain, September 5, 1778, Stevens, *Facsimiles,* no. 1145.

[2]Commissioners to Germain, September 21, 1778, ibid., no. 1161.

[3]Germain to Knox, October 29, 1778, *Various Collections,* 6:152.

[4]Bute to Stuart, November 1778, Bute, *A Prime Minister and His Son,* p. 140.

[5]*An Ode to the Scotch Junto and Their American Commission on the Late Quarrel between Commissioner Ed-n and Commissioner J-hnst-ne.*

[6]Granby to Johnstone, October 31, 1778, Laing MSS, La. II. 73/142.

[7]Johnstone to Granby, November 29, 1777, *Rutland MSS,* 3:11.

[8]Cobbett, *Parl. Hist.,* 19:1346–53.

[9]Ibid., 19:1354.

[10]Ibid., 19:1401.

[11]Ibid., 20:26.

[12]Germain to Knox, January 7, 1779, *Various Collections,* 6:155.

[13]Gordon to Rockingham, n.d., Fitzwilliam MSS.

[14]Robinson to North, January 31, 1779, *Abergavenny MSS,* p. 24.

[15]Cobbett, *Parl. Hist.,* 20:140.

[16]Eden to North, February 19[?], 1779, Stevens, *Facsimiles,* no. 559.

[17]Cobbett, *Parl. Hist.,* 20:163, 834. Scaramouch was originally a stock character in Italian farce, a cowardly boaster; later, as a common noun, it was used more loosely as a contemptuous epithet for a rascal.

[18]A particularly trenchant critique of Johnstone's arguments was published in pamphlet form by Democraticus (Hugh Boyd), for which see Hugh Boyd, *The Miscellaneous Works of Hugh Boyd with an Account of His Life and Writings,* pp. 115–28. Later critics were John Charnock in *Biographia Navalis* and James Ralfe in *Naval Biography.*

[19]Cobbett, *Parl. Hist.,* 20:348–57.

[20]Ibid., 19:915.

[21]Sandwich to the king, April 4, 1779, Fortescue, *George III,* 4:320.

[22]Wedderburn to Eden, n.d., Stevens, *Facsimiles,* no. 2103.

[23]Sandwich to the king, April 3, 1779, Fortescue, *George III,* 4:320.

[24]The king to Sandwich, April 5, 1779, Earl of Sandwich, *The Private Papers of John, Earl of Sandwich,* 2:245; Jenkinson to the king, April 8, 1779, Fortescue, *George III,* 4:323.

[25]Johnstone to Germain, June 19, 1779, *Various Collections,* 6:158–9. For the wretched condition of West Florida, see Gray, "Elias Durnford, 1739–1794," p. 60.

[26]Mackesy, *War for America,* pp. 279–80.

[27]*London Magazine* 48 (July 1779):330.

[28]Johnstone to Admiralty, June 10, 29, July 10, 1779, Adm. 1/387, ff. 302, 303, 305.

[29]Walpole to Lady Ossory, July 14, 1779, Walpole, *Correspondence,* 33:109.

[30]Johnstone to Sandwich, June 29, 1779, Sandwich, *Papers,* 3:31.

[31]*London Magazine* 48 (Aug. 1779):378.

[32]Johnstone to Admiralty, June 29, 1779, and Conway to Johnstone, July 12, 1779, Adm. 1/387, ff. 303, 311–2.

[33]Conway to Johnstone, July 13, 1779, Laing MSS, 2:67. By the time he abandoned his Channel duty to Captain Finch in August, Johnstone's flotilla included also the *Amazon*, the *Hydra*, the brig *Cabot*, and the cutters *True Briton* and *Pheasant*. Johnstone to Finch, August 1, 1779, Adm. 1/387, ff. 315–7.

[34]Johnstone to Admiralty, Jersey, July 31, 1779, Adm. 1/387, f. 306, and Sandwich to Hardy, August 3, 1779, Sandwich, *Papers*, 3:55. Johnstone's intelligence, which he was wise enough to send directly to the Admiralty by the fastest means, was fairly accurate. The allied fleets united on July 23, spent a week organizing signals and, even as he wrote, were attempting to round Cape Ushant. Contrary winds prevented their entry into the Channel until August 15, A. Temple Patterson, *The Other Armada*, p. 168.

[35]Johnstone to William Johnstone Pulteney, August 3, [1779], Pulteney Papers, no. 458.

[36]Bowater to Denbigh, September 3, 1779, Balderston and Syrett, *The Lost War*, p. 193, Mackesy, *War for America*, pp. 293–7.

[37]Sandwich to the king, September 5, 7, 1779, Fortescue, *George III*, 4:424, 428.

[38]Johnstone to Pulteney, September 3, 1779, Pulteney Papers, no. 459.

[39]Johnstone to Finch, July 21, 1779, Adm. 1/387, ff. 319–20.

[40]Johnstone to Admiralty, September 26, 1779, ibid., f. 324. Johnstone's fellow "nine-pin," Lord Macartney, had surrendered Grenada to Admiral d'Estaing on July 3, 1779. What other Johnstones may have owned in the island is unknown, but George Johnstone, jointly with William Dalrymple, had purchased the Upper Letante estates there in 1774, Maclean, *Reward Is Secondary*, p. 439n.

[41]Johnstone to William Johnstone Pulteney, September 26, 1779, Pulteney Papers, no. 460.

[42]Johnstone to Sandwich, November 3, 1779, Sandwich, *Papers*, 3:103.

[43]Mackesy, *War for America*, pp. 272–8; Johnstone to Sandwich, September 23, October [?] and 19, 1779, Sandwich, *Papers*, 3:145–8, 182–4.

[44]Schaw, *Lady of Quality*, pp. 250, 252.

[45]Beatson, *Naval and Military Memoirs*, 6:295.

[46]Admiralty to Johnstone, November 9, 1779, Adm. 1/387, f. 330.

[47]Walpole to Mann, April 24, 1779, Walpole, *Correspondence*, 14:465.

[48]Lord Pembroke to Lord Herbert, May 20, 1779, Herbert, *Henry, Elizabeth, and George*, p. 183.

[49]Johnstone to Admiralty, January 19, 1781, Adm. 1/387, f. 624, in which Johnstone applied for his pay as commodore from the Admiralty. It is possible but unlikely that he would have been paid a second salary as an envoy, since there was already one at Lisbon, Robert Walpole, nephew of his more famous namesake. He served in Portugal as minister plenipotentiary and envoy extraordinary from 1771 to 1800. He was very sociable and his taste for the sexual double entendre scandalized the puritanical (Schaw, *Lady of Quality*, p. 241), but not, we may assume, Johnstone, whose humorous taste inclined in the same direction.

[50]See Samuel F. Bemis, *The Hussey-Cumberland Mission and American Independence*.

[51]Johnstone to Sandwich, December 10, 1779, Sandwich, *Papers,* 3:190:

[52]Bemis, *Hussey-Cumberland,* p. 26.

[53]Ibid., pp. 26, 37, 53, 59.

[54]Richard Cumberland, *Memoirs,* p. 236.

[55]Cobbett, *Parl. Hist.,* 16:1322.

[56]William Coxe, *Memoirs of the Kings of Spain of the House of Bourbon,* 5:72.

[57]Bemis, *Hussey-Cumberland,* p. 63.

[58]Johnstone's diplomatic dabbling may possibly have been a blind. It is quite certain that Cantofer was not simply a diplomatic go-between but also a supplier of military intelligence picked up in Madrid. See Johnstone to Robert Walpole, July 16, 1780, Adm. 1/387, f. 580.

[59]Coxe, *Memoirs of the Kings of Spain,* p. 75.

[60]Intelligence memorandum, November 30, 1779, enclosing a letter from Marquis Gonzalez de Castejon to Don Joseph Diez, October 30, 1779, Adm. 1/387, ff. 349, 386.

[61]Johnstone to the Gentlemen of the Oporto Factory, November 28, 1779; Johnstone to Whitehead, December 6, 1779, and December 7, 1779, Adm. 1/387, ff. 370, 400, 402.

[62]Johnstone to Admiralty, February 29, 1780 (wrongly dated 1779 in MS), ibid., f. 299.

[63]English prisoners broke out of a Brest jail, seized a brig and sailed it back to England with similar information, Mackesy, *War for America,* p. 324.

[64]Probably he was the same as the John M'Laurin who carried news of the Spanish declaration from Johnstone to Rodney in 1762.

[65]Johnstone to Admiralty, May 7, 1780, Adm. 1/387, f. 460.

[66]Sandwich to Johnstone, July 17, 1780, Sandwich, *Papers,* 3:286.

[67]Johnstone to Admiralty, June 9, 1780, Samuel Barrington, *The Barrington Papers,* 2:343.

[68]Mackesy, *War for America,* p. 357.

[69]Johnstone to Admiralty, August 15, 1780, Adm. 1/387, f. 588.

[70]Loughborough to Robinson, September 8, 1780, *Abergavenny MSS,* p. 302.

[71]*Scots Magazine* 42 (Aug. 1780):442–3, 545. He had presumably kissed hands with George III on becoming a member of the Carlisle commission and would attend a royal levee in 1783. Archibald to Andrew Dalzel, March 6, 1783, Edinburgh University Library, D.K.7.52/103.

[72]For the complex changes in the aims and details of this scheme, see G. Rutherford, "Sidelights on Commodore Johnstone's Expedition to the Cape," pp. 189–308.

[73]Fortescue, *George III,* 5:145, 155–6, 173–4.

[74]Cited by Rutherford, "Sidelights," p. 200.

[75]Admiral to Lady Rodney, December 10, 1780, February 7, 1781, in Lord Rodney, *The Life and Correspondence of the Late Admiral Lord Rodney,* 1:457 and 2:20.

[76]Lord Rodney, *Letter Books and Order Book of Admiral Lord Rodney, 1780–1782,* 1:50–1, 52, 64.

77Johnstone to Andrew Stuart, January 9, 1781, MS 6:8256, f. 13, National Library of Scotland.

78Cobbett, *Parl. Hist.,* 21:1130–8.

79Walpole to W. Mason, February 3, 1781, Walpole, *Correspondence,* 29:100.

80W. Fawkener to Carlisle, March 2, 1781, *Carlisle MSS,* p. 468.

81Wraxall, *Memoirs,* 2:70.

Chapter 7

1Rutherford, "Sidelights," pp. 201, 203, 204.

2A good general account may be found in Harlow, *Second British Empire,* 1:108–21. The account of one of his captains favorable to Johnstone is in Thomas Pasley, *Sir Thomas Pasley's Sea Journals, 1778–1782,* while two other eyewitness descriptions, by Benjamin Slacke and Patrick Ross, of the battle itself form a large part of William B. Willcox's "The Battle of Porto Praya, 1781." If allowance is made for his obvious biases Johnstone's own account in the *London Gazette* of June 8, 1781, is helpful, while Raoul Castex, *La Manoeuvre de La Praya,* is valuable for its use of French sources, particularly Suffren's logs. Useful too are the unpublished descriptions of Captains Douglas and Metcalfe, who were aboard East Indiamen in La Praya bay when Suffren attacked and who wrote down their impressions only days later. They may be read in the Orme MSS, vol. 197, ff. 153–74, India Office Library and Records, London. Rutherford's excellent article, "Sidelights," is the best and most comprehensive account.

3A full list, complete with details of guns and commanders may be found in Pasley, *Sea Journals,* p. 21. Corresponding information about their French opponents may be found in Castex, *La Praya,* pp. 217-22.

4In fact only one of Suffren's ships of war, the *Annibal,* was without copper, Rutherford, "Sidelights," pp. 204, 206.

5Rockingham to Hardwicke, n.d., Fitzwilliam MSS.

6Johnstone to Admiralty, February 17, 19, 21, and 23, 1781, Adm. 1/54.

7Johnstone to Admiral Darby, March 13, 1781, Add. MSS, 38681, f. 75.

8Johnstone to Admiralty, April 16, 1781, Adm. 1/54. Dated on the day of battle, it was clearly written before its outbreak.

9Castex, *La Praya,* p. 214.

10Pasley, *Sea Journals,* pp. 124, 129.

11This anecdote and various others illustrating verbatim Johnstone's humor and invective on this expedition are from a letter written on board the *Monmouth,* evidently by an officer who was no friend of Johnstone. An extract from this letter (hereinafter referred to as *Monmouth Letter*) was found in a clipping from an unidentified newspaper of October 1781, which was stuck in the flyleaf of Duke University's copy of Blake, *Remarks.*

12Rutherford, "Sidelights," p. 206. A year later Johnstone alleged that the *Jupiter* and *Active* were sent ahead to prepare a reception at La Praya for the ships following (Adm. 1/5319), but at the time, Pasley wrote in his journal that he had been sent with the possibility that "chance might throw something in our way," Pasley, *Sea Journals,* p. 130.

[13]Adm. 1/5319.

[14]Rutherford ("Sidelights," p. 206) says the fifteenth, but one of the few things on which Johnstone and Captain Darby (who was one of those who made the trip from Mayo to La Praya) could agree at Darby's court-martial was that it was the fourteenth. Adm. 1/5319.

[15]Patrick Ross to Lord George Germain, March 6, 1782, and Benjamin Slacke, "Transactions of the Squadron and Convoy Commanded by Commodore Johnstone on a Secret Expedition," in Willcox, "Porto Praya," pp. 68, 72.

[16]Pasley, *Sea Journals,* p. 137.

[17]His attempts at justification were flimsy. He claimed that (a) when the latecoming ships arrived, the smaller vessels were ordered to anchor inside the arc of larger ones, but he was disobeyed; (b) in any case stiff winds made rearrangement of ships in the crowded harbor difficult; (c) he had ordered a lookout to station himself on the high point five miles from the harbor to signal enemy approaches, but that the man could not land on the point on the day of battle because of rough surf; and (d) he did not persist in sending a lookout to the point because the frigate *Isis* was about to put out to sea when the French attacked. These excuses emerged during the course of Darby's court-martial, Adm. 1/5319. Even if they had been believable, nothing could disguise the absence of that urgency which should have informed his defensive preparations.

[18]Pierre André de Suffren (1729–88) was born in Provence, entered the navy at fourteen, fought against the British in the War of the Austrian Succession and in the Seven Years War, toward the end of each of which he was taken prisoner. During the American Revolution he fought in the West Indies and off Gibraltar, before the battle at La Praya. He went on to fight five masterly actions against Sir Edward Hughes in the Indian Ocean, after which he was made a vice-admiral in 1784. A. T. Mahan called him "a very great man" in *The Influence of Sea Power upon History,* p. 466; Michael Lewis in *The Navy of Britain,* p. 487, describes him as "something of a genius." Johnstone, who was neither, was unlucky to have had to face the greatest French sailor of the age.

[19]Mahan, *Influence of Sea Power,* pp. 326, 426, 478.

[20]William Hickey, *Memoirs of William Hickey,* 3:51, 56–7.

[21]This interpretation is at variance with the interpretations of Castex, La Praya, p. 253, who considered that Suffren attacked because he foresaw beneficial strategic consequences, and of Mahan, *Influence of Sea Power,* p. 424, who quotes Suffren's own words presumably for consumption by the French ministry of marine, to make the same point. Neither mentions the desire for mercantile prizes as any part of his motivation.

[22]Johnstone to Hillsborough, April 30, 1781, quoted in the *London Gazette* of June 8, 1781.

[23]Castex, *La Praya,* pp. 275, 290.

[24]Wilcox, "Porto Praya," p. 69.

[25]Castex, *La Praya,* p. 295.

[26]Willcox, "Porto Praya," p. 69.

[27]Beatson, *Naval and Military Memoirs,* 5:321.

[28]Adm. 1/5319 and *London Gazette (* June 8, 1781), p. 29.

[29]*Monmouth Letter.* Sir John Macpherson (1745–1821), cousin to the author of *Ossian,* first went to India as a purser on an East Indiaman in 1767, returning in 1768 as agent for the

nawab of the Carnatic. After another tour in India he became M.P. for Cricklade, then a member of the Calcutta Council in 1781, and finally governor general in 1786.

[30]Orme MSS, vol. 197, ff. 153–4.

[31]Orme MSS, vol. 197, ff. 162–3.

[32]Castex *La Praya,* pp. 313, 315.

[33]Hickey, *Memoirs,* 2:379. Burnaby commanded the frigate *Diana* in the battle.

[34]Pasley, *Sea Journals,* pp. 136, 138; Sir Herbert W. Richmond, *The Navy in India, 1763–1783,* p. 148.

[35]Willcox, "Porto Praya," p. 70; Pasley, *Sea Journals,* p. 319.

[36]Rutherford, "Sidelights," pp. 295–6.

[37]*London Gazette* (June 8, 1781), p. 33.

[38]Sutton to Thomas Thoroton, July 27, 1781, *Rutland MSS,* p. 42.

[39]*London Gazette* (June 8, 1781), p. 33.

[40]Orme MSS, vol. 197, f. 166.

[41]Rodney, *Life and Correspondence,* 2:248–9.

[42]Walpole, *Correspondence,* pp. 531–2.

[43]Rutherford, "Sidelights," p. 298.

[44]Hickey, *Memoirs,* 3:58.

[45]William Pulteney to James Johnstone, n.d., C. L. Johnstone, *History of the Johnstones,* p. 329.

[46]Pasley, *Sea Journals,* p. 140.

[47]*Monmouth Letter.*

[48]Pasley, *Sea Journals,* p. 144.

[49]Johnstone had the gall to demand salvage money for the recapture of the *Hinchingbrook* from the East India Company. The authorities at Fort William, Calcutta, accepted the claim and, subject to Admiralty court approval, assessed compensation due to Johnstone at 36,056 rupees, Governor-General and Council at Fort William to the Court of Directors, October 23, 1783, B. A. Saletore, ed., *Fort William–India House Correspondence,* 9:405.

[50]One journal *(London Magazine* 50 [Sept. 1781]:455) confidently asserted that Johnstone had sailed directly from Porto Praya to the River Plate with the conquest of Buenos Aires as one of his objects. It would be interesting to know on what evidence the report was based—possibly the gossip of the crew of the sloop *Porto,* which brought Johnstone's dispatches from Santiago.

[51]Pasley, *Sea Journals,* pp. 156, 167.

[52]Charles Stedman, *The History of the Origin, Progress, and Termination of the American War,* 2:339. Rutherford ("Sidelights," p. 200) believed that Johnstone had no written instructions, but Stedman's account, to me at any rate, conveys a different impression. Although R. Kent Newmyer, in "Charles Stedman's History of the American War," found evidence of

plagiarism in the final volume of Stedman's work, he considered the second volume more reliable.

[53]The Chairs to Hillsborough, August 19, 1780, Home Miscellany, 146, f. 133, India Office Library and Records, London.

[54]The *Annual Register,* 25:110. The "brave Woltemaade," after whom the ship was named, had, by swimming his horse, twice carried a line to a wrecked Dutch ship in Table Bay and saved the passengers' lives at the expense of his own. Hickey, *Memoirs,* 3:224–5.

[55]Stedman, *History,* 2:340.

[56]Henry Kirke, *From the Gun Room to the Throne,* p. 46; *Annual Register,* 25:111; Pasley, *Sea Journals,* p. 174.

[57]*Monmouth Letter* and Pasley, *Sea Journals,* p. 174.

[58]Walpole to Mann, October 18, 1781, Walpole, *Correspondence,* 25:194; Mackesy, *War for America,* pp. 416–7; *Town and Country Magazine* 13 (Oct. 1781):514.

[59]*Political Magazine* (Aug. and Sept. 1781), pp. 479–80, 521. Courtenay was a Northite M.P. for Tamworth with views on the American war almost identical with Johnstone's; Eyre, another Northite, represented Morpeth.

[60]Pasley, *Sea Journals,* pp. 175–6.

[61]*Monmouth Letter* and Pasley, *Sea Journals,* pp. 182–3.

[62]Beatson, *Naval and Military Memoirs,* 5:328–9. Johnstone probably got more from the proceeds of the *Sévère* than from the *Neckar,* since prize money was payable only on merchantmen. See Lewis, *Social History of the Navy,* pp. 316–33.

[63]Rutherford, "Sidelights," p. 308, and Pasley, *Sea Journals,* p. 178.

[64]With the unlooked-for result that the settlers were stranded there until December 1782. The French included three officers, sixteen dangerously ill men, and five attendants. They had been on board the *Philippine,* a rich prize taken by the *Jupiter* on the way to Trinidada. Pasley, *Sea Journals,* p. 185.

[65]Rutherford, "Sidelights," p. 307.

Chapter 8

[1]*Town and Country Magazine* 13 (Oct. 1781):515.

[2]Hickey, *Memoirs,* 2:380. Arthur Aspinall has stated that the boys' mother was Martha Ford, Arthur Aspinall, *The Later Correspondence of George III,* 3:337.

[3]Johnstone to Warren Hastings, June 24, 1785, Add. MSS, 29:168, f. 309; Delacombe to Johnstone, Montreuil-sur-mer, July 2, 1776, Laing MSS, 2:73.

[4]Prob. 11/1154; Suresh Chandra Ghosh, *The Social Conditions of the British Community in Bengal, 1757–1800,* p. 40; C. L. Johnstone, *History of the Johnstones,* p. 50.

[5]Aspinall, *The Later Correspondence of George III,* 1:319.

[6]Thomas Graham to William Drummond, October 27, 1789, *Report on the Laing MSS,* La. II. 534; Hickey, *Memoirs,* pp. 379–80. Johnstone arrived at Portsmouth on board the frigate *Diana* on February 28, *Gentleman's Magazine* 52 (Mar. 1782):145. The same report suggests

that his stay in Lisbon may have been prolonged by the arrival there of some of his men who had been shipwrecked.

[7]Rutherford, "Sidelights," p. 307; *Gentleman's Magazine* 52 (Mar. 1782):145.

[8]Pasley, *Sea Journals,* p. 174.

[9]William M. Clowes, *The Royal Navy;* 3:350.

[10]Sutton to Thomas Thoroton, July 27, 1781, *Rutland MSS,* 3:42–3.

[11]Sandwich to Lord Hillsborough, June 8, 1781, S.P. 42/56, P.R.O., London.

[12]Most of the correspondence relating to the affair was reproduced in a sixpenny pamphlet, *Letters Which Passed Between Commodore Johnstone and Capt. Evelyn Sutton in 1781 with Respect to Bringing Captain Sutton to Trial* (London, 1782), a copy of which is in the British Library. The rest may be read in Adm. 1/54.

[13]Adm. 1/5323.

[14]*The Speeches of the Judges of the Court of the Exchequer upon Granting a New Trial in the Case of Captain Evelyn Sutton . . .* , pp. 2–6. *London Magazine,* n.s. 2 (June 1784):505; 3 (July 1784):79; 3 (Dec. 1784):487.

[15]*Scots Magazine* 49 (May 1787):210–1.

[16]Daniel Pulteney to Rutland, May 25, 1787, *Rutland MSS,*3:391. William Murray, earl of Mansfield, and Alexander Wedderburn, Lord Loughborough, were both Scots.

[17]Clowes, 3:350.

[18]*Scots Magazine* 49 (May 1787):259.

[19]Johnstone's Memorandum on Trinidada, November 18, 1781; Johnstone to Pasley, November 22, 1781; Johnstone to Shelburne, May 11, 1782; [Nepean?] to Admiralty, May 16, 1782; Johnstone to Admiralty, May 25, 1782, H.O. 28, vol. 2, ff. 79–80, 82, 85, 136, P.R.O., London, and Adm. 1/54.

[20]Johnstone to Stephens, May 27, 1782, Adm. 1/54.

[21]Cobbett, *Parl. Hist.,* 23:359.

[22]Ibid., 23:245, 1039, and 24:357.

[23]Ibid., 23:244, 599, and 24:252, 311.

[24]Henry Dundas (1742–1811) was M.P. for Midlothian and lord advocate of Scotland. North looked to him to make himself responsible for all Indian business, although, unlike North, Dundas opposed Warren Hastings. For many years he was Pitt's treasurer of the navy until he became successively, in 1791 and 1794 secretary of the treasury, then of war. In 1802 he became Viscount Melville.

[25]Sutherland, *East India Company,* pp. 389–90.

[26]North to Robinson, October 27, 1782, *Abergavenny MSS,* pp. 55–6.

[27]Sutherland, *East India Company,* p. 395.

[28]John Ehrman, *The Younger Pitt,* pp. 121–2.

[29]Cobbett, *Parl. Hist.,* 23:1286.

[30]John Holland Rose, *William Pitt and National Revival,* p. 143.

[31]Holland Rose, *William Pitt,* p. 146; Johnstone to Pitt, November 25, 1783, P.R.O. 30/8/148.

[32]Sutherland, *East India Company,* p. 405.

[33]C. H. Philips, "The New East India Board and the Court of Directors, 1784," pp. 439–40.

[34]Johnstone to [?], January 13, 1784, Benson J. Lossing, Field Book of the Revolution, vol. 7, MS no. 5947, New York Public Library, New York.

[35]Johnstone to Pulteney, February 8, [1784], Pulteney Papers, no. 466.

[36]C. H. Philips, "The East India Company 'Interest' and the English Government, 1783–4," p. 94.

[37]Johnstone to Pulteney, February 5, 1785, Pulteney Papers, no. 470.

[38]*Eleventh Report,* p. 53.

[39]Johnstone to Pulteney, February 5, 1785, Pulteney Papers, no. 470.

[40]Atkinson to Dundas, [June?] 1784, Philips, "New East India Board," p. 445; Atkinson to Dundas, January 31, 1785, Holden Furber, "The East India Directors in 1784," pp. 490, 494.

[41]Arnold to Johnstone, July 18, 1784, Johnstone to Arnold, July 21, 1784, Isaac N. Arnold, "Something New of Benedict Arnold and His Descendants in England," pp. 314–6.

[42]Johnstone to Pulteney, January 8, [1778], Pulteney Papers, no. 465; Cobbett, *Parl, Hist.,* 20:347; Johnstone to Pulteney, July 26, 1782, Pulteney Papers, no. 456.

[43]Johnstone to Pulteney, n.d., Pulteney Papers, no. 462; Johnstone to Hastings, June 24, October 6, 1785, Add. MSS., 29:168, f. 309; 29:169, f. 56. The elephant reference derives from a famous cartoon by James Sayer, who depicted Fox riding an elephant with the features of Lord North, preceded by a trumpeter resembling Edmund Burke.

[44]C. L. Johnstone, *History of the Johnstones,* p. 240.

[45]I am indebted for this suggestion to Drs. Emil Wright and William Mock of the Opelika Medical Arts Center.

[46]Johnstone to Wilkes, January 10, 1786, Add. MSS., 30:873, f. 4; George Staunton to Johnstone, December 7, 1786, MS 9246, National Library of Scotland. Irving was Johnstone's solicitor. He had chambers in the Temple, and he was from Auchinbridge, Scotland. James Boswell thought him "an agreeable and a sensible man who brought Scotch ideas fully into London." Boswell, *Boswell in Search of a Wife,* p. 290.

[47]Henry Poellnitz Johnston, *The Gentle Johnstones and Their Kin,* p. 24; John Burke, *History of the Commoners of Great Britain and Ireland,* 3:209.

[48]Prob. 11/1154.

[49]*Scots Magazine* 49 (May 1787):259.

Chapter 9

[1]The phrase is that of R. M. S. Pasley, the editor of Pasley's journals, Pasley, *Sea Journals,* p. 302.

[2]Walpole to Mann, April 24, 1779, Walpole, *Correspondence,* 14:465.

[3]Walpole to Richard Mason, April 8, 1778, Walpole, *Correspondence,* 28:300.

[4]Wraxall, *Memoirs,* 2:68.

[5]Charles Townshend to George Selwyn, November 6, 1778, *Selwyn,* 3:347.

[6]Pasley, *Sea Journals,* p. 124.

[7]Alistair Cooke to the U.S. House of Representatives, September 25, 1974, printed in *The Listener* (September 26, 1974), p. 399.

[8]Johnstone to Hastings, May 11, 1784, Add. MSS., 29163, f. 390.

Bibliography

This bibliography is grouped into three parts, each separately alphabetized: manuscripts, published primary sources, and secondary sources. Published articles are not grouped separately but are included in either published primary sources or secondary sources as seems most appropriate.

Abbreviations

Add. MSS	Additional Manuscripts
Adm.	Admiralty
C.M.	Court-Martial
C.O.	Colonial Office
H.M.C.	Historical Manuscripts Commission
H.O.	Home Office
MPAED	Mississippi Provincial Archives, English Dominion
Prob.	Probate
P.R.O.	Public Record Office
S.P.	State Papers
T.	Treasury

Manuscript Materials

Blair Castle, Blair Atholl, Perthshire.

Atholl MSS 49 (6) 99 (Gordon).

British Museum (British Library), London.

Add. MSS 14034 (Florida); 29163, 29168–9, 29193 (Hastings); 30872–3 (Wilkes); 34419 (Eden); 36133 (commissions); 38681 (Darby).

Edinburgh University, Library, Edinburgh.

Laing MSS La. II. 67 (Conway); La. II. 73 (Johnstone family papers); La. II. 78 (naval dispatches); La. II. 91, 214 (James Johnstone); La. II. 509 (Archibald Campbell).

D. K. 7.52 (Dalzel).

Glamorgan Central Library, Cardiff, Wales.

Bute Correspondence.

Huntington Library, San Marino, California.

Pulteney Papers (Johnstone's letters to Pulteney).

India Office Library and Records, London.

Orme MSS, vol. 197 (Praya).

B/256–9 (General Court minutes).

European MSS, G37 (Powis; i.e., Clive MSS).

Home Miscellany, 146, 154 (company/government letters).

Baxter Transcripts from the East India Company Stock Ledgers.

Library of Congress, Washington, D.C.

Miscellaneous MSS Collection (Johnstone's commissions).

Peter Force Papers, series 9 (peace commission).

Mississippi Provincial Archives, Jackson, Mississippi.

A miscellany of papers relating to West Florida transcribed from various sources. Of ten projected volumes based on them only one was published (referred to below under Rowland, Dunbar). The unpublished remainder are cited in this text as Mississippi Provincial Archives, English Dominion.

National Library of Scotland, Edinburgh.

MSS nos. 1:580 (letters to Johnstone); 1:1006 (Alexander Johnstone); 6:8256 (letters from Johnstone); 6:9246 (letters to Johnstone).

National Maritime Museum, Greenwich.

Adm/L/A235, B8, C39, H164, L29, T217, V77, W4 (lieutenants' logs).

New York Public Library, New York.

Benson J. Lossing, Field Book of the Revolution, MS 5947.

Nottingham University Library, Nottingham.

Newcastle MSS, NCC 2 (Clinton).

Pennsylvania Historical Society, Philadelphia.

Thomas Willing Papers: F–118 (Howe).

Simon Gratz Collection: case 2, box 30/4 (Eden); case 4, box 29 (Willing); case 16, box 14 (Ferguson)

Penn MSS, vol. 5 (Lafayette).

Public Record Office, London.

Adm. 1/54 (1781, 1782); 1/387 (1779, 1780); 1/511 *(Biddeford);* 1/1985 (1760, 1763); 1/5296, part 1 (Johnstone's C.M., 1757); 1/5298 (Thompson's C.M.); 1/5299, part 4 (Johnstone's C.M., 1760); 1/5319 (Darby's C.M.); 1/5323 (Sutton's C.M.); 2/1338 (naval intelligence); 12/22 (C.M. Digest); 51/458, part 5 *(Hornet);* 107/4 (lieutenants' certificates).

C.O. 5/65–68 (West Florida and Indian tribes); 5/574 (Board of Trade correspondence); 5/582 (Forbes); 5/601 (Florida Land Register).

H.O. 28, vol. 2 (Trinidada).

P.R.O. 30/8/3 (Shelburne); 30/8/148 (Pitt); 30/47/14/3 (West Florida before British colonization).

Prob. 11/1154 (Johnstone's will).

S.P. 42/56 (Sandwich).

T.I. 437 (West Floridian economy).

Wentworth Woodhouse Muniments, Sheffield City Libraries, Sheffield.

Burke Correspondence.

Fitzwilliam MSS.

Primary Published Materials

Abergavenny, Marquess of. *Abergavenny MSS.* H.M.C., London, 1887.

Adair, James. *History of the American Indians.* 1775. Reprint. Edited by Samuel C. Williams. Johnson City, Tenn., 1930.

Alvord, Clarence W., and Clarence E. Carter, eds. *Illinois Historical Collections.* Vols. 10 and 11. Springfield, Ill., 1915–16.

American Archives. See Force, Peter, ed.

An Appeal to the Public in Behalf of George Johnstone, Esq., Governor of West Florida. London, 1763.

Annual Register, First Series, 1758–1862. 104 vols. London, 1777–1863.

An Ode to the Scotch Junto and Their American Commission on the Late Quarrel between Commissioner Ed-n and Commissioner J-hnst-ne. London, 1778.

Anson, Lord. *Lord Anson's Voyage Round the World, 1740–1744.* Edited by Richard Walter. West Drayton, 1947.

Aspinall, Arthur. *The Later Correspondence of George III.* 5 vols. Cambridge, 1962–70.

Aspinall, Arthur, and E. Anthony Smith, eds. *English Historical Documents.* Vol. 11. London, 1959.

Balderston, Marion, and David Syrett, eds. *The Lost War: Letters from British Officers during the American Revolution.* New York, 1975.

Baretti, Joseph. *A Journey from London to Genoa through England, Portugal, Spain, and France.* 1770. Reprint. New York, 1970.

Barrington, Samuel. *The Barrington Papers.* 2 vols. Edited by D. Bonner Smith. Navy Records Society. London, 1941.

Bartram, William. *Travels.* 1791. Reprint. Edited by Francis Harper. New Haven, 1958.

Bathurst, Earl of. *Bathurst MSS.* H.M.C. London, 1923.

The Beauties of the British Senate. Vol. 1. London, 1786.

Bentham, Jeremy. *The Works of Jeremy Bentham.* 11 vols. 1838–43. Reprint. Edited by Sir John Bowring. New York, 1962.

Berdt, Dennys De. *Letters of Dennys De Berdt, 1757–1770.* Cambridge, Mass., 1911.

Blake [pseud.]. *Remarks on Commodore Johnstone's Account of his Engagement with a French Squadron under the Command of Mons De Suffrein on April 16, 1781, in Porto Praya Road in the Island of St. Jago.* London, 1782.

Boswell, James. *Boswell for the Defence, 1769–1774.* Edited by William K. Wimsatt and Frederick A. Pottle. New York, 1959.

_____. *Boswell in Search of a Wife, 1766–1769*. Edited by Frank Brady and Frederick A. Pottle. New York, 1956.

_____. *Boswell's London Journal, 1762–1763*. Edited by Frederick A. Pottle. New York, 1950.

Boyd, Hugh [Democraticus]. *The Miscellaneous Works of Hugh Boyd with an Account of His Life and Writings*. Edited by Lawrence D. Campbell. London, 1800.

Burke, Edmund. *The Correspondence of Edmund Burke*. 9 vols. General editor, Thomas W. Copeland. Chicago, 1958–70.

Burnett, Edmund C., ed. *Letters of Members of the Continental Congress*. 8 vols. Washington, D.C., 1921-36.

Bute, Earl of. *A Prime Minister and His Son; From the Correspondence of the 3rd Earl of Bute and of Lieutenant-General the Hon. Sir Charles Stuart K.B.* Edited by E. Stuart-Wortley. London, 1925.

Calder, Isabel M., ed. *Colonial Captivities, Marches, and Journeys*. Port Washington, N. Y., 1967.

Carlisle, Earl of. *Carlisle MSS*. H.M.C. London, 1897.

Carlyle, Alexander. *Autobiography of Alexander Carlyle*. Edinburgh, 1860.

Chastellux, Marquis de. *Travels in North America in the Years 1780, 1781, and 1782*. 1786. Reprint. Edited by Howard C. Rice, Jr. Chapel Hill, 1963.
Cobbett, William. *The Parliamentary History of England from the Norman Conquest in 1066 to the Year 1803*. 36 vols. London, 1806–20.

Considerations on the Question in Litigation between Commodore Johnstone and Captain Sutton in the Form of an Address. London [?], 1785 [?].

Correspondence of King George the Third. See Fortescue, Sir John, ed.

The Critical Review. August 1768.

Cumberland, Richard. *Memoirs*. New York, 1806.

Dempster, George. *Letters of George Dempster to Sir Adam Ferguson, 1756–1813*. Edited by James Fergusson. London, 1934.

Eighth Report. H.M.C. Darlington, 1881.

Eleventh Report, Appendix. Part 7. H.M.C. London, 1888.

Fitzmaurice, Lord. *Life of William, Earl of Shelburne*. 2 vols. London, 1912.

Force, Peter, ed. *American Archives*. 4th and 5th series. 9 vols. Washington, D.C., 1837–53.

Fortescue, Sir John, ed. *Correspondence of King George the Third*. 6 vols. London, 1927–8.

Franklin, Benjamin. *Letters and Papers of Benjamin Franklin and Richard Jackson, 1753–1785*. Edited by Carl Van Doren. Philadelphia, 1947.

_____. *The Works of Benjamin Franklin*. 10 vols. Edited by Jared Sparks. Boston, 1836–40.

Gage, Thomas. *The Correspondence of General Thomas Gage*. 2 vols. Edited by Clarence E. Carter. New Haven, 1931.

Gentleman's Magazine, 1745–87.

Gibbon, Edward. *Memoirs of My Life.* 1796. Reprint. Edited by George Bonnard. New York, 1966.

Grafton, Duke of. *Autobiography and Political Correspondence of Augustus Henry, Third Duke of Grafton.* Edited by Sir William R. Anson. London, 1898.

Grenville, George. *The Grenville Papers.* 4 vols. Edited by W. J. Smith. London, 1852–5.

Henry, Tenth Earl of Pembroke. *Letters and Diaries.* Edited by Henry Herbert. London, 1950.

Herbert, Henry, ed., *Henry, Elizabeth, and George.* London, 1939.

Hickey, William. *Memoirs of William Hickey.* 4 vols. Edited by Alfred Spencer. London, 1950.

Hill, S. C. *Bengal in 1756–7: A Selection of Public and Private Papers Dealing with the Affairs of the British in Bengal during the Reign of Siraj-Uddaula.* 3 vols. London, 1905.

Hooker, Richard J., ed., *Carolina Backcountry on the Eve of the Revolution.* Chapel Hill, N.C., 1953.

Hume, David. *The Letters of David Hume.* 2 vols. Edited by Y. T. Greig. Oxford, 1969.

Hutchins, Thomas. *An Historical Narrative and Topographical Description of Louisiana and West Florida.* 1784. Reprint. Edited by Joseph G. Tregle, Jr. Gainesville, Fla., 1968.

Jenkinson, Charles. *Jenkinson Papers, 1760–1766.* Edited by Ninetta Jucker. London, 1949.

Johnstone, George. *A Letter to the Proprietors of East India Stock.* London, 1769.

———. *Letters Which Passed between Commodore Johnstone and Capt. Evelyn Sutton in 1781.* London, 1787.

———. *Speech of Mr. George Johnstone in the General Court of Proprietors of East India Stock upon the Subject of Restitution for Private Losses in the War against Cossim Ali Cawm.* London, 1768.

———. *Thoughts on Our Acquisitions in the East Indies.* London, 1771.

Journal of the Commissioners for Trade and Plantations from January 1754 to December 1763. London, 1936.

Journal of the Commissioners for Trade and Plantations from January 1764 to December 1767. London, 1936.

Journals of the Continental Congress (1777 and 1778). Philadelphia, 1778–9.

Lafayette, Marquis de. "Letters from the Marquis de Lafayette to the Hon. Henry Laurens, 1777–1780." *South Carolina Historical and Genealogical Magazine* 9 (1908).

Laurens, Henry. See Lafayette, Marquis de. For letters from Laurens' son, see *South Carolina Historical and Genealogical Magazine* 6 (1905).

Lee, William. *Letters of William Lee, 1766–1783.* Edited by Washington Chauncey Ford. Brooklyn, 1891.

London Gazette, 1743–1782.

London Magazine, 1760–1785.

Lonsdale, Earl of. *Lonsdale MSS.* H.M.C. London, 1893.

Macartney, Lord. *The Private Correspondence of Lord Macartney, Governor of Madras (1781–85).* Edited by C. Collin Davies. London, 1950.

Mereness, Newton D., ed. *Travels in the American Colonies.* New York, 1961.

Miller, David Hunter. *Treaties and Other International Acts of the United States.* 8 vols. Washington, D.C., 1931–48.

The Monmouth Letter. Part of a clipping from an unidentified newspaper of October 1781 stuck into Duke University's copy of Blake's pamphlet cited below.

Montbéraut, Chevalier Montault de. *Mémoire justificatif.* Translated and edited by Milo B. Howard and Robert R. Rea. Tuscaloosa, Ala., 1965.

Montesquieu, Baron de. *The Spirit of Laws [L'esprit des lois* (1748)]. Edited by J. V. Prichard. Translated by Thomas Nugent. London, 1878.

Monthly Review, November 1763.

New York Gazette, 1771–5.

New York Historical Society. *Collections for 1872.* New York, 1873.

North Briton, February 19, 1763.

Oswald, James. *Memorials of the Right Hon. James Oswald.* Edinburgh, 1825.

Padgett, James A., ed. "Commission, Orders, and Instructions to George Johnstone, British Governor of West Florida, 1763–1767." *Louisiana Historical Quarterly* 21 (1938).

Palk, Robert. *Report on the Palk MSS.* H.M.C. London, 1922.

Pasley, Thomas. *Private Sea Journals, 1778–1782.* Edited by R. M. S. Pasley. London, 1931.

Pembroke, Tenth Earl of. See Henry, Tenth Earl of Pembroke.

Pennsylvania Gazette, 1764–7.

Political Magazine, 1781.

Providence Gazette, 1770–5.

Public Record Office. *Calendar of Home Office Papers of the Reign of George III.* Vol. 2. London, 1879.

Pulteney, William. *Thoughts on the Present State of Affairs with America and the Means of Conciliation.* London, 1778.

Reed, Joseph. *Life and Correspondence of Joseph Reed.* 2 vols. Edited by William B. Reed. Philadelphia, 1847.

————. *Remarks on Governor Johnstone's Speech.* Philadelphia, 1779.

Report on the Laing MSS. Vol. 2. H.M.C. London, 1926.

Reports on American MSS in the Royal Institution of Great Britain. Vol. 1. H.M.C. Dublin, 1906.

Reports on MSS in Various Collections. Vol. 6. H.M.C. Hereford, 1909.

Robertson, Archibald. *Archibald Robertson: His Diaries and Sketches in America, 1762–1780.* Edited by Harry Miller Lydenberg. New York, 1930.

Rodney, Lord. *Letter Books and Order Book of Admiral Lord Rodney, 1780–1782.* 2 vols. New York Historical Society. New York, 1932.

———. *The Life and Correspondence of the Late Admiral Lord Rodney.* 2 vols. Edited by Godfrey Mundy. London, 1830.

Romans, Bernard. *Concise Natural History of East and West Florida.* 1775. Reprint. Gainesville, Fla., 1962.

Rowland, Dunbar. *Mississippi Provincial Archives, 1763–1766: English Dominion.* Vol. 1. Nashville, Tenn., 1911.

Rutland, Duke of. *Rutland MSS.* Vol. 3. H.M.C. London, 1894.

Saletore, B. A., ed. *Fort William–India House Correspondence.* Vol. 9. Delhi, 1959.

Sandwich, Earl of. *The Private Papers of John, Earl of Sandwich.* 3 vols. Edited by G. R. Barnes and J. H. Owen. Navy Records Society. London, 1932.

Schaw, Janet. *Journal of a Lady of Quality, 1774 to 1776.* Edited by Evangeline W. Andrews and Charles M. Andrews. New Haven, 1923.

Scots Magazine, 1763–87.

Selwyn, George. *George Selwyn and His Contemporaries.* 1882. Reprint. 4 vols. Edited by John Jesse. London, 1949.

Serle, Ambrose. *The American Journal of Ambrose Serle, 1776–1778.* Edited by Edward H. Tatum, Jr. San Marino, Calif., 1940.

Smith, William. *Historical Memoirs from 16 March, 1763, to 9 July, 1776, of William Smith.* New York, 1956.

Smollett, Tobias. *Peregrine Pickle.* 1751. Reprint. Edited by James Clifford. London, 1964.

Sparks, Jared, ed. *Correspondence of the American Revolution.* 4 vols. Boston, 1853.

The Speeches of the Judges of the Court of Exchequer upon Granting a New Trial in the Case of Captain Evelyn Sutton. . . . London, 1787.

Steel, David. *Royal Navy List.* London, 1783–1811.

Stevens, Benjamin F., ed. *Facsimiles of Manuscripts in European Archives Relating to America, 1773–1783.* 25 vols. London, 1889–95.

Stopford-Sackville, Mrs. *Stopford-Sackville MSS.* 2 vols. H.M.C. London, 1904–10.

Town and Country Magazine, 1763–87. See especially the issue for October 1781, which contains a short life of Johnstone to 1781.

Trumbull, John. *M'Fingal: An Epic Poem.* 1782. Reprint. Edited by Benson J. Lossing. New York, 1881.

Walpole, Horace. *Correspondence of Horace Walpole.* 42 vols. Edited by W. S. Lewis. New Haven, 1934–80.

———. *The Last Journals of Horace Walpole.* 2 vols. Edited by A. F. Steuart. London, 1910.

———. *Memoirs of the Reign of George III.* 4 vols. Edited by Sir Denis Le Marchant. London, 1851.

Washington, George. *The Writings of George Washington, 1745–1799.* 39 vols. Edited by John C. Fitzpatrick. Washington, D.C., 1931–44.

Wharton, Francis, ed. *The Revolutionary Diplomatic Correspondence of the United States.* 6 vols. Washington, D.C., 1889.

Willing, Thomas. *Willing Letters and Papers.* Edited by Thomas Willing Balch. Philadelphia, 1922.

Wraxall, Sir Nathaniel W. *Memoirs.* 5 vols. London, 1884.

Secondary Works

Alden, John R. *John Stuart and the Southern Colonial Frontier.* Ann Arbor, Mich., 1944.

———. *The South in the Revolution, 1763–1789.* Baton Rouge, La., 1957.

Alvord, Clarence W. *The Mississippi Valley in British Politics.* 2 vols. 1916. Reprint. New York, 1959.

Arnold, Isaac N. "Something New of Benedict Arnold and His Descendants in England." *Magazine of American History* 11 (October 1883).

Atkinson, William C. *A History of Spain and Portugal.* Harmondsworth, 1960.

Beaglehole, J. C. *The Life of Captain James Cook.* Stanford, Calif., 1974.

Beatson, Robert. *Naval and Military Memoirs of Great Britain from 1729 to 1783.* 6 vols. London, 1790.

Bemis, Samuel F. "British Secret Service and the Franco-American Alliance." *American Historical Review* 29 (1924).

———. *The Diplomacy of the American Revolution.* Bloomington, Ind., 1957.

———. *The Hussey-Cumberland Mission and American Independence.* Gloucester, Mass., 1968.

Bence-Jones, Mark. *Clive of India.* London, 1974.

Bleakley, Horace. "Tête à Tête Portraits in 'The Town and Country Magazine.'" *Notes and Queries,* 10th series, 4 (Sept. 23, 1905).

Bonsall, Brian. *Sir James Lowther and Cumberland and Westmorland Elections, 1754–1775.* Manchester, 1960.

Born, John D., Jr. "Charles Strachan in Mobile: The Frontier Ordeal of a Scottish Factor, 1764–68." *Alabama Historical Quarterly* 27 (1965).

———. *Governor Johnstone and Trade in British West Florida, 1764–1767.* Wichita, Kans., 1968.

Boxer, Charles R. *The Portuguese Seaborne Empire, 1415–1825.* London, 1969.

Brown, Alan S. "The British Peace Offer of 1778." *Papers of the Michigan Academy of Science, Arts, and Letters* 40 (1955).

Brown, Weldon A. *Empire or Independence.* Baton Rouge, La., 1941.

Burke, John. *History of the Commoners of Great Britain and Ireland.* 4 vols. London, 1833–8.

Cannon, Richard. *Historical Record of the 70th of Foot.* London, 1836.

Caraccioli, Charles. *The Life of Robert, Lord Clive.* 4 vols. London, 1775–7.

Carter, Clarence E. "The Beginnings of British West Florida." *Mississippi Valley Historical Review* 4 (1917).

_____ . "Some Aspects of British Administration in West Florida." *Mississippi Valley Historical Review* 1 (1914).

Castex, Raoul. *La Manoeuvre de La Praya.* Paris, 1913.

Charnock, John. *Biographia Navalis.* 6 vols. London, 1798.

Christie, Ian. *The End of North's Ministry, 1780–1782.* London, 1958.

Claiborne, John F. H. *Mississippi as a Province, Territory, and State.* Jackson, Miss., 1880.

Clowes, William M. *The Royal Navy: A History from Earliest Times to the Present.* 7 vols. 1897–1903. Reprint. London, 1966.

Cone, Carl B. *Burke and the Nature of Politics.* Lexington, Ky., 1957.

Cooke, Alistair. Speech to the U.S. House of Representatives, September 25, 1974. *The Listener* (September 26, 1974).

Corbett, Sir Julian. *England in the Seven Years War: A Study in Combined Strategy.* 2 vols. London, 1907.

Coxe, William. *Memoirs of the Kings of Spain of the House of Bourbon.* vol. 5. London, 1815.

Davies, A. Mervyn. *Clive of Plassey.* London, 1939.

Derry, John W. *Charles James Fox.* New York, 1972.

Dictionary of National Biography. 4th ed.

Donoughue, Bernard. *British Politics and the American Revolution: The Path to War, 1773–75.* London, 1964.

Ehrman, John. *The Younger Pitt.* Vol. 1. New York, 1969.

Fabel, Robin F. A. "George Johnstone and the 'Thoughts Concerning Florida'—A Case of Lobbying?" *Alabama Review* 29 (1976).

_____ . "Governor George Johnstone of British West Florida." *Florida Historical Quarterly* (1976).

Fabel, Robin F. A., and Robert R. Rea. "Lieutenant Thomas Campbell's Sojourn among the Creeks, November 1764–May 1765." *Alabama Historical Quarterly* 36 (1974).

Feiling, Keith. *Warren Hastings.* London, 1954.

Ferguson, Richard S. *Cumberland and Westmorland M.P.'s* London, 1871.

Fisher, H. E. S. "Anglo-Portuguese Trade, 1700–1750." *Economic History Review* 16 (1963).

Furber, Holden. "The East India Directors in 1784." *Journal of Modern History* 5 (1933).

———. *John Company at Work*. Cambridge, Mass., 1951.

Gauld, Charles A. "A Scottish View of West Florida in 1769." *Tequesta* 29 (1969).

Ghosh, Suresh Chandra. *The Social Conditions of the British Community in Bengal, 1757–1800*. Leiden, 1970.

Gipson, Alice Edna. *John Home: His Life and Works*. New Haven, 1916.

Gipson, Lawrence H. *The British Empire before the American Revolution*. 15 vols. New York, 1936–70.

Gray, Robert E. "Elias Durnford, 1739–1794: Engineer, Soldier, Administrator." Master's thesis, Auburn University, 1971.

Hallward, N. L. *William Bolts: A Dutch Adventurer under John Company*. Cambridge, 1920.

Hamilton, Peter J. *Colonial Mobile*. Mobile, Ala., 1952.

Harlow, Vincent T. *The Founding of the Second British Empire, 1763–1793*. 2 vols. London, 1952, 1964.

Holland Rose, John. *William Pitt and National Revival*. London, 1915.

Holzman, James M. *The Nabobs in England: A Study of the Returned Anglo-Indian, 1760–1785*. New York, 1926.

Howard, Clinton N. *The British Development of West Florida, 1763–1769*. Berkeley, 1947.

———. "Colonial Pensacola: The British Period." *Florida Historical Quarterly* 19 (1940–1).

———. "Governor Johnstone in West Florida." *Florida Historical Quarterly* 18 (1938–9).

———. "The Interval of Military Government in West Florida, 1763–4. *Louisiana Historical Quarterly* 22 (1939).

———. "The Military Occupation of British West Florida, 1763." *Florida Historical Quarterly* 18 (1938–9).

———. "Some Economic Aspects of British West Florida, 1763–1768." *Journal of Southern History* 6 (1940).

Humphreys, R. A. "Lord Shelburne and a Projected Recall of Colonial Governors in 1767." *American Historical Review* 37 (1931–2).

James, W. M. *The British Navy in Adversity*. London, 1926.

Johnson, Cecil. *British West Florida, 1763–1783*. New Haven, 1943.

———. "Pensacola in the British Period: Summary and Significance." *Florida Historical Quarterly* 37 (1958–9).

———. "West Florida Revisited." *Journal of Mississippi History* 28 (1966).

Johnston, Henry Poellnitz. *The Gentle Johnstones and Their Kin*. Birmingham, Ala., 1966.

Johnstone, Catherine L. *The Historical Families of Dumfriesshire and the Border Wars*. Dumfries, Scotland, 1889.

———. *History of the Johnstones, 1191–1909*. London, 1909.

_____ . *Supplement to History of the Johnstones*. Glasgow, 1925.

Jones, Thomas. *History of New York during the Revolutionary War*. 2 vols. New York, 1879.

Kerr, Wilfred B. "The Stamp Act in the Floridas, 1765–1766." *Mississippi Valley Historical Review* 21 (1934–5).

Khan, Abdul Majed. *The Transition in Bengal, 1756–1775: A Study of Sayd Muhammed Reza Khan*. Cambridge, 1969.

Kirke, Henry. *From the Gun Room to the Throne*. London, 1904.

Labaree, Leonard W. *Royal Government in America*. New York, 1930.

Lewis, Michael. *The Navy of Britain*. London, 1948.

_____ . *A Social History of the Navy, 1793–1815*. London, 1960.

Lossing, Benson J. *Field-Book of the Revolution*. 2 vols. New York, 1860.

McGovern, James R., ed. *Colonial Pensacola*. Pensacola, Fla., 1972.

McGuffie, Tom H. *The Siege of Gibraltar, 1779–1783*. London, 1965.

Mackenzie, Henry. *An Account of the Life and Writings of John Home, Esq*. Edinburgh, 1822.

Mackesy, Piers. *The War for America, 1775–1783*. Cambridge, Mass., 1964.

Maclean, James N. M. *Reward Is Secondary*. London, 1963.

Mahan, A. T. *The Influence of Sea Power upon History*. London, 1894.

Mahon, R. H. *Life of General the Hon. James Murray*. London, 1921.

Malcolm, John. *The Life of Robert, Lord Clive*. 3 vols. London, 1836.

Morris, Richard B. *The Peacemakers: The Great Powers and American Independence*. New York, 1965.

Mossner, E. C. "New Hume Letters to Lord Elibank, 1748–1776." *Texas Studies in Literature and Language* 4 (1962–3).

Mowat, Charles L. "The First Campaign of Publicity for Florida." *Mississippi Valley Historical Review* 30 (1943).

_____ . "The Southern Brigade." *Journal of Southern History* 10 (1944).

Murray, A. C. *The Five Sons of "Bare Betty."* London, 1936.

Namier, Sir Lewis B., and John Brooke. *England in the Age of the American Revolution*. London, 1930.

_____ . *The House of Commons, 1754–1790*. 3 vols. London, 1968.

Newmyer, R. Kent. "Charles Stedman's History of the American War." *American Historical Review* 63 (1958).

Norris, John. *Shelburne and Reform*. New York, 1963.

Norton, Mary Beth. *The British-Americans: The Loyalist Exiles in England, 1774–1789*. Boston, 1972.

Olson, Alison. *The Radical Duke*. Oxford, 1961.

Pares, Richard. *King George III and the Politicians*. Oxford, 1953.

Patterson, A. Temple. *The Other Armada*. Manchester, 1960.

Philips, C. H. *The East India Company, 1784–1834*. Manchester, 1961.

————. "The East India Company 'Interest' and the English Government, 1783–4." *Transactions of the Royal Historical Society,* 4th series 20 (1937).

————. "The New East India Board and the Court of Directors, 1784." *English Historical Review* 55 (1940).

Pitman, Frank W. *The Development of the British West Indies, 1700–63*. New Haven, 1967.

Pryde, George S. *Scotland from 1603 to the Present Day*. 2 vols. London, 1960.

Ralfe, James. *The Naval Biography of Great Britain*. 4 vols. London, 1828.

Ramsay, John. *Scotland and Scotsmen in the Eighteenth Century from the MSS of John Ramsay, Esq. of Ochertyre*. 2 vols. Edited by Alexander Allardyce. Edinburgh, 1888.

Rea, Robert R. "Belles Lettres in British West Florida." *Alabama Review* 13 (1960).

————. "Graveyard for Britons: West Florida, 1763–1781." *Florida Historical Quarterly* 47 (1969).

————. "John Eliot, Second Governor of British West Florida." *Alabama Review* 30 (1977).

————. "The King's Agent for British West Florida." *Alabama Review* 16 (1963).

————. "Military Deserters from British West Florida." *Louisiana History* 9 (1968).

————. "A Naval Visitor in British West Florida." *Florida Historical Quarterly* 40 (1961).

————. "Outpost of Empire: David Wedderburn at Mobile." *Alabama Review* 7 (1954).

————. "Pensacola under the British (1763–1781)." In *Colonial Pensacola,* ed. James R. McGovern. Pensacola, Fla., 1972.

————. "The Trouble at Tombeckby." *Alabama Review* 21 (1968).

Reid, Loren. *Charles James Fox: A Man for the People*. Columbia, Mo., 1969.

Richmond, Sir Herbert W. *The Navy in India, 1763–1783*. London, 1931.

Ritcheson, Charles R. *British Politics and the American Revolution*. Norman, Okla., 1954.

Roche, John F. *Joseph Reed: A Moderate in the American Revolution*. New York, 1968.

Russell, Jack. *Gibraltar Besieged*. London, 1965.

Rutherford, G. "Sidelights on Commodore Johnstone's Expedition to the Cape." *The Mariner's Mirror* 28 (1942).

Shaw, Helen L. *British Administration of the Southern Indians, 1756–1783*. Lancaster, Pa., 1931.

Shy, John W. *Toward Lexington*. Princeton, N.J. 1965.

Smelser, Marshall. *The Winning of Independence*. Chicago, 1952.

Sosin, Jack. *The Revolutionary Frontier, 1763–1783*. New York, 1967.

_____. *Whitehall and the Wilderness*. Lincoln, Nebr., 1961.

Starr, J. Barton. "Campbell Town: French Huguenots in British West Florida." *Florida Historical Quarterly* 54 (1975).

Stedman, Charles. *The History of the Origin, Progress, and Termination of the American War*. 2 vols. Dublin, 1794.

Sutherland, Lucy. *The East India Company in Eighteenth-Century Politics*. Oxford, 1952.

_____. "Lord Shelburne and East India Company Politics, 1766–9." *English Historical Review* 49 (1934).

Thomas, Peter D. G. *The House of Commons in the Eighteenth Century*. Oxford, 1971.

Turberville, A. S. *A History of Welbeck Abbey and Its Owners*. Vol. 2. London, 1939.

Valentine, Alan. *Lord North*. 2 vols. Norman, Okla., 1967.

Van Doren, Carl. *Secret History of the American Revolution*. New York, 1941.

Vorsey, Louis De. *The Indian Boundary in the Southern Colonies, 1763–1775*. Chapel Hill, N.C., 1966.

Watson, J. S., ed. *Cicero's Oratory and Orators*. London, 1889.

Watson, J. Steven. *The Reign of George III, 1760–1815*. London, 1964.

Willcox, William B. "The Battle of Porto Praya, 1781." *American Neptune* 5 (1945).

_____. *Portrait of a General*. New York, 1964.

Index